Creativity and Cultural Production

Creativity and Cultural Production

Issues for Media Practice

Phillip McIntyre

First published 2012 by
PALGRAVE MACMILLAN

Palgrave Macmillan in the UK is an imprint of Macmillan Publishers Limited,
registered in England, company number 785998, of Houndmills, Basingstoke,
Hampshire RG21 6XS.

Palgrave Macmillan in the US is a division of St Martin's Press LLC,
175 Fifth Avenue, New York, NY 10010.

Palgrave Macmillan is the global academic imprint of the above companies
and has companies and representatives throughout the world.

Palgrave® and Macmillan® are registered trademarks in the United States,
the United Kingdom, Europe and other countries.

ISBN 978–0–230–27228–6

This book is printed on paper suitable for recycling and made from fully
managed and sustained forest sources. Logging, pulping and manufacturing
processes are expected to conform to the environmental regulations of the
country of origin.

A catalogue record for this book is available from the British Library.

A catalog record for this book is available from the Library of Congress.

10   9   8   7   6   5   4   3   2   1
21 20 19 18 17 16 15 14 13 12

Printed and bound in Great Britain by
CPI Antony Rowe, Chippenham and Eastbourne

Contents

Acknowledgements

A book like this, about a topic like this, could not have been made without the contribution of quite a number of people. I would like to thank some of them here. Firstly, let me say that all the professionals I have dealt with at Palgrave Macmillan have been a pleasure to work with. For granting me the leave to write, while others were slaving over a lectern and computer, the University of Newcastle also has my heartfelt thanks. This institution has given me such a privileged existence. All my colleagues in the School of Design, Communication and IT should be thanked for their support, advice and kindness over the years. The undergrads who have been challenged by my ideas deserve a very large vote of thanks for debating them with me. They have been a tough audience, a hard set of critics and a great pleasure to engage with. I would especially like to thank the honours and postgraduate students who have taken up the opportunities a topic like this presents. For their constant encouragement of my work, I would particularly like to thank Judith Sandner, Susan Kerrigan, Janet Fulton, Chloe Killen, Gaye Sheather, Sarah Coffee, Harry Criticos and, especially, Michael Meany. I have also been fortunate to have had the benefit of John Tulloch's years of experience, which came at just the right moment. His guiding hand has been particularly helpful in bringing this book to completion. He has been a mentor, colleague, critic and friend. Mihaly Csikszentmihalyi also graciously answered my queries and Keith Sawyer, in particular, deserves thanks for not only leading the way but also providing the space for me to contribute. While I was on leave in the United Kingdom working on this book, there were many who, firstly, took my work seriously and, secondly, provided laughter and friendship when it was needed. These friends include Bob Davis, Paul Thompson, Steve Kilpatrick, Rees Archibald and Steve Parker, all from Leeds Metropolitan University. In particular, it is Justin Morey who took my family under his wing and made our stay in England the most memorable we have had. I'd also like to thank Sarah Cohen at Liverpool University, Keith Negus at Goldsmiths College and David Hesmondhalgh at Leeds University for taking the time to engage in dialogue and for giving me the space to present these ideas. Dinners with Phil Tagg were engaging, stimulating and rewarding. I'd also like to thank all the scholars from the Art of Record Production (ARP) who provided welcome conversations and critical input when it was needed. Pam Burnard from Cambridge University was especially encouraging, and I would like to thank her for her contagious enthusiasm and intellectual energy. My children, Kylie, Zoe, Elizabeth, Alexander, Isaac and Benny, keep me in my place and remind me what all this effort is really about. Isaac has willingly taken up the challenge a scriptwriter's life presents and Elizabeth, especially, took on the idea of creativity and made it her own. She writes the way I would like to write. Mum and Dad – I hope it was worth it. Finally, but never last, I want to tell Julie this could not have been done without her love, her constant encouragement and her faith in me. Her willingness to take journeys to all sorts of places makes her the most cherished of all those I love.

This book is based, in part, on some of my previous writings. I would like to thank the various publishers for permission to use parts of the following articles:

McIntyre, P. (2006a) 'Radio Program Directors, Music Directors and the Creation of Popular Music', in S. Healy, B. Berryman & D. Goodman (eds) *Radio in the World: Radio Conference 2005* (Melbourne: RMIT Publishing), pp. 449–60.

McIntyre, P. (2007) 'Copyright and Creativity: Changing Paradigms and the Implications for Intellectual Property and the Music Industry', *Media International Australia Incorporating Cultural Policy*, 123, 82–94.

McIntyre, P. (2008) 'Creativity and Cultural Production: A Study of Contemporary Western Popular Music Songwriting', *Creativity Research Journal*, 20(1), 40–52.

McIntyre, P. (2009a) 'Rethinking the Idea of the Mainstream/Alternative Dichotomy in Contemporary Western Popular Music in the Light of Recent Research into Creativity', in C. Strong & M. Phillipov (eds) *Stuck in the Middle: The Mainstream and Its Discontents, Selected Proceedings of the 2008 IASPM-ANZ Conference* (Brisbane: International Association for the Study of Popular Music), 28–30 November 2008, pp. 142–51.

McIntyre, P. (2009b) 'Rethinking Communication, Creativity and Cultural Production: Outlining Issues for Media Practice', in T. Flew (ed.) *Communication, Creativity and Global Citizenship: Refereed Proceedings of the Australian and New Zealand Communications Association Annual Conference*, Brisbane, July 8–10, http://www.proceedings.anzca09.org. (This work is licensed under the Creative Commons Attribution-Share Alike 2.5 Australian License. To view a copy of this license, visit http://creativecommons.org/licenses/by-sa/2.5/au/ or send a letter to Creative Commons, 171 Second Street, Suite 300, San Francisco, California, 94105, USA.)

Part I

Theories about Creativity and Cultural Production

1
Introductory Perspectives on Creativity

Creativity is not what most people think it is. The creativity I am about to discuss has been researched from a number of perspectives by a number of disciplines. What each of them has had to contend with is a set of common-sense understandings that often colour the way people deal with their own creative action. None more so than in the case of media practice. This disparity between what the research world thinks creativity is and what the rest of the population thinks is one of the problems researchers strike in using the word 'creativity', and then further problems occur in turning that phenomenon of creativity into an object of study. It is one of those words that many people tuck into their lexicon and use as if everybody they encounter understands exactly what they mean. This assumption, that creativity is an unproblematic given, is rarely questioned. In fact it often never occurs to many media scholars or media practitioners, in particular, to question the cultural assumptions on which their understandings of creativity are based.

So how is one to approach creativity? Given many of the views that are current, it would seem to be a daunting task: a task that some argue we shouldn't even attempt as it could possibly take the mystery out of the very thing we are investigating. This is the case especially when the word creativity is associated with artistic activity, so much so that the two terms *artistic* and *creative* are conflated and then used interchangeably and, once again, unproblematically. As Duncan Petrie asserts, artistic activity is 'the popular locus of discussions of creativity, although the idea can and does extend to all forms of human activity' (1991, p. 2). What the research into creativity reveals is that there is overwhelming evidence that all walks of human life, including the sciences, have been involved in creative activity. A simple enough conclusion but one that seems to be difficult to grasp if we continue to

3

follow, and believe in, the common conflations, assumptions and the continuing existence of the *inspirationist* and *Romantic* frames of reference: frames that inform most popular thinking on creativity. From this position the creative process is largely seen as inexplicable and mysterious.

Like the master creator in the Genesis story, or the muse invoked in aspects of the Greco-Roman tradition, creators are seen to have the extraordinary ability to bring into being an idea or an object out of what appears to be nothing. These 'divine' and 'inspirational' ideas of creativity are firmly embedded in Western culture. They can be exemplified by the use of popular images such as the lightning bolt striking, the electric light turning on at the moment the creative idea appears or the use of popular expressions relating to creativity, such as 'a gift from god', or 'a bolt from the blue' or 'tapping into the muse'. These ideas link creativity to the supernatural and suggest that creativity comes about in some way from extraordinary beings conjuring extraordinary things from non-existence.

However, if we take these above views seriously, creativity would seem to be 'not only beyond any scientific understanding, but also impossible' (Boden 1994, p. 75). The existence of extraordinary beings is doubtful and, more practically, it can be seen that the idea that things arise from nowhere is itself highly problematic. The truth is that all matter arises from a set of antecedent conditions. But if there are doubts to be cast on the perspectives that populate the public imagination, the implication must be that there is an adequate alternative perspective that can be reasonably employed to explain creativity.

To begin putting an alternative view in place, one can start by simply stating that when a person is to be creative they must start from somewhere and with something in order to create something. This view also owes much to the Greco-Roman tradition. Writing on 'being' in his *Metaphysics* (1960), Aristotle argued that '...whatever comes to be is generated by the agency of something, out of something, and comes to be something' (1960, p. 142). With this assertion Aristotle's work proved to be 'seminal to the rationalist as well as the naturalist tradition of interpretation' (Rothenberg & Hausman 1976, p. 28) as for him creative acts:

> like other natural and human processes, are explicable in terms of antecedent conditions. It is important to emphasise that Aristotle, unlike Plato, views the resources with which the creative artist begins as both necessary and sufficient to account for all that is found in the created product. (ibid.)

As a more recent and by no means isolated example of this Aristotelian line of reasoning, the definition of creativity provided by Linda Schiffer includes 'the ability to take existing objects and combine them in different ways for new purposes' (Schiffer 1996). She uses the example of Gutenberg and how he, in the process of inventing the printing press, took the mechanisms of the already existing wine press and, combining this with the common die/punch of leatherworkers, concocted his revolutionary printing machine. Through examples such as this Schiffer reinforces the idea that 'creativity is the action of combining previously uncombined elements. From art, music and invention to household chores, this is part of the nature of being creative' (ibid.). She expands this basic definition by stating that creativity can also be seen as 'playing with the way things are interrelated. Creativity is thus the ability to generate novel and useful ideas and solutions to everyday problems and challenges' (ibid.). Putting these ideas together one can say that the generation of novel products is reliant on a series of antecedents.

However, when something is recognised as creative a judgement of some sort must be involved in making that recognition. Judgements, of course, do not occur in a vacuum. The decisions made about what is creative or not creative are always made against a background body of knowledge. It is the value attributed to the novel and unique combination of antecedents by the society creativity occurs within and by the social organisation specifically concerned with the knowledge in which the creativity occurs that eventually accords an act of creativity creative status. Novel objects and ideas which are generated from antecedent conditions are thus only creative within a specific sociocultural framework.

This idea is at the heart of one of the central debates in studies on creativity. The arguments surrounding the debate can be traced, in part, to the idea of consensual validation in preadolescence first suggested by Harry Stack Sullivan during the 1940s (1955, p. 43). Using this idea as a springboard, Morris Stein published an article called 'Creativity and Culture' in *The Journal of Psychology* in the early 1950s in which he worked his way through a definition of creativity that was phrased as follows – 'The creative work is a novel work that is accepted as tenable or useful or satisfying by a group in some point in time' (Stein 1953, p. 311). His general argument suggests that if the only criteria to judge whether a person, product or process is creative or not is that we simply amalgamate past experiences or products to produce something new, then any idea or product, no matter how absurd or bizarre, would qualify as being creative. As many theorists since have contended (Gardner 1993a,

Boden 1994, Csikszentmihalyi 1997), as did Stein, this way of looking at creativity provides no access to what makes the creative product
distinctive in relation to other ideas, products or objects.

Rothenberg and Hausman (1976) also suggest it is the mechanism of
social validation that allows for the differentiation between creative persons, ideas and objects and other merely eccentric or banal entities and
experiences. Simply because a set of ideas or artefacts is combined in a
novel way, this new amalgamation, in and of itself, does not make the
combination creative or interesting. A judgement, based on knowledge
of pre-existing work, needs to be made to distinguish one work from
another. Rothenberg and Hausman suggest that creativity thus:

> involves the translation of our unique gifts, talents and vision into
> an external reality that is new and useful (but) we must keep in
> mind that creativity takes place unavoidably inside our own personal,
> social, and cultural boundaries...Subsumed under the appropriate-
> ness criterion are qualities of fit, utility, and value. (1976, p. 8)

This idea that a creative act, product or process is of value to a society helps explain the way that some creative products are not always
seen as such on their initial introduction to the world. It also helps
explain why one generation will rediscover, and value, what a prior generation saw as merely ordinary. Therefore with the addition of social
confirmation of the originality of a work as a necessary component of a
workable definition of creativity, creativity must then be recognised as
being spatio-temporally dependent and thus contextually based. What a
particular society values in innovation will influence the decisions being
made about what is seen as creative, and the fundamental operation of
this value distinction within a society also makes creativity itself culturally relative, 'since what is valued by one person or social group may or
may not be valued – praised, preserved, promoted – by another' (Boden
1994, p. 77).

Putting aside this relativist argument for a moment, it can also be
seen that if one sees some creative work as extraordinary, one must
also make a distinction between this work and the ordinary processes
you or I undertake in being creative. This concern with differentiating
between socially or culturally validated forms of creativity and creativity that is individually based has led to sets of distinctions being used by
researchers which differentiate between what are perceived as extraordinary forms of creativity and those that seem to be more mundane.
Commenting on these distinctions, Rothenberg and Hausman assert

that if creativity is conceptualised as being equal to general qualities such as spontaneity and openness, then we should be looking at creativity as an aspect of all individuals. However, if creativity is thought of as 'requiring radical change, productive of far-reaching new-value, then we should confine our study to special talent or genius' (Rothenberg & Hausman 1976, p. 8). This dilemma has led to a number of bipolar oppositions being used to account for the difference between 'ordinary' creativity and 'extraordinary' creativity. Sometimes these differences are characterised as ordinary versus extraordinary, paradigm-shifting versus garden-variety or big 'C' versus little 'c' creativity.

Looking at the same set of differentiations Margaret Boden (1994) applied a further set of names to the same phenomena. For her the first form is what she labels P-creativity and for her it is psychological in basis. P-creativity is valuable if that person hasn't had that idea before. It is irrelevant to the individual if other people have had the idea and how many times they've had the idea. On the other hand, Boden's second category, historical creativity, or what she calls H-creativity, possesses value if it is both P creative and if no-one in human history has ever had the idea before.

It should be noted that H-creativity is thus the most difficult to pin down as many ideas attributed to one person have in fact been partially attributable to others (Charles Darwin's work on evolution being a prime example) and as some creative ideas have been lost or simply misunderstood at one point in time and then resurfaced later (Bach's musical pieces and their eventual recognition as significant works serves as an example here). However, Boden makes the pertinent observation that it is these vagaries of recognition that make it hard to systematically explain H-creativity. Nonetheless, the most important aspect of her ideas can be seen in the statement that 'there can be no psychological explanation of this historical category. But all H-creative ideas, by definition, are P-creative too' (Boden 1994, p. 77). Boden's distinctions not only give a useful framework for explaining paradigm shifting examples of creativity, but they also importantly highlight the similarities that exist between what were thought to be supposedly different ways of being creative. In doing so she does away with the bipolar oppositions that see extraordinary creativity as somehow being both quantitatively and qualitatively different to ordinary creative acts. By explaining H-creativity as a related extension of normal everyday personal creativity, Boden adds support to the idea that creativity may not be simply the result of operating within some universally transcendent process but is, in part, a matter of selection through a process of judgement that is contextually dependent and is thus a grounded and therefore more fathomable process.

With these assumptions on board it is still, nonetheless, desirable to also make an analytical distinction between the contexts of discovery, the origin of an idea as it were, as opposed to its social validation, in order to concentrate on the mechanisms of the introduction of novelty. In doing so the concern then becomes primarily oriented towards asking how an idea actually arose. Was the idea generated from pre-existing forms or did it arrive via some other means? Without going too far into the field of computational psychology, or even revisiting the idealist philosophies of Plato (1937), it could be stated that Boden's position, in particular, holds to the idea that form is a precursor to creativity. She asserts that exemplary creativity deals not only with rearranging the elements within the form in some unique way but also in actually rearranging the form. From this point she not only argues that it is possible to distinguish between first-time novelty and radical originality without resorting to bipolar oppositions, but she also asserts that, given the dependence of antecedent condition in the creative process, what were previously seen as constraining factors must also be seen as enabling ones. She argues:

> the ascription of creativity always involves tacit or explicit reference to some specific generative system. It follows, too, that constraints – far from being opposed to creativity – make creativity possible. To throw away all constraints would be to destroy the capacity for creative thinking. Random processes alone, if they happen to produce anything interesting at all, can result only in first-time curiosities, not radical surprises. (This is not to deny that, in the context of background constraints, randomness can sometimes contribute to creativity [Boden 1990, ch 9].) (1994, pp. 78–9)

Evans and Deehan (1988), in also attempting to come to grips with how to characterise creativity, indicate that there is an abundance of ways to tackle the problem. However, to make matters a little easier, they suggest that creativity has generally been looked at from two basic directions. Firstly, there is that associated with 'product' or 'output'. Creativity is simply what creative people do and can thus be seen in the objects made by creative people. 'We use intelligence and the imagination to make up something new, fresh and lasting, transforming the old into something better' (Evans & Deehan 1988, p. 37). Creators in this sense replace what has gone prior with something new, innovative and improved.

The second way to conceptualise creativity, as Evans and Deehan suggest, is based on the notion of personal potential. The self-actualising individual is creative. This notion includes a wide range of individuals, not just those normally accepted as creative. It goes beyond looking at artists and inventors to include anyone 'who fulfils his or her potential, who expresses an inner drive or capacity, (and) who strikes out into unknown psychological territory' (Evans & Deehan 1998, p. 37) as creative individuals. This latter appraisal however doesn't aid greatly in isolating what it is to be creative as it can be argued that all individuals in order to grow and learn, eventually, it is hoped, become self-actualising (Maslow 1968).

Despite some of the evident problems with these ways of seeing creativity they can both be categorised as person-centred. Adopting the person-centred perspective often leads to questions about whether the creative individual is gifted or whether they are simply exercising acquired skills. Or to put it another way, as Evans and Deehan do, can creativity be seen as a matter of perspiration or inspiration? In their view:

> creativity and creative ways of thinking are skills that can be developed and refined; conscious application is needed, not the vagaries of 'inspiration', in order to achieve a creative output; creative people tend to view their work in its cultural, intellectual or historical context; originality is not novelty for its own sake, and to qualify for the description 'creative' a product must have inherent value. (1988, pp. 38–9)

The characteristics of creativity included in the above extract certainly provide an alternative to the inspirational view. Rothenberg and Hausman, however, provide a few additions. They state that 'minimally... creativity consists of the capacity for, or state of, bringing something into being' (1976, p. 6). In addition this 'bringing something into being involves at least three separable components: an agent, a process, and a product' (ibid.). One could also claim that there are at least three aspects of creativity which correlate closely with those components listed by Rothenberg and Hausman. Schiffer argues:

> The creative process, receiving the most attention, focuses on the mechanisms and phases involved as one partakes in a creative act. A second aspect of creativity is the creative person. Here, personality traits of creative people are central. The environmental atmosphere

and influence are concerns of a third aspect, the creative situation. Lastly, the criteria or characteristics of creative products have been sought. (1996)

These divisions therefore give any study of creativity corresponding foci of interest: the creative person, the creative process and the created object. Many studies focus on more than one area and as would be expected there are subdivisions within these basic three. For instance, in terms of process it is possible to look at different (but interrelated) dimensions or levels of dynamics with which one can create. The first is:

> ... the system which may be a particular medium (e.g. oil painting or a particular musical form), or a particular process (like a problem solving agenda, or an approach to creativity like Synectics). The creative person manipulates that means to a creative end. The second dimension is described by the conceptual 'content' which the medium describes. Again, the creative person depicts, changes, manipulates, expresses somehow the idea of that content. (Schiffer 1996)

Howard Gardner takes these ideas a step further by proposing that to investigate creative persons, products or processes, each can be looked at in what he terms four distinct disciplinary perspectives. He lists these as the subpersonal, the personal, the impersonal and the multipersonal.

Firstly, the creative individual can be investigated in terms of neurobiological factors, that is, on a subpersonal level. Secondly, a psychological investigation can be made, focusing on cognitive aspects, personality, motivation, will and other psychological features of the human person. Thirdly, the domain of knowledge that a creative individual interacts with can be explored. Gardner explains that 'so long as there exists structures of knowledge and/or of performances, which can be so specified that a novice can acquire expertise' (1993a, p. 34), it is these structures that can be labelled domains. They are impersonal in as much as they can be contained in a non-living entity like a textbook. Lastly, he describes what he terms the multipersonal. This level looks at the 'complex of individuals and institutions which pass judgement on the various products in the domain' (Gardner 1993a, p. 35).

Another way to frame a typology of creativity is to use Gardner's ideas as a base and see a continuum leading from an emphasis on the individual through to an emphasis on the contextual, and the role each plays in the creative process. This way of analysing the available perspectives on creativity becomes particularly useful when examining the literature, as most ideas contained there can be categorised within one or two of these particular areas on the continuum from individual to contextual responsibility. For example, work has begun to be accomplished in neurobiology on the connection between the way the brain works and the experience of creativity. In addition, psychological approaches to the nature of extraordinary creators can be linked back to earlier evolutionary work and the psychological state of remarkable innovators linking genius, for example, to insanity. The refutation of these ideas, and the developments within cognitive, personality and social psychology, has been particularly useful in the study of creativity. Sociology has not been idle in this area either with some challenging work being conducted on the nature of creativity itself disputing, for example, the investigation of the myth of individual genius. This work has laid the foundation for an increasingly Copernican and thus contextual interpretation of creativity. Furthermore, the notion that creation needs to be reconceptualised goes hand in glove with many post-structuralist points of view which have loudly cried for the 'death of the author'. Needless to say the reconceptualisation of the author, or creator, was an attempt to displace the Romantic view where the responsibility for creativity was seen to be centred solely on the individual. This is best exemplified by the creator-genius model. Since all of these perspectives, these ways of defining and analysing creativity, need to be examined in some detail and since the genius model has persisted for some time we will firstly turn our attention to it.

2
The Creator as Genius

Robert Albert and Mark Runco, when investigating the history and research into creativity, assert that:

> By the end of the eighteenth century, it was concluded that whereas many persons may have talent of one sort or another and that this talent would be responsive to education, original genius was truly exceptional and by definition was to be exempt from the rules, customs and obligations that applied to the talented. (Sternberg 1999, p. 21)

Robert Weisberg concurs stating that:

> the literature on creativity was until recently dominated by what one could call the 'genius' view of creativity, which also pervades our society. This view, which has many sources, ranging from Plato to Koestler to Osborn to psychometric theorists such as Guildford, assumes that truly creative acts involve extraordinary individuals carrying out extraordinary thought processes. These individuals are called geniuses, and the psychological characteristics they possess – cognitive and personality characteristics – make up what is called genius. (Sternberg 1999, p. 148)

This idea of genius is underpinned by two widespread views of creativity still in common use in the West. One of these is labelled the *inspirationist* view while the other has been labelled the *Romantic* view (Boden 2004, p. 14). Many times there is such a deeply held belief in these views that a reasoned investigation of creativity appears to be not only wrong-headed but almost sacrilegious. Margaret Boden, for one, contends that 'these views are believed by many to be literally true. But they are rarely critically examined. They are not theories, so much as *myths*: imaginative constructions' (ibid.).

If this is the case, where did they come from? To answer that question we need to firstly cast our minds back to the world of the Greeks. Plato, writing about inspiration in the fourth century BC, set the stage for what became a persistent belief in a complex relationship of creativity with the supernatural or the divine. He himself believed that inspiration came from beyond the individual and did so usually when that individual was out of their senses or working beyond reason. Noting that Greeks believed poetry to be one of the highest forms of human expression, Plato stated in his 'Dialogue with Ion' that the muse was the lodestone all poets were searching for and the source of inspiration they had to be intimately connected to:

> She first makes men inspired, and then through these inspired ones others share in the enthusiasm, and a chain is formed, for the epic poets, all the good ones, have their excellence, not from art, but are inspired, possessed, and thus they utter all these admirable poems.... A poet is a light and winged thing, and holy, and never able to compose until he has become inspired, and is beside himself, and reason is no longer in him. So long as he has this in his possession, no man is able to make poetry or to chant in prophecy...these lovely poems are not of man or human workmanship, but are divine and from the gods, and that poets are nothing but interpreters of the gods, each one possessed by the divinity to whom he is in bondage. (Plato 1971, p. 220)

This inspirationist view, that a creator must be undisciplined and almost mad while waiting to be divinely inspired, is still with us today. From this inspirationist perspective, it must be the extraordinary being with extraordinary gifts who is more likely to have access to the muse and thus to creativity. It is from this narrative that the genius model arises.

If one traces the etymology of the word 'genius', it can be seen that it shifted meaning over a number of centuries, from being a literal term derived from Latin for the spirits that inhabit people and places, to become a description of a spirit, similar to the muse, that influences a person in both good and evil ways, to then becoming a term for a person endowed with a particular spirit or power, most often thought to be exceptional intellectual or creative powers (OED 2010). This latter power is ascribed to individuals 'who are esteemed greatest in any department' (ibid.). It is little wonder then that genius figures are associated with God-given or spirit-like talents evident in the work they produce and the lives they lead. Despite all the arguments and evidence to the contrary, this perception appears to still be embedded in Western common-sense belief systems.

One of the dominant discourses in the West is that of the Judeo-Christian tradition. One of the fundamental tenets of this belief system is that the world was bought into being from non-existence. There are not too many in the West who are not familiar with the story that starts, 'in the beginning, God created the heavens and the earth . . . '. This story is fundamental to centuries of understanding. It recognises the possibility of all things being able to be made or created from non-existence. Once the notion of genius can be seen as analogous to that of the creator myth, then it also becomes acceptable that creativity itself can be conceived of as a spiritual and mystical process directly connected to extraordinary individuals with god-like powers. These individuals have, for a number of largely unknowable reasons, access to that process. Since God also 'created man in his image' it is a small enough step to take, and then accept, that a few rare individuals working under divine inspiration can create astounding objects, ideas and concepts that have their genesis in a realm beyond mere mortals.

However, for Immanuel Kant (1982), whose name has become inextricably tied to the field of aesthetics and thus for our purposes to the notion of genius, there is a disconnection with the biblical or Platonic idea that the source of a creator's genius comes from a divine external source. He instead insisted that the locus of creativity could be found internally, in:

> a unique and spontaneous act that introduces a leap in ordinary natural processes . . . the creator gives the rule to his work; he generates his style and the significance of the product in accordance with his freely functioning imagination. [Furthermore] creation of art is not only independent of prior procedures or rules, but it is independent of all conditions other than spontaneous activity made possible through faculties in the creator's consciousness. (Rothenberg & Housman 1976, p. 29)

This move away from creativity being driven by an external force working on the individual, such as a muse, a tutelary spirit or indeed the Christian God, towards an emphasis on the unknowable internal landscape of the creator was a powerful one.

By the 1700s there was a growing rejection in some circles of ratio-
nalism and a move towards the idea that intuition and emotion may be
the best way into a 'real' experience of the world, and according to Peter
Watson (2005), the West is still living with the ramifications of this rejection. For him 'the rival ways of looking at the world – the cool, detached
light of disinterested scientific reason, and the red-blooded, passionate creations of the artist – constitute the modern incoherence' (2005,
p. 610). Elizabeth Paton summarises much of this strong intellectual
tradition, which valorised the passionate above the rational, in her own
research into creativity and fiction writing. She suggests that a number
of philosophers vital to Romanticism, including Kant, Rousseau, Goethe
and Schiller, 'proposed a return to nature and authenticity and a reliance
on feelings, instinct and subjective thought ... [but] the Romantic movement did not explicitly oppose rationality' (2008, p. 23). She cites the
examples of Coleridge who, in his *Biographia Literaria*, incorporated elements of empiricism and foreshadowed the work of Freud. However,
Paton notes that 'despite the inherent complexities of the Romantic movement, a distinction between reason and instinct/intuition has
persisted' (2008, p. 24).

In pushing reason aside with the idea that 'creativity bubbles up from
an irrational unconscious, and that rational deliberation interferes with
the creative process' (Sawyer 2006, p. 15), the emphasis shifted from
discovering the truth of experience rationally towards thinking that
individual artists were motivated by an 'inner muse that was beyond
conscious control' (ibid., p. 16). For the nineteenth-century Romantics
in particular, who did not want to be shackled to the de-humanising
and apparently deterministic world they saw in the increasingly indus-
trialised world around them, the desire for self-determination had given
way to self-expression and self-discovery, leaving the individual at the
heart of the creative process. The question then arose for them as to
what makes one individual different from the other in terms of creative
capability. What, in essence, marked artists off as special? Since many
Romantics distanced themselves from a society they perceived to be utilitarian and philistine, it was this very distancing and ensuing isolation
'that served to fuel ideas of split personality and opposing selves, an
allusion to popular notions of artistic creativity as intrinsically linked to
pain, suffering and madness' (Petrie 1991, p. 3):

> The notion of creativity driven by feelings and intuition was main-
> tained in later forms of Romanticism, drawing on the lives and works
> of earlier artists who came to represent stereotypes of artistic genius.

Commemorated in work by Wordsworth, Coleridge, Shelley, Keats and Rossetti, the English poet Thomas Chatterton became a symbol of the suffering of misunderstood genius after his suicide in 1770; a related stereotype of highly sensitive and passionate genius was influenced by Goethe's ([1774] 1990) fictional hero Werther who relied on pure feeling but was also driven to suicide; although disdainful of many of the central tenets of Romanticism, Byron embodied another aspect of the stereotypical Romantic genius, that of the social deviant permitted to live and act outside the realm of accepted social behaviour because of his artistic contributions. (Paton 2008, p. 24)

From the Romantic point of view, 'it is the artist who creates, who expresses himself, who creates values. The artist does not discover, calculate, deduce, as the scientist (or philosopher) does. In creating, the artist invents his goal and then realises his own path toward that goal' (Watson 2005, p. 609). For the Romantic artist, as Margaret Boden suggests, 'intuitive talent is innate, a gift that can be squandered but cannot be acquired – or taught' (2004, p. 15). However, she believes that this way of seeing creativity is defeatist as it implies that 'the most we can do to encourage creativity is to identify the people with this special talent, and give them room to work. Any more active fostering of creativity is inconceivable' (ibid.).

Both positions, the inspirationist and the Romantic, have led to the stereotypical view of the quasi-neurotic artist existing in their garret waiting for the muse to arrive or inspiration to strike (Zolberg 1990, pp. 109–10). However, this is a conception of a creative person, and from there, creative activity, that is difficult to sustain when one examines in detail the lives of those our own particular social and cultural grouping considered to be exceptionally creative. This examination has been carried out a number of times but is best exemplified in the work of Howard Gardner, as set out in his book *Creating Minds: An Anatomy of Creativity Seen through the Lives of Freud, Einstein, Picasso, Stravinsky, Eliot, Graham and Gandhi* (1993). While Gardner's, and many others' (e.g. Howe 1999), ideas have moved much closer to seeing creativity emanating from a multifactorial process, the general acceptance of the inspirational and Romantic view led, in part, to scientific work during the nineteenth century which concentrated on the question of what made the creative individual different to other individuals. Explanations were pursued to reveal the character of the phenomenon of genius with an assumed belief that since genius was extraordinary the next logical place to look for it would be in deviant behaviour and, of course, the most deviant form of behaviour was insanity. Cesare Lombroso (1891) was a central figure in this process.

Lombroso, a psychiatrist and Professor of Legal Medicine at the University of Turin writing at the turn of the nineteenth century, approached his research on genius utilising the biological theories in vogue at the time. He believed that the physical degeneration of the brain was the cause of abnormal functioning in the individual. Since by definition genius was certainly 'abnormal', then logically the two, genius and insanity, must be connected. Lombroso then set about documenting the abnormal behaviour of 'men of genius'. He argued there was a 'resemblance between insanity and genius' (1984, p. 66) and thus one could conclude that the thought processes of genius were not rational but generally instinctive and unconscious. Despite the dubiousness of some of these claims the link between deviance, insanity and creativity was thought to be established.

This idea was not lost on Sigmund Freud. In his paper 'Creative Writers and Day-Dreaming' (Freud in Strachey 1953, p. 75), Freud attempted to explain what gifted individuals do in terms of quasi-neuroses. He proposed that writers, and by implication all creators, were like children at play. He argued that the creative writer:

> creates a world of phantasy which he takes very seriously – that is, which he invests with large amounts of emotion – while separating it sharply from reality. Language has preserved this relationship between children's play and poetic creation. It designates certain kinds of imaginative creation concerned with tangible objects and capable of representation. As 'plays'; the people who present them are called players. (Freud quoted in Rothenberg & Hausman 1976, p. 49)

He adds that 'every child at play behaves like a creative writer. In that he creates a world of his own, or, rather, rearranges the things of his world in a new way which pleases him' (ibid.). Freud claimed that this activity on the part of the creative writer is driven by wish fulfilment. According to Arthur Berger, Freud argued that in many creative productions 'the original daydream that generated the story is greatly disguised' (1995, p. 159). However, in the end, 'the creative production can be traced back to some strong experience, usually had in childhood, that generated a wish that eventually is fulfilled in the creative work' (ibid.). In essence, the 'Freudian tradition in psychology sees the artist driven by unconscious motivations – a quasi-neurotic who channels his near-pathology into a socially permissible path' (Zolberg 1990, pp. 109–10).

Duncan Petrie however calls Freud's explanation for creativity into question and argues that Freud was working under the sway of the Romantic ideal. In regarding the artist as a neurotic:

> Freud was merely adopting a popular belief of his age – an expression of industrial rationalisation and bourgeois philistinism. In relating the creative powers of the artist to neurosis, Freud is effectively providing what amounts to a medicalised re-reading of the Romantic agony. (Petrie 1991, p. 5)

Petrie further argues that Freud can be criticised for thinking of art as existing *only* in its relation to 'the individual who produced or contemplated a particular work. The objective role of social conditions and the process of production itself are practically ignored' (Petrie 1991, p. 5). Furthermore, since the Freudian view suggests that 'creative individuals are inclined (or compelled) to sublimate much of their libidinal energy' (Gardner 1993, p. 24) to creative activity, and since it is assumed that this activity is an unconscious process, it can be asserted that the individuals involved do so with little intention. However, as will be argued later, this position strips them of their freedom to make artistic choices, that is, it strips them of their creative agency. It also leaves little room for distinguishing the 'effective artist or scientist from the ineffective or banal one' (Gardner 1993, p. 25).

In attempting to resolve this problem Robert Weisberg argues that there is no distinction to be made between the thought processes of ordinary individuals and that of the extra-ordinary figures who make startling and unusual leaps in creativity. In his book *Creativity: Beyond the Myth of Genius* (1993), Weisberg set out four areas of creative thought that, to his mind, explain the similarities rather than the distinctions. Firstly, Weisberg argued that all 'attempts to solve problems are based on past experience' (Weisberg 1993, pp. 152–3). People engaged in creative activity initiate work on problems by matching the problem to their knowledge base and solutions come about in an evolutionary way not a revolutionary way. Secondly, he asserts the process 'based on local memory search is set in motion by feedback concerning the inadequacy of some proposed solution' (ibid.). Thirdly, the new information brought into existence alters the arena in which the problem now occurs, and this new information presents the possible new solution. Finally, he goes on to say that if solutions to problems are 'creative' because 'they are novel and they meet the demands of the problem, then the capacity to think creatively must be a basic human capacity, and not the exotic trait or skill envisioned by the "genius" view' (Weisberg 1993, pp. 152–3).

Using these four steps as a guide Weisberg then explores in some detail the work of a few noted 'genius' figures. He examines Watson and Crick's discovery of the double helix model of DNA which set off a revolution in molecular biology, Darwin's theory of evolution, Edison's invention of the kinetoscope and Picasso's painting of Guernica. Through an appraisal of these selected examples he presents documentary evidence of the thought processes of these noted creators. He contends that while these discoveries and works were highly important for their fields, in all these cases 'one sees nothing like the creative leaps postulated by the genius view' (Weisberg 1993, p. 168). Instead novel products, be they paintings, scientific theories or inventions, started out as simple extensions of what had preceded them. 'The initial conception then underwent modification, until something new emerged' (ibid.). Weisberg sees the idea of the flash of genius, the leap of creative insight, the lightning bolt of divine inspiration as nothing more than a slowly evolving and incremental cognitive process, only recognised at the moment of illumination. Strokes of genius 'are firmly embedded within an extended process of becoming one with and synthesising from existing elements' (Negus and Pickering 2004, p. 158). Consequently, if only the illumination aspect of creativity is consciously recognised, then it would seem appropriate to explain creativity in terms of this alone. But once creativity is seen as an evolving process involving a complex set of factors, then it would seem that remarkable insights are within the grasp of all given the right circumstances.

In many ways, Weisberg's ideas accord with the neo-Darwinian view of creativity presented by Dean Keith Simonton (Brockman 1993). Simonton also attempts to explode the view of the mythic genius figure. He argues that ideas, concepts, memories, feelings and so on are subject to the same sorts of permutations and variations that occur in biology in genetic mutations. These permutations or variations happen haphazardly and the 'blind variations are then subject to a consistent selection process which eliminates those ideas, thoughts and so on that lack adaptive fitness' (Simonton in Brockman 1993, p. 178). Simonton suggests that, 'there must exist within the creator's mind some stable criteria by which to winnow out the true, beautiful, or useful variations from those that are false, ugly or impractical' (ibid.). Here they make judgements drawing on pre-existing sets of social and cultural knowledges. Once judgements have been made the variations have to be preserved and reproduced, that is, they have to be retained. Therefore, there is a two-step process that occurs in creative thinking. Firstly, blind variation produces the possible permutations and, secondly, selective retention chooses and stores the information. Simonton cites cases of highly creative individuals ruminating, pondering and worrying at problems for extended periods and suggests that in this rumination there is not one dominant style of thinking taking place. According to Simonton it is freely associational since, in order to produce as many variations as possible, creative cogitation must encompass a significant range of thought processes. This process not only occurs internally, that is, within the mind of the creator, but once an object or idea is manifest in the world it too follows the same evolutionary process. All of the papers, products, ideas and artworks that are produced are selected by 'appreciators, audiences, patrons, or colleagues' (Simonton in Brockman 1993, p. 184). Some works will convince this field of their worth and others will simply fail in this endeavour. It follows, argues Simonton, that a creative individual must be prolific in order to merit 'genius' status, since one exceptional feature that marks a genius 'is there astonishing productivity' (Brockman 1993, p. 185). This productivity not only increases the chances of their work being selected but it also increases the fallibility of these genius figures and thus rehumanises them in their willingness to make mistakes (Negus & Pickering 2004, p. 159). They do so many times in the trial-and-error process which produces the one idea that will lead to exceptional creativity or, using the older conception, gain them the status of 'genius'.

What these arguments tend to indicate is that there may not be as radical a disjuncture between what ordinary people do and the supposed extraordinary powers of the astonishing genius. This assertion confirms Margaret Boden's characterisation of H-creativity, that is, creativity deemed to be historically important, as an extension of P-creativity, the type that ordinary people personally engage in. Nonetheless, if we pursue for a moment the idea that the experience of genius may be qualitatively different from other forms of creativity, an examination of where an assumption of the veracity of this idea has led will expose the supposed connection between, for example, intelligence and the notion of genius. Pursuing this idea will then lead us to another. That is, above-average intellectual ability is thought to be a significant distinguishing factor between P-creativity and H-creativity or personal creativity and paradigm shifting creativity. If this is the case, then one would expect that there would be a direct correlation between high intelligence and 'genius'. But this assertion doesn't appear to be the case.

The problem with linking high intelligence and so-called 'genius' can be exemplified by investigating an organisation like MENSA. MENSA, a club for highly intelligent people, was founded in England in 1946 with 'the idea of forming a society for bright people' (MENSA 2010). The only qualification for membership is to have an IQ in the top 2 per cent of the population. MENSA has around 110,000 members in 100 countries throughout the world, and there are active MENSA organisations in over 40 countries on every continent except Antarctica. One would expect to see in an organisation such as this a high proportion of what have been termed genius figures. However, there is simply no one prevailing characteristic among these members:

> The range is staggering. Mensa has professors and truck drivers, scientists and firefighters, computer programmers and farmers, artists, military people, musicians, laborers, police officers, glassblowers – the diverse list goes on and on. There are famous Mensans and prize-winning Mensans, but there are many whose names you wouldn't know. (MENSA 2010)

If an organisation like this can't boast a significant number of genii on its roster, then it would seem that the direct correlation made between genius and intelligence may be somewhat tenuous. However, the idea that high intelligence and genius are linked can also be problematised by investigating the notion of intelligence itself. Intelligence, according to Haralambos and Holbern, has been defined as 'abstract reasoning ability' and it is argued that it is 'a selection of just one portion of the total spectrum of human mental abilities' (1995, p. 746). They go on to state that it is 'the ability to discover the rules, patterns, and logical principles underlying objects and events, and the ability to apply these discoveries to solve problems' (ibid.). They also point out that IQ tests, of the type initially proposed by Binet in the nineteenth century, have become questionable measures of this facility and instead measure knowledge and memory, not the ability to reason. While there are also a number of cross-cultural problems with these measurements it is usually agreed that intelligence is attributable to both genetic and environmental factors (1995, p. 747). Robert Sternberg and Linda O'Hara, after summarising over a century of work in psychology on the relationship between creativity and intelligence, including their own research, conclude that:

> ... psychologists still have not reached a consensus on the nature of the relation between creativity and intelligence, nor even of exactly what these constructs are. All possible set relations between creativity and intelligence have been proposed, and there is at least some

evidence to support each of them. The negative side of this state of affairs is that we can say little with certainty about the relation between creativity and intelligence. (Sternberg & O'Hara in Sternberg 1999, p. 269)

This conclusion indicates that there may indeed be other factors apart from intelligence that can be used to account for exemplary creators. One of these may be talent.

H.J. Walberg, writing in a paper entitled 'Creativity and Talent as Learning' (Sternberg 1988), makes a subtle distinction between creativity and talent, but nonetheless sees creativity being dependent on talent no matter whether that talent is constitutional or acquired. Talent, in this view, is malleable and can be enhanced and developed by practice and persistence. The corollary is that 'genius', the possession of exceptional intellectual or creative power or other natural ability or tendency, can be at least partially learned. Walberg argues that highly creative individuals have been exposed to the field they have become experts in and they continually practice the knowledges and operations within that field. As he contends:

Creativity may involve rare rather than unique accomplishments, and it may be useful to think of it as being on one end of a continuum of performance or learning that is attainable by nearly anyone with sufficient instruction and perseverance ... Linguistic and other environments, especially if they are enduring and powerful, strongly shape accomplishments; societies and individuals, moreover, can choose or determine their environments. Contrary to the notion of instant creativity that was popular in the 1960's, distinguished accomplishment seems partly a matter of continuous and concentrated effort over a decade or more. (Walberg in Sternberg 1988, p. 345)

Walberg then goes on to state that simple perseverance, which Negus and Pickering also characterise as 'obsessive powers of concentration' (2004, p. 158), may not be adequate in and of itself to achieve exceptional creativity. However, while other abilities such as good problem-solving techniques, aesthetic ability and originality may play a part, this does not mean that perseverance and practice can be entirely negated. Walberg also asserts that most people are talented but usually only in one or two specialised areas, a notion supported by Weisberg (1993), Gardner (1993) and Csikszentmihalyi (1997). There also seems to be an application in terms of creativity of the 'Matthew Effect'. This concept, proposed by R.K. Merton (1968), was a simple adaptation from the Gospel of St Matthew. It functions on 'the principle of cumulative advantage' (Gorny 2007) and in effect states that 'the rich get richer'. If a person is given the right start and their specialised talents are encouraged and enhanced, by practice, and they also persevere with their access to these specialised knowledges, they will develop their creativity commensurately. In essence Walberg's position is that 'environments affect growth and growth affects environments' (Sternberg 1988, p. 350). In the end it may simply be that 'geniuses' are those who have been presented with opportunities and, given the necessary talent and characteristics adequate to the task, presumably taken those opportunities.

Weisberg concurs with these observations when he concludes his work on what he calls the 'myth of genius' by stating that commitment and expertise are essential to creative insight. He asserts that 'great innovations in science and the arts were almost invariably produced by individuals who possessed strong motivation and persistence' (Weisberg in Sternberg 1988, p. 173). These individuals include a list of notable individuals such as Darwin, Picasso, Edison, Einstein and Beethoven, among many others. Weisberg rightly argues that each of these people spent lifetimes effectively operating in their respective fields and their extraordinary achievements, the thing that earned them the title 'genius', came about at least in part as a result of that lifetime of commitment to their work. For Weisberg 'commitment provides sufficient time for the small changes that occur as one gathers experience in some domain to evolve into something truly original and innovative'(1988, p. 173). He goes on to say that 'creative products are firmly based on what came before. True originality evolves as the individual goes beyond what others had done before' (ibid.). The paradox here is, of course, that the instigation of a novel product, idea or process, harking back to Aristotle's formulation of what constitutes being, is dependent on what pre-exists it. The new is in fact dependent on the old. If this is the case, anyone wishing to be creative should first of all make themselves as familiar as they can with the old, that is, all of the accumulated material that pre-exists, and could contribute, to their idea. This immersion in what precedes them will aid in providing the necessary background to allow the individual to undertake work in that area, and it also serves to suggest possibilities for modifying and altering earlier products. Weisberg asserts that, in reality, 'all scientists and artists have extensive training either formally or informally, and very few individuals make a mark in the world without a relatively long commitment to an area beyond their actual training' (Weisberg in Sternberg 1988, p. 173). If this is the case, one must then turn to the acquisition of skill, the mastering of skill and from there the ability to see beyond the paradigms of the rules, forms and structures the creator works within in order to explain exemplary creativity.

According to Sharon Bailin (1988) once the symbol system the creator is engaged with is mastered, the truly creative individual is capable of paradigm shifting innovation. In this regard Bailin argues, in a manner similar to Weisberg, that 'new ground is broken in a field by critical judgement, but this judgement is itself based upon a repertoire of acquired and assimilated skills in the discipline' (Bailin 1988, p. 96). She insists:

> there is not a real discontinuity between achieving highly within the rules of a discipline and achieving highly when it entails going beyond or changing some rules. The latter is, rather, an extension of the former. It would be incorrect to view any discipline or creative activity as taking place within rigid boundaries and being totally delimited and defined by rules. Instead, the possibilities for what can be achieved are really open-ended. Furthermore, one never breaks down all the rules, since to do so would be to abandon the discipline. (1988, p. 96)

It appears then that the distinction to be drawn between creative and uncreative works is that a creative individual who produces these works must have a genuine understanding of the skills techniques, conventions and traditions of the discipline they are working in (Bailin 1988, p. 97). In this case the skills base would also encompass critical judgement and, as Bailin argues, in order to shift the creative paradigms of a discipline the artist or creator must be highly skilled, at the leading edge of the discipline and possess a real understanding of that discipline (ibid.).

This position, it could be argued, also leaves little room to account for what has been termed naive or primitive art, or for the existence of child prodigies. However, in an article entitled 'Creativity and Knowledge: A Challenge to Theories', Robert Weisberg (Sternberg 1999) once again presents evidence that even so-called child prodigies immerse themselves in the domains in which they have been acclaimed rather than simply arriving fully formed, cognisant and competent within a particular domain. He cites the case of Mozart. Weisberg argues that most of Mozart's early work, the work that gives him his reputation as a child prodigy, was not creative in the sense that it broke new ground. According to Weisberg:

> Mozart's first masterwork as identified by Hayes (1989) was the Piano Concerto no.9 K.271. This piece was composed more than ten years into Mozart's career, when he was 21 years old. Mozart's first four piano concertos (K. 37, 39, 40, 41) were produced in June–July, 1767; Mozart's age was 11. However, calling these works piano concertos by Mozart is misleading, since they contain no original music by him...they were merely arranged by Mozart for a new combination of instruments.... This pattern of development indicates that Mozart's earliest musical experiences involved immersion in the work of others, and probably involved use of the earlier composers' works as models for how certain compositional problems could be handled. This activity could be considered deliberate practice, under the direction of Mozart's father, an established musician of some renown, who could be considered a master teacher. In addition, since the young Mozart was also a performer, he probably played these works in his performances, producing still deeper immersion. (Weisberg in Sternberg 1999, pp. 235–6)

These details are confirmed by Michael Howe in his book *Genius Explained* (1999, pp. 3–7). At the seemingly opposite end of the spectrum naive or primitive artists are generally seen to be ignorant of the academic rules pertaining to the professional artist. This ignorance, however, may only be partial since they could not be ignorant of the entirety of the conventions and codes of art. They must take on board enough knowledge of the domain of art to engage with the skills required to manipulate the paints, the canvas and the subjects that in themselves entitle them to be called 'artists'. Oto Bihali-Merin contends that 'all art is naive to begin with' (1984, p. 17) and it is when 'those artists who are sufficiently talented to achieve a certain mastery' (1984, p. 18) do so that they cease to be classified as naive artists. From this it can be argued that while naive artists exhibit a certain decorative art-lessness and display rudimentary skills in relation to professional artists they, nonetheless, still possess skills. They therefore must at some stage have immersed themselves in the domain of art to a degree that enabled them to engage with it in the first place. In this way craft and art, amateur and professional, draw on the same skills base albeit with differing expertise. The recognition that these are not separate and isolable activities once again reinforces the idea P-creativity proceeds along the same continuum as H-creativity. It could thus be proposed that 'the ordinary is not at odds with the exceptional, but continually open to the possibility of becoming exceptional' (Negus & Pickering 2004, p. 158).

In summing these ideas up it can be said that both Bailin's and Weisberg's views, outlined briefly above, correspond to the conception that creativity is the use of imagination, expertise and perseverance to make something new and fresh, transforming the old into something novel or original which may then lead to astounding cultural works. It is the conception of creative genius as an unknowable, mystical process, a view aligned with both the inspirational Platonic view and the Romantic ideal, which is problematic here. This is not to say that extraordinary work does not happen. It just means there is a necessity to think of it differently. We need to go beyond the idea of the artist as a specially gifted individual creative worker, engaged in some supra-human task, a conception that can be seen as historically based and the product of a particular society. However, regardless of this necessity, it has been the case that many researchers, particularly in psychology, have not considered to any great extent the social or cultural aspects of creativity and focused their work instead on investigating this phenomenon at the level of individual biology and psychology.

3
Bio-Psychological Perspectives

Individual-based notions of creativity are buried deep within the Western Greco-Roman Judeo-Christian intellectual tradition. They are exemplified in the myths associated with ideas of genius (Sawyer 2006, pp. 18–27), and it can be seen, for example, that these myths informed early work on creativity by figures such as Lombroso and Freud. The central narratives implicitly held in these intellectual traditions draw in some instances on notions of the muse and a belief in god-like powers and have led to an idea of creativity that is metaphysical and at times mystical in basis. They have become associated with a self-expressive, freely thinking individual genius, a conception that has led in some quarters to the idea of the quasi-neurotic compelled through various states of creative agony to starve in their artist's garret.

Embedded in the research, however, are significant counter propositions to what have become known as *inspirationist* and *Romantic* positions (Boden 2004, p. 14). This research has come from a number of fields. It includes work from sociology (e.g. Zolberg 1990, Stillinger 1991, Wolff 1993, Howe 1999, Alexander 2003) some of which has been concerned primarily with art practice (Becker 1982) and cultural production (Bourdieu 1977, 1990, 1993, 1996). The field of literary criticism (Pope 2005) and the poststructuralist notions of Barthes (1977) and Foucault (1979), as well as the media studies arm of communication and cultural studies (Petrie 1991, Negus & Pickering 2004), have also been active in understanding notions of creativity. However, psychology, as a broad discipline focused on understanding the workings of individual psyches, has produced a significantly large body of work in this area (Runco & Pritzker 1999, Sternberg 1999, Bergquist 2006, Sawyer 2006), and it serves our discussion well to briefly outline some of it here.

Firstly, before we proceed, it needs to be briefly stated here that there have been a number of speculative and commercially successful training methods, many of which have come out of the advertising world, applied to the notion of creativity, but for many of them 'there is almost no solid experimental evidence that any of these methods work' (Sawyer 2006, p. 300). The ideas of lateral thinking (de Bono 1971, 1992), brainstorming and creative problem solving (e.g. Osborn 1953) and other assertions (von Oech 1983, 1986) have been, as Robert Sternberg asserts, subject to minimal empirical scrutiny (1999, pp. 5–6). However, the psychodynamic school operating inside the discipline of psychology, seen in works by Freud (1959), Vernon (1970), Rothenberg (1979) and others (see Sternberg 1999), has explored tensions between conscious and more primitive unconscious drives. This school of thought no longer believes, however, that creative people are more likely to be mentally abnormal. For example, Rothenberg (1979) claimed that the creative process is 'not only *not* primitive but [is] consistently more advanced and adaptive than ordinary waking thought' (Sawyer 2006, p. 52). Meanwhile, Skinner and the behaviourists, while they saw creativity as a cognitive behaviour pattern unconscious to the individual (Bergquist 2006), only studied those behaviours they could literally see. They left alone what was occurring inside the brain. The increasingly positivist turn in psychology also produced a series of psychometric approaches which attempted to measure aspects of creativity. Torrance (1974), building on Guildford's (1950) stimulus, produced a number of these tests for creativity, underscoring the fact that the research focus had shifted towards measuring a set of supposedly objective features of creativity. The one thing, apart from considerations of what became known as convergent and divergent thinking, that was measured more than anything else was intelligence, as this was thought to be the basis of creativity. As discussed earlier, there were problems associated with this approach. Personality was also studied deeply in order to find a distinguishing set of characteristics that would enable creative individuals to be accurately pin-pointed. Researchers have so far failed to discover these personality traits; traits that could:

> distinguish creative people from ordinary people, to develop a test that could identify exceptional talent early in life, and to design educational techniques that could improve a student's creativity. Part of the reason for this failure was that they were too willing to accept our creativity myths; personality psychologists weren't aware that their own conceptions of creativity were socially and historically unique (Raina, 1993; Stein, 1987). (Sawyer 2006, p. 55)

The problematics of these ideas led, in part, to the development of focused approaches to the study of creativity which sought an explanation by grappling with the cognitive processes thought to underpin creativity (Ward et al. 1997). As Keith Sawyer describes, cognitive psychologists began to examine 'the representational structures of the mind, their interconnections, and the mental processes that are shared by individuals' (2006, p. 57). Examples may be seen in the work of Finke (1989), Sternberg & Davidson (1995) and Howard Gardner (1993) as well as the models developed by Johnston Laird (Boden 1994) and many others. Robert Weisberg (1993), for one, proposed that ordinary cognitive processes, those that are applicable in everyday situations rather than unusual or unique ones, could be the most appropriate solution.

Alongside this work from the cognitive school, social-personality approaches also developed. This school of thought asserted that personality variables (e.g. Maslow 1968), motivation (e.g. Amabile 1983) and the sociocultural environment were also important sources of creativity and could no longer be neglected. We shall return to their ideas shortly. However, the more recent work in neuropsychology, focused squarely on the brain, appears to insist on a monist version of the alleged brain/mind duality, with some in this school explaining aspects of creativity in terms of the relationships between neurochemical processes and certain cognitive states (see Ashby et al. 1999, Marr 2006).

The relatively new field of neuroscience has begun exploring empirically the connection between the biological mechanism of the brain and the activities of the creative mind. In an abstract to their article 'The Creative Brain/The Creative Mind', Newberg and D'Aquili claimed that:

In the past few decades, neuroscience research has greatly expanded our understanding of how the human brain functions. In particular, we have begun to explore the basis of emotions, intelligence, and creativity. These brain functions also have been applied to various aspects of behavior, thought, and experience. We have also begun to develop an understanding of how the brain and mind work during aesthetic and religious experiences. Studies on these topics have included neuropsychological tests, physiological measures, and brain imaging. These different techniques have enabled us to open up a window into the brain. It is by understanding the functioning of the creative brain that we begin to understand the concept of the creative mind. It is through the use of emotions and other higher cognitive functions that the brain and mind can create ideas, music, literature,

and ultimately our entire repertoire of behaviors. How these different creative abilities are derived can also be traced to various parts of
the brain and how they function. Modern neuroscience allows us to
begin to understand the creative aspect of the brain and mind and
perhaps can take us one step further toward understanding the most
profound types of aesthetic and religious experiences. (Newberg &
D'Aquili 2000, p. 53)

Added to these claims, in a keynote address entitled 'Creating Creative Brains' given to the CCI conference on creativity, Susan Greenfield
(2008) remarked that creativity will be the commodity of the twenty-
first century. She went on to predict that there were some questions
neuroscience could answer, such as what happens in the brain when
a person is creative, and suggested that this discipline could help to
answer the question 'what is the creative mind set?' She then set about
giving an abbreviated description of neuroscience as a discipline outlining the nested layers of research that move in from consciousness and
eventually arriving at the genetic composition of the brain.

She affirmed that neuroscience's concerns were focused, at the outside
level of this nested process, on consciousness. Remembering that the
mind is a personalisation of the brain, this concern with consciousness
has led, typically, to a concentration in research on dysfunction. This
can be seen in studies of depression and schizophrenia which are themselves umbrella terms that include a range of impairments rather than
just one. The next layer of enquiry for neuroscience then focuses on
functions of the brain such as memory or vision that may be impaired
by these larger sets of dysfunctions. Underpinning these functions is a
further set of sub-functions including the mechanism that allows the
perception of, for example, colour, form and movement. As an instance
of this, it has been found that there are 30 brain regions that process
how humans understand colour. And, of course, the next layer down
of research looks specifically at these brain regions and what they do.
What the study of these brain regions reveals is that the whole is more
than the sum of its parts. Brain regions are themselves composed of
networks and circuits that allow neuronal connections to operate. The
concern at this level of enquiry is, predominantly, with the operation of
the synapse. Synapses are part of the gap that neurotransmitters operate within, providing the ground for electrical signals to operate across
these connections. Neuroscience then concerns itself with the component parts of the synapse and peels these away until the discipline is
focused on the study of genetic make-up. It should be seen from this

brief description that neuroscience is a nested process with each area of concern nested one inside the other from consciousness right on down to genetics. The critical observation is that, as Greenfield was at pains to point out, this process worked very much in the opposite direction as well. That is, the environment was just as important in shaping synaptic activity as synaptic activity was in shaping the environment. More on these nested connections shortly.

Meanwhile, keeping in mind all of this activity occurring in the research, I would like to focus for a brief period on the underlying set of concepts that inform many of these research approaches. It should allow us to fully appreciate what is being dealt with here. In order to understand the connection between the biological brain and the creative mind, many researchers have been attempting to isolate a biologically related mechanism in the brain that explains the workings of the mind and thus creativity. These ideas are premised on conceiving of the mind as being related directly to the biological mechanism of the brain. This 'monist' position on the mind/body problem asserts that 'all mental events are identical to physical events, and that the only laws that govern the relations between events are physical, not psychological, laws' (Eliasmith n.d.. However, as Chris Eliasmith suggests:

> If a convincing rejection of dualism can be formulated, the classic mind-body problem will be solved by its becoming a non-problem and the materialist approach of modern science will be vindicated. If, conversely, dualism can be convincingly maintained, it is by no means obvious that empirical evidence will suffice for a thorough understanding of the mind – in other words, understanding the brain may not be enough for understanding the mind. (Eliasmith n.d.)

Nonetheless, the sort of analysis which centres one's ability to be creative within the biological attributes of the brain is, as Eliasmith points out, the most common one (e.g. Tokoro & Mogi 2007). Sitting alongside Plato, Aristotle, Kant and Freud, Sir Francis Galton is recognised as the producer of one of the seminal works in this area of the study of creativity. Galton's claim to be in the distinguished company listed immediately above lies with the proposition that he was one of the first to assert that there is a 'general biological factor in genius and, by implication, in creativity' (Rothenberg & Hausman 1976, p. 12). He lay part of the groundwork for further work based on explaining creativity through natural mechanisms, and as such many biologically and psychologically centred accounts of creativity owe their basis to Galton's ideas. Writing in 1869, he proposed that genius and talent are inherited and that:

> men [sic] who are gifted with high abilities...easily rise through all the obstacles caused by the inferiority of social rank [and] men who are largely aided by social advantages, are unable to achieve eminence, unless they are endowed with high natural gifts. (Galton 1950, p. 38)

His ideas were an attempt to extend Charles Darwin's theory of evolution 'to the transmission of human faculties' (Rothenberg & Hausman 1976, p. 42). Galton collected, collated and analysed a significant amount of data on eminent men in England and their families and histories. With the information from this study of over three hundred families, he set out to show 'that a man's [sic] natural abilities are derived by inheritance, under exactly the same limitations as are the form and physical features of the whole organic world' (1950, p. 1). One problem facing Galton was that he selected eminent people that were commercially successful, seeing this as a hallmark of genetic inheritance, while neglecting to see the role financial inheritance, a socially constructed advantage, would have on his results. As Colin Martindale asserts 'recent studies of the heritability of creative test performance have yielded contradictory results...contrary to Galton, there is no evidence that creativity runs in families' (1999, p. 148).

Martindale (1999) also states that a group of researchers, these include Waller, Bouchard, Lykken, Tellegen and Blacker, have put forward a mechanism that appears to account for the contradictory positions relating to biological inheritance of creativity. These researchers argue that creativity is characterised by what has been termed emergenesis. This term refers to what they call higher-order traits, such as creativity, emerging only if a number of other traits, such as perseverance or intelligence, or as others suggest, the right social and cultural environment, are in place. According to this proposition, 'emergenic traits can be highly heritable, but do not run in families, because family members are unlikely to have *all* of the required traits' (Martindale 1999, p. 148). And yet, despite the evident problems with Galton's work, the notion that there is some deeper connection between biology and creativity has not diminished in popularity.

Joseph and Glenda Bogen, working in the late 1960s, looked well beyond Galton's work on evolutionary patterns and, as a precursor to the work developing in neuroscience, focused their attention specifically on the structure of the brain. Bogen and Bogen were also deeply concerned with the biological factors underlying the thoughts that manifested themselves in the mind. They considered that there were two divisions in the mind. One they called a 'propositional mind' and the other they termed an 'appositional mind'. The first was responsible for logical and linguistic function and the second concerned with non-rational and visio-spatial functions. Creativity, in Bogen and Bogen's view, 'results from the coordinated function of these two types of mind' (Rothenberg & Hausman 1976, p. 13). They then put forward the proposition that 'creativity depends on the connecting brain fiber structure called the corpus callosum and on co-ordination of the distinct functions of the two hemispheres' (ibid.). Importantly, they also reinforced the necessity for both hemispheres to be operative in the creative process. They argued, for example, that:

> ... interhemispheric collaboration need not be restricted to verbal-visuo-spatial interaction; if the right hemisphere has a special capacity for tonal, timbre and other aspects of music, interhemispheric communication could clearly contribute to musical creativity. Indeed, we can easily entertain the notion that artistic creativity in general benefits from interhemispheric collaboration. (Bogen & Bogen in Rothenberg & Hausman 1976, p. 258)

Despite these caveats on the Bogens' part and the complexity involved in what they were attempting to explain, many took the idea that there was specialised activity in the left and right hemispheres of the brain as the complete story and neglected what the Bogens had to say on interhemispheric collaboration.

In addition, Roger Sperry (1974) also pointed out in the early 1970s that there appears to be two types of thinking: one being verbal and the other non-verbal, separately represented in the left and right hemispheres. In a series of noted experiments, he and his students were able to split the brain into two and argued from the results he achieved, which won him a Nobel Prize, that 'both the left and the right hemisphere may be conscious simultaneously in different, even in mutually conflicting, mental experiences that run along in parallel' (Sperry 1974, p. 11). He went on to suggest that the differences in hemispheres could be seen in the characteristics of each. The right hemisphere, according to Sperry, seems to be:

> holistic and unitary rather than analytic and fragmentary, and orientational more than focal, and to involve concrete perceptual insight rather than abstract, symbolic, sequential reasoning. However, it yet

remains for someone to translate in a meaningful [i.e., physiological] way the essential right-left characteristics. (1974, p. 11)

The general understanding of this approach, taken to be true by the study's popularisation, is that certain behavioural patterns may emerge dependent on which side of the brain is physically dominant. This idea gave rise to the notion of lateral dominance, a concept generally taken out of context and used to both extend the ideas beyond what the actual research work indicated and profit from its unintentional misapplication. Two examples will suffice.

Betty Edwards, in a famous book entitled *Drawing on the Right Side of the Brain: A Course in Enhancing Creativity and Artistic Confidence* (1979), suggested ways that people could enhance their creativity by focusing on what was seen to be the imaginative, synthesising, artistic, holistic and conceptual side of the brain. This was presumed to be the right hemisphere. The left side of the brain was thought to be involved in analytical, mathematical, technical and problem-solving activity. Apart from the problems of associating creativity solely with artistic activity and an underlying perception that it had little to do with analysis and problem solving, a view that has more to do with Romanticism than science, the more general understanding of this approach is that certain behavioural patterns will emerge dependent on which side of the brain is physically dominant. Ned Herrmann, as another example amongst many others, asserted that 'the evidence of human dominance shows that wherever there are two of anything in the body, one is naturally dominant over the other. Therefore like we are right or left handed, we are also naturally "footed", "eyed", "kidneyed", etc. We can also be thought of as "brained" ' (Herrmann 1998). The simplistic correlation appended to these ideas was to then list which side of the brain controlled or produced specific characteristics and behaviours. For example, music was thought to be specifically a right brain activity, neglecting of course to note the technical, analytical and synthetic abilities which are necessary for music to become part of anyone's activities. This over-reliance on the basic duality of left or right brain functioning led many to 'extrapolate wildly from fairly restricted data until every human polarity is ascribed to hemispheric difference' (Truax 1984, p. 52).

Despite the popular adoption of left brain/right brain curriculums, there appears to be little in the current research to support them (Hellige 2001, Boden 2004, O'Boyle & Singh 2004). Under a short section entitled 'Myths of "right" and "left" brain, and "divergent" and "convergent" thinking' in his book *Creativity: Theory, History, Practice* (2005), Rob Pope asserts:

> It is still common in casual conversation about creativity to talk of two supposedly distinct capacities corresponding to the brain's two hemispheres: 'right brain' as the creative and imaginative side; and 'left brain' as the critical and analytical side. This often gets mixed up with equally casual, and similarly binary, appeals to two supposedly distinct styles of thinking and, by extension, thinker: 'divergent' (creatively open) and 'convergent' (critically focused). Such terms may be handy as a crude and largely symbolic shorthand; but they derive from early behavioural and substantially superseded studies of learning styles in 1960s and 1970s (see Vernon 1970: 371–84 and compare Sternberg 1999: 48–9, 145–9). Certainly they bear little resemblance to the complexly integrated workings of the brain as described in the foregoing pages. Nowadays, cognitive psychologists would tend to talk of brain activity in terms of *multilevel, parallel* and *recursive processing*. And the kinds of electronic and chemical 'mapping' referred to above are increasingly showing that the brain has *complex networks of complementary activity all over*, as well as localised response to stimulus in a specific area (see Dennett 1991, Calvin 1997, Damasio 2000, Boden 2004, Geake and Dodson 2004 and Greenfield 2004). (Pope 2005, p. 115)

With this in mind, neuropsychologists Michael O'Boyle and Harnam Singh claim that, as suggested by Joseph Hellige (1993), 'having learned so much about hemispheric differences (and independence), it is now time to "put the brain back together again" (p. 206)' (2004, p. 371). One result of their studies into mathematically gifted (MG) adolescents was to contend that 'notably, the MG showed no reliable left-right differences when processing global or local information on unilateral trials' (O'Boyle & Singh 2004, p. 376). These results are not surprising in the light of recent comments from Joseph Hellige (1993, 2001), a leading researcher in this area. He argues that the differences and divisions we ascribe to the brain are more often than not metaphorical rather than real. Hellige tends to qualify when presented with questions about focusing certain definitive properties on individual hemispheres:

> My thinking is that in most domains the two hemispheres make complementary contributions. Let me give you a couple of examples: Even in language when we say the left hemisphere is dominant for

language we usually mean the ability to produce overt speech, the ability to understand individual words, the ability to handle grammar and so forth. But there are other aspects of language such as inferring the meaning or inferring the emotion based on the tone of voice which allows us to determine whether the speaker is angry or happy or sad. Those things are often overlooked as part of language but they constitute a very important part of what allows us to communicate. And there's good evidence that the right hemisphere not only contributes to those aspects of language but may, in some instances, even be more important than the left hemisphere. (Hellige in Mitchell 2004)

Despite these indications of the complexities involved in ascribing particular attributes of the mind to specific aspects of the brain, the search for the connection between the brain and creativity appears to have created just as many doubts about these ideas as it has provided answers to the complex research questions involved.

As a further example, in following the basic premise that the brain is the organ devoted to the activities of the mind, it appears to follow that if we alter the activity of the brain we can alter the way the mind works. The corollary for creative individuals is that they may be able to view the world differently by biologically manipulating the centres of sense perception. As David Suzuki indicates in his audiovisual summary of the science involved, 'neurotransmitters modify and shape human behaviour. A few in particular even help scientists understand the biological basis of sadness and joy, love and violence and the way we see the world through a particular human spectrum' (Suzuki 1994). One of these, serotonin, has been labelled the brain's workhorse, managing mood, appetite and, importantly for this study, memory and learning, both of which have been connected to creativity. Serotonin acts as both an inhibitor and enhancer depending on which part of the brain it is active in. The foremost areas that it deals with are the frontal lobes and the thalamus. The frontal lobes, as Suzuki explains, are the 'smart' parts of the brain where decision making and planning takes place. The thalamus has the task of controlling the sensory information that is distributed to various areas of the brain, including of course the frontal lobes. Serotonin acts on the thalamus influencing the sensory information that reaches the decision-making areas in the brain.

It appears that many societies and cultures over a long period of time have undertaken, albeit without this precise information, to trigger this biological activity so as to alter the perceptions of the world around them. Religious rites, hallucinogens and sensory deprivation have been historically the principle methods of altering the brain activity to literally change the mind's view of the world around it. Many of the techniques used to do this are explored at length in the literature and myths of artists and metaphysicists in the twentieth century. For example, W. Somerset Maugham in *The Razor's Edge* (1963) chronicles one man's attempt to find the path to self-awareness and enlightenment by experimenting with a number of these techniques. Jack Kerouac's short story 'Alone on a Mountaintop' (1972) gives an account, through the eyes of a participant, of the alterations to the mind that a change in sensory input can induce. The Sun Dance ritual of the North American Indians is a good example of the sensory deprivation practised as part of religious rituals to induce an altered perception of reality. The autobiography of Chief Buffalo Child Long Lance (1976) gives an eyewitness account of these rituals and an insight into the results, for this culture, of conducting them. The intake of particular hallucinogens for altering perception is also graphically described in Carlos Castaneda's anthropological narrative *The Teachings of Don Juan: A Jacqui Way of Knowledge* (1968). As the title suggests, these mind-altering substances were used as a tool in the quest for differing ways of seeing. However, it has been discovered that all of these activities in the long run result in the action of similar biological mechanisms. By controlling or altering the levels of serotonin, decision making, memory, learning and planning may all be influenced, sometimes dramatically. Since it has been argued that decision making, memory, learning and planning are critical activities in the creative process, it is not surprising a deep belief in the idea that there is a biological connection between sensory deprivation and creativity itself is still current. But there are other factors to consider.

For example, low levels of the neurotransmitter, dopamine, in the frontal lobe of the brain may result in a poor working memory, but higher levels of dopamine are 'thought to produce feelings of bliss. It's sometimes referred to as the pleasure chemical' (Suzuki 1994). Once again, bliss may be experienced as a result of sensory deprivation. The fasting associated with the more ascetic sides of Hindu religion in India, for example, often leads to states of bliss indicating the biological connection between this activity and levels of dopamine in their practitioners. More pertinently, for us the connection between bliss and creativity has been explored at length in the more recent work of Mihaly Csikszentmihalyi and has resulted in his conclusion that every creative act takes place within a state of what he terms 'flow' (Csikszentmihalyi & Csikszentmihalyi 1988). Csikszentmihalyi (1991) contends that 'flow' or more correctly 'autotelic experience', a concept that will be explored more fully later, operates as a prime motivator in most creative activity. This state has been compared to Eastern ideas on creativity (Niu & Sternberg 2006) where the Taoist idea of achieving high creativity can be accessed through entering a 'state where everything breaks through the shell of itself and fuses with every other thing' (2006, pp. 31–2). Niu and Sternberg suggest that this state is seen as the most significant stage of creativity that people can pursue. As they suggest, this Eastern belief system holds to the idea that 'once one has this great sympathy, he or she can be absolutely free to connect with the universe, and all he or she does is highly creative' (2006, p. 32).

> The Taoist idea of returning and losing oneself has had a great impact on Chinese literati and their creative activity throughout Chinese history, especially in the domains of poetry and painting. The great Chinese poets and artists who, through meditation and self-cultivation, penetrated to this great sympathy produced a large amount of truly great works. They are thought to owe a great debt to ancient Taoist theory and its methods (Chang, 1970). Interestingly, a modern psychologist, Csikzentmihalyi (1988, 1997), has proposed a similar theory about the creative process. He has said that when people are engaged in highly creative activity, they tend to be in a state of 'flow,' in which they are highly focused on their work without noticing events happening outside. Csikzentmihalyi has also mentioned that people can experience this 'flow' during the utilization of many Eastern styles of meditation. (Niu & Sternberg 2006, p. 32)

The examples given above of the ways humans have attempted to induce these states of creative bliss refer often to mystical or metaphysical experiences but, as indicated, they may well be grounded in more mundane truths and may not, despite the belief that they do, lead directly to creative activity.

Colin Martindale, summarising the research into the bio-psychological bases to creativity, asserts that there are a number of agreed traits recorded during creative activity but 'creative people do not exhibit all of these traits in general but only while engaged in creative activity' (1999, p. 149). One of the possible conclusions that could be drawn from these accounts is that it is difficult to decide what is cause and what is effect. In other words, all of the biological markers of brain activity occur during the act of being creative and are thus measurable during this act. On the evidence this is not disputed. As Hennessey and

Amabile argue, 'neuroimaging methods can provide information about neural activity during insight' (2010, p. 574). However, is the evidence produced of brain activity the result of the subject being creative, or is the activity a precursor to being creative with these conditions needing to be in place before the activity occurs? None of these questions appear to have been resolved as yet. Hennessey and Amabile assert that those concerned with the neurological basis of creativity may have a lengthy wait before researchers in this area are prepared to reach consensus:

> The possibilities are promising, but we are not anywhere near the point of being able to image the creative process as it unfolds in the human brain. Even cutting-edge instruments mask the order in which various brain areas become activated in the massive parallel processing that results in high-level creativity. (2010, p. 574)

Furthermore, as could be argued, a biological base for creativity may not completely and fully account for the exceptional production of creativity by extraordinary individuals since it does not account for the decisive connection value distinction plays in the creative process both historically and culturally. The biological precursors for creativity, explored above, may simply be just that – avenues for setting the right environment for acts of creativity to occur in.

It is at this point that I want to return to the nested aspects of neuroscience as suggested by Susan Greenfield (2008). Her claim is that neuroscience has a number of concerns that are intimately connected one within the other. The influence that consciousness has on brain functions such as perception, to brain regions, networks, circuits, neuronal connections, neurotransmitters and synapses, right on down to genetic material, is just as important as the connections that run the other way. In this case Greenfield argues that to say that a person's genetic make-up determines their creativity would be entirely misleading as there is evidence that there is a two-way interaction between the 100 billion or so neurones most people possess and the actions those people undertake in their operations in the world. She argues the neurones themselves adapt to and are changed by the individual's personal experience. As interaction with the environment occurs for individuals, the brain grows more connections. This dynamic interactive process allows greater growth of connections and this occurs in an exponential way. There is not simply a one-to-one link between genes and consciousness and thus creativity. From this information she argues that genes are a *necessary but not sufficient condition* for creativity to occur.

She suggests that in order to understand meaningful experience, of the type typically seen in creative activity, one needs to examine all of the things neuroscience is concerned with, but these alone are not enough to explain creativity. In short, there are additional things involved other than just a person's neurological or biological activity.

This position is supported and extended somewhat by Antonio Damasio who, according to Rob Pope (2005, p. 114), emphatically opposes any suggestion that creativity can simply be read off inherited genes or be solely ascribed to the neural networks embedded in a creative individual's brain. He insists that creativity emerges from the interaction that occurs between an individual and the environment. Damasio asserts:

> The sort of brain activity that leads to creative behaviour involves three functional levels: a genome-specified level of brain circuitry, an activity-specified level of brain circuitry, and then something that results from the interactions of the brain with physical, social and cultural environments. That is why extremely reductionist views cannot capture all the issues we wish to understand when we discuss creativity (Damasio in Pfenniger and Shubik 2001: 59–60). (Quoted by Pope 2005, p. 114)

It can thus be argued that, by and of themselves, neurobiological factors, or the behavioural traits ascribed to them, may not be able to, in and of themselves, induce specific cases of creativity. They will, at best, simply provide exceptional conditions for differing thought patterns, which is ultimately only one of the many necessary elements needed to be active in the creative process. Other important factors are those concerning the creative individual's environment where the actions of creative individual are socially, culturally and historically located. It is the basis for these latter conceptions and the notion that creativity may be socially produced within specific cultural contexts that now deserves some consideration.

4
Creativity and the Social

Creativity is an activity that manages to make something from something, as opposed to making something from nothing. In addition, the new idea, process or product that is created must be original and be judged to be so in at least one social setting. This of course implies that the context in which creativity occurs is critically important. Why? The answer is that for an object to be judged to be unique or original it must be judged to be so against some criteria that pre-exists the newly created object. The framework for that judgement is provided by the social grouping. If this is the case, it would be apposite to briefly examine the idea that the creative process occurs in stages as it also has some relevance to the idea that the social is indeed critical to an understanding of creativity.

Graham Wallas (1945) proposed, firstly in the 1920s, that the creative process followed a series of stages. Wallas outlined four stages encompassing what he labelled preparation, incubation, illumination followed by verification. The preparation stage, according to Wallas, involves the gathering of information necessary to the process. The problem is defined as well at this early stage. Incubation, which Wallas admits he first heard about through a speech given in 1891 by the physicist Helmholz, is a stage where the person may not necessarily be consciously thinking about the problem. The person steps back from the problem and lets their mind contemplate and work through all aspects of it. This stage may be temporally discontinuous in as much as it may occur very briefly and take mere minutes. It may also occur over a much longer period lasting for weeks and even years. The illumination stage consists of 'the appearance of the "happy idea"' (Wallas 1945, p. 41). Unlike the other stages this one may come very quickly, all in a rush as it were. Wallas asserts that the final stage, verification, is a period in which the idea is tested and 'reduced to exact form' (ibid.).

While Wallas' ideas about creativity being a staged process have been heavily contested, which we will come to in more depth shortly, the aspects that constitute these stages have, nonetheless, been identified to exist. In this case, if verification is part of creativity it would be difficult to continue to see creativity and innovation as distinct phenomenon. At times creativity has been reduced to the notion that it is solely to do with generating ideas while innovation is perceived as successfully applying those ideas. However, as Nemiro argues, to say that creativity is just 'thinking up new things' and innovation is 'doing new things' is far too simplistic a view. It suggests that 'creativity is largely cognitive and innovation largely behavioral' (Nemiro 2004, p. 14). There is, for Nemiro, a problem with seeing these as two separate processes. In a paper Nemiro and Mark Runco presented, they argued that:

> Surely innovation requires some thought, and creative insights may follow from actual activity. Just as surely there can be some interplay; a creative idea may suggest an innovation, which in turn suggests new and creative possibilities. Part of the problem is the either-or assumption, the dichotomy that artificially separates creativity and innovation. (Nemiro & Runco quoted in Nemiro 2004, pp. 14–5)

Nemiro contends that the two concepts are 'intertwined, as ideas are generated, developed, finalized, and then evaluated' (2004, pp. 14–5). If ideas are finalised and evaluated, then they must also be manifest at some point in order for this process to happen. The idea must be produced, either as an abstraction or a literal manifestation, in order to be verified as creative. If it is verified, as Wallas proposes it must be, then it must at this point be both creative and innovative.

Robert Weisberg, however, contends that it is difficult to categorise each creative step in a universal set of stages, and he can find little evidence, particularly of incubation, apart from self-reportage from creative individuals. It should be noted that, even though Wallas's stages were based on 'his own introspection and scattered observations', they have been, if not entirely accepted, at least widely considered by many theorists (Rothenberg & Hausman 1976, p. 69). As Csikszentmihalyi argues, despite the criticisms they do provide a useful set of markers or areas one can use to begin enhancing understandings of creativity. He, however, attaches a fifth step, elaboration, to Wallas's original four but adds that:

The five-stage view of the process may be too simplified, and it can be misleading, but it does offer a relatively valid and simple way to organise the complexities involved.... It is essential to remember...that the five stages in reality are not exclusive but typically overlap and recur several times before the process is completed. (Csikszentmihalyi 1997, p. 83)

While I will take up the merits or not of these ideas in more depth later when we discuss intuition, it is the first and last phases of this conception of creativity that I wish to concentrate on here. The argument would be that if both preparation and verification are indeed vital parts of the creative process, then one cannot avoid admitting that there are deep connections to structures of knowledge existing external to the individual that are also important. Nor can one avoid a necessarily social connection in making judgements about the merit of the work produced, as the work doesn't exist in a vacuum. Judgements are always made against pre-existing knowledge structures; in which case, both value distinction and social validation, as suggested prior, are indeed important considerations.

If this situation is the case, then it would be wise in any exploration of the phenomenon of creativity to look at the social and cultural contexts in which creative art and innovative science operate. It should therefore also be recognised that the field of sociology's contribution to the study of creativity has been at least as influential in understanding creativity as the biological or psychological approaches have been. However, one caveat needs to be added here. Rather than seeing creativity as a phenomenon applicable to all human activity, be it art or science, as most psychologists do (e.g. Sawyer 2006), sociologists have largely tended to see creativity predominantly in relation to art practice, following the more common view that creative practice *is* art practice, and have thereby generally conflated the two.

In this regard Forster and Blau indicate that 'bio-psychological approaches have little use for anyone who wants to understand art as something which acts in society and, in turn, is influenced and shaped by society' (1989, p. 6). Nonetheless biological, psychological or sociological perspectives need not be antagonistic. They can be, as I will conclude by arguing, quite complementary. However, before we reach that conclusion, the social and cultural theories that apply to creativity in general, and in particular, the arts, bear some investigation.

According to Vera Zolberg (1990), those interested in the social features of creative activity are generally aware of three aspects to it: the constructedness of the art object, the process aspect of creation and the contextually bound nature of the artist. She asserts that:

> From a sociological standpoint, a work of art is a moment in a process involving the collaboration of more than one actor, working through certain social institutions, and following historically observable trends. Because [sociologists] assume that, like other social phenomena, art cannot be fully understood divorced from its social context, and because whatever else it is, an art work has monetary value, they accept the fact that the value attached to it derives, not solely from aesthetic qualities intrinsic to the work, but from external conditions as well. (Zolberg 1990, p. 9)

As an illustration of the assumption that 'external conditions' (and by that phrase is meant conditions external to the individual's contribution) are connected to creativity, there is at least some conjecture that if a society provides the right conditions, then a positive influence on creative activity can take place.

This is the basic premise that underpins social and economic theorist Richard Florida's book *The Rise of the Creative Class* (2002). Florida contends that rather than economic development being driven by the classic economic motors of efficiency and organisation it is creativity that has in fact been the engine of growth. He argues that the future of cities around the planet will depend on these agglomeration's ability to attract and maintain the creative talent necessary to drive an economy along. He suggests that a new class of what he calls 'super creatives' have developed. These include engineers, architects, scientists, designers, mathematicians, musicians and many others, who have the function of creating new ideas, objects, technologies and cultural content, all of which are necessary for a modern economy to keep achieving. Appended to this group are those he sees as 'creative professionals'. This secondary group are those involved in law, business, finance and so on, who convert the work of the 'super creatives' for exploitation and use in the broader economy. Florida then argues that public policy should be about setting up the necessary environment for these creative classes to thrive in. These environments would be necessarily bohemian and certainly culturally diverse as these appear to be the ones that develop around these creative groups. Underlying Florida's argument are a number of assumptions. Firstly, a functionalist view of society and, secondly, a predominantly Western post-industrial view of the world. There also appears to be a relatively minor assumption of the Romanticist view of creativity. However, the major assumption underpinning the views expressed in his proposals, at least from the perspective of the work being presented here, is the idea that context is vitally influential on creative activity.

One of the broadest of the contextual views of creativity which has been presented in the literature is that of Vytautus Kavolis. Drawing on the expansive work of Pitirim Sorokin, Kavolis' work in the 1960s and 1970s also 'attempted to identify the social conditions which provide the seedbed for outbreaks of artistic creativity in history' (Forster & Blau 1989, p. 7). There is in Kavolis' thinking a link between artistic creativity and the level of prosperity in a society. He proposes that there is evidence to suggest that the cycles a society goes through, that is periods of growth, climax and decline, correspond to the need for achievement on an individual level. This need occurs particularly strongly during the growth cycle of a society. The general interpretation is that increases in prosperity tend to reduce the motivation for achievement, but this is often a simplistic reading of the data especially when the sociological phase-cycle theory, first put forward by Bales and Parsons, is looked at more deeply. Firstly, according to phase-cycle theory:

> all social systems have a number of basic functional problems to solve. Among these, instrumental *adaptation* to the external environment, organisation of the legal-institutional machinery for *goal attainment*, internal social-emotional *integration*, and tension reduction (and latent pattern maintenance) are of paramount importance. (Kavolis in Foster & Blau 1989, p. 383)

Secondly, social systems produce only limited amounts of resources whether it is wealth, disposable time or administrative power, and they can only mobilise a portion of these resources for problem-solving activity. Specialisation tends to circumscribe the action necessary for the solution to other problems and efforts can be dissipated while concentrating on central issues. Thirdly, and leading directly from the prior two, problem solving tends to take place in a cyclical manner since not all problems can be solved at once. A lot of emphasis will be focused on one type of problem, and other problems will tend to be neglected, at any one time. Once this functional problem has been resolved, 'resources are increasingly recommitted to previously neglected tasks which the solution of this problem has made salient' (Kavolis in Foster & Blau 1989, p. 387).

In *History on Art's Side: Social Dynamics in Artistic Efflorescences* (1972), Kavolis argues that all societies go through a series of regular and predictable psychoeconomic phase cycles. He contends that:

> ... artistic creativity tends to be stimulated by a disturbance of a condition of relative equilibrium; reduced during the period of intense goal-directed action; increased during the normally integrative phase, when the social system is settling down to a new equilibrium; and again reduced when the new equilibrium is taken for granted. (Foster & Blau 1989, p. 7)

Kavolis asserts that it is during the phase of social–emotional integration, typically more necessary in periods of disturbance, that artistic activity will be increasingly stimulated and, consequently, relatively inhibited during any other form of large-scale social activity. However, after studying the historical data of a number of societies with information drawn from a number of sources but predominantly utilising Pitirim Sorokin's *Social and Cultural Dynamics* (1937), the best that Kavolis is prepared to say definitively is that 'artistic creativity may in general be linked with changing patterns of motivation' (Foster & Blau 1989, p. 384) in a society.

Though he is not a sociologist, but has been one of the figures in psychology who have pushed that discipline towards accepting social and cultural perspectives, Dean Keith Simonton has also made significant contributions to understanding creativity from the point of view of cultures, nations and civilisations. He has written extensively on the topic and applied a methodological process known as historiometry to his research. In doing so he argues that in order to understand the efflorescence of creative individual activity in various times and places one also needs to understand 'the changes in the cultural, social, political and economic circumstances that determine the extent to which the resulting milieu nurtures the development of creative potential and the expression of that developed potential' (Simonton 2003, p. 304). This conclusion is supported by a wealth of research detail where Simonton variously examines the socio-cultural context of individual creativity (1975), the causal relationship between war and scientific discovery (1976), techno-scientific activity and war (1980), and individual genius and cultural configurations (1996). Working across the grain of psychology Simonton also suggests:

> Psychologists have tended to view creativity as an individual-level phenomenon. That is, they have tended to concentrate on the cognitive processes, personality traits, and developmental antecedents

associated with individual creators. This focus follows naturally from the very nature of psychology as a scientific enterprise dedicated to understanding individual mind and behavior. Yet this tradition of 'psychological reductionism' has also inspired an antithetical conception of creativity as an exclusively societal-level event. In the extreme form, that of a complete 'sociocultural reductionism,' the individual becomes a mere epiphenomenon without any causal significance whatsoever. (Simonton 2003, p. 304)

Recognising that there has been a predominant focus on the individual in the study of the production of art in particular, Janet Wolff (1981), like Simonton, also argues that creativity may have less to do with the individual than it does with the operation of society. However, she argues on a somewhat less macro-functional level than Sorokin or Kavolis, or indeed Simonton, tending towards a more traditional conflict-based sociological perspective.

Using the premise that 'the cultivation of the five senses is the work of all previous history' (Marx 1980, p. 353), in that all artistic sensibilities are derived in some way from the socialisation of the individual, Wolff argues that much of what the West takes to be creative activity, and therefore what the West presumes an artist to be, is itself historically based. She argues that the more recent conception of what an artist is, largely related as it is to Romantic conceptions, initially emerged from the period of the Renaissance. It has been linked, as others have argued (Wiesner, Ruff & Wheeler 1993), to the rise of humanism from out of the Medieval period. One of the features of:

> ... humanism is its emphasis on individualism. Medieval society was corporate – that is, oriented toward, and organised around people acting in groups. Medieval political philosophy dictated that the smallest component of society was not the individual but the family. An individual ruler stood at the top of Medieval society, but this ruler was regarded as tightly bound to the other nobles by feudal alliances and, in some ways, as simply the greatest of the nobles. Workers banded together in guilds; pious people formed religious confraternities; citizens swore an oath of allegiance to their own city. Even art was thought to be a group effort, with the individual artist feeling no more need to sign a work than a baker did to sign each loaf of bread (We know the names of some medieval artists from sources such as contracts, bills of sale, and financial records, but rarely from the paintings or sculptures themselves). (Wiesner, Ruff & Wheeler 1993, p. 224)

Wolff asserts in her book *The Social Production of Art* (1981) that prior to the Renaissance in Europe, artists worked in much the same way as other workers did. They were seen as artisans and craftsmen who were collectively committed and shared the responsibility for the work they produced; 'though there were master builders and builders to whom others were apprenticed, they were not yet seen as sole producer and the single genius behind the work' (Wolff 1981, p. 17). This point is reinforced by cultural historian Deborah Haynes who asserts that 'before about 1500 there were no artists as we know them today, and there was no distinction between artist and artisan' (1997, p. 103). As these European societies developed, the position of artisan, a person who owned their own tools and sold the commodities they produced, became more specialised. Deborah Haynes contends that:

> in the ancient world, a hierarchical social structure placed artisans and craftspeople below traders and merchants, but above slaves. In this system, occupations and the status they represented were hereditary. The earliest specialised craftspeople were probably itinerant, but as market demands grew, they became more stationary and specializations developed. In the making of weapons and tools, for instance, artisans included metalworkers, patternmakers, smelters, turners, metal chasers, gilders, goldsmiths and silversmiths. (Haynes 1997, p. 76)

Particularly in Europe, Haynes argues, as populations grew and societies became more stable, guilds had developed which regulated all of the conditions of work for their members as well as the process of production. The guilds did this by setting wages and hours as well as prescribing the tools and techniques their members could use. They oversaw both quality and price. 'In this way, they functioned to preserve traditions; but beyond that, they also carried a certain mystique that may have contributed to the developing status of the artist' (Haynes 1997, p. 76). With the shift away from what were essentially city communes towards the rise of private patronage around the fourteenth and fifteenth century, as Haynes explains, a division began to appear between highly skilled artists who could afford to disregard the guilds and the guilds themselves. Many of these artists became the subject of hero worship and, as Haynes contends, many began to see 'their work not in terms of economic gain (or loss) but as a calling. Thus the artist *qua* artist began to emerge' (Haynes 1997, p. 104).

These 'artists' then became affiliated with the courts of late medieval and early modern Europe, which worked to their benefit. 'Artists began to be viewed, and to view themselves, as irreplaceable, which was supported by the notion that artistic genius was unmistakably individual' (Haynes 1997, p. 104). Individual creators began to differentiate themselves from the conception that they were mere artisans and became to be seen as men [*sic*] of intellect and vision, as Kenneth Clark (1969) has identified. Leonardo da Vinci, Michelangelo and Raphael were the exemplaries of this figure and provided the apogee of the artist as hero.

It can be seen then that the processes of professionalisation, secularisation and patronage were important features in the development of the conception of artists that has become entrenched in current ways of seeing these figures. Thus with the concomitant rise of the merchant class in Europe during the late Middle Ages and early modern period, coupled with the advent of the liberal humanist conception of the individual, the notion of artists as unique individuals began to be established. The difference between art and work became distinct and the idea of the similarity between the two began to be lost. Over the intervening centuries, Wolff (1981) argues, the artist figure was increasingly conceptualised as an individual with little or no institutional ties whatsoever, which, in conjunction with the Romantic ideals of the nineteenth century, in the end gave rise to the popular image of the 'artist in a garret' that the West is familiar with. In other words the Western notion of 'the artist' and the way they are expected to behave is itself a historically specific construction.

Wolff goes on to argue that prior to this conception of the artist as being outside, as it were, the constraints of society, it was common practice for an artist to work to orders from the very society itself, as an instrument of that society. They were in fact central figures within society. It was not uncommon, and certainly not seen as reprobate, for an artist to tailor the cultural product they were making to the wishes of their benefactor or 'to change one's allegiance without apology' (Wolff 1981, p. 27). Furthermore, she argues that 'it has *never* been true that the artist has worked in isolation from social and political constraints' (ibid.), whether these are of a direct or an indirect kind. 'The idea of the artist as sole originator of a work obscures the fact that art has continued to be a collective product' (ibid.). As a result she concludes that if this is indeed the case, the cultural product associated with these figures:

loses its character as transcendent, universal fact, whose 'greatness' is unanalysable, but somehow mysteriously and inherently present.

It is seen instead as the complex product of economic and ideological factors, mediated through the formal structures of the text (literary or other), and owing its existence to the particular practice of the located individual. (Wolff 1981, p. 139)

Art in this sense is truly a product of the social.

Relying less on conflict-based theorists such as Marx and more on the interactionist approach of John Dewey, one of the other central figures in the sociological firmament dealing with creativity, Howard Becker has re-introduced the idea of the artist as a team player. In doing so he also challenged the conception of the artist as genius holding sole responsibility for the produced cultural artefact (Becker, 1982). His symbolic interactionist thesis is outlined succinctly by Vera Zolberg declaring that his book *Art Worlds* (1982) was the summation of his thought on the arts in society:

He starts from the perspective of microscopic interaction among participants, moving gradually to increasingly larger sociational patterns that serve as the basis of, and eventually coalesce, into large, complex societies encompassing a variety of art worlds. The 'worlds' in which artists' work exist as more or less institutionalised subcultures that normally have little to do with one another. Each centres around one of four principal types of artists: integrated professionals, mavericks, folk artists, naif artists. This subcultural analysis presents the arts as relatively self-contained and segmented one from the other, more like a mosaic than a collage. In the tradition of the Chicago school of urban sociology, art worlds are like neighbourhoods making up a city. (Zolberg 1990, p. 124–5)

Initially, Becker looked at the idea of art as an activity in an attempt to answer the question: what occurs when an artist brings their ideas to fruition? He decided that there were myriad activities to be undertaken for an art work to exist as it does (1982, pp. 2–6). From inspiration to idea, then on to the execution of that idea and finally to its manufacture and distribution, the work of art is subject to a reliance upon a network of many players or workers (Alexander, 2003). The division of labour in art, according to Becker, lies somewhere between an individual doing everything involved in creative production and every small detail of activity being done by a separate person. Becker decided that 'to analyse an art world we look for its characteristic kinds of workers and the bundle of tasks each one does' (Becker 1982, p. 9).

Becker argues that not all divisions of labour are 'natural' however (ibid. pp. 9–10), although we come to recognise them as so. For instance, it does not follow that the division of labour in popular music must be organised in the way that it is. For example, Greil Marcus argues that since Lennon and McCartney established themselves as pre-eminent creators in the popular music field, songwriters have been expected to be multiskilled as writers, recording artists and performers (Marcus 1980, p. 185). He asserts that prior to this change it was acceptable and even desirable for these functions to be kept separate. The function of songwriters was to supply material for those performing and recording the material. However, post Lennon and McCartney there is now established a normative practice where an individual is expected to perform an amalgam of tasks. Thus in rock music it is currently expected that performance and composition go hand in hand, which is the reverse of the more recent historical position. In addition, in terms of the division of labour in contemporary popular music, it does not always follow that an audio engineer's tasks and a record producer's tasks should be divided, although in rock music this has often been the case. In the field of electronic dance music the reverse predominates, where the engineer, producer and songwriter can be conflated into a single persona. Becker contends that 'each kind of person who participates in the making of art works, then has a specific bundle of tasks to do' (Becker 1982, p. 11), but nonetheless while each art world rests on these extensive divisions of labour, the allocation of tasks is arbitrary. As Becker argues, and as was pointed out above by both Wolff and Haynes, the appearance of autonomy of the individual artist is 'superficial' (ibid. p. 16). However, there is still an ideological commitment to a belief in the requirement of a unique individual possessing special talent. These individuals are accorded special privileges and rights. They are seen as gifted, given the moral latitude accorded to those who are gifted, and in return we believe society receives works of invaluable quality (ibid p. 16). Becker then exposes this position by suggesting that since it is believed that extreme skill is required for carrying out aspects of some artworks, distinctions as to who is an artist and who isn't can be seen in the divisions of labour. These divisions, different from activity to activity, have become necessary to ensure that not all receive the privileges and benefits of those labelled 'artists'.

Becker (1982, p. 19) argues that in making these divisions of labour within art worlds there is also a spurious distinction made between what he labels core activities as art and all other activities which are carried out by support personnel, and this distinction is dependent on the perceived degree of skill required. This perception, Becker argues, leads to a polarised view where one set of activities is seen to possess the characteristic of 'art', with all its connotations of genius, and any other associated set of activities can be labelled 'craft', with its connotations of workaday industry. Becker (ibid.) argues that position is therefore a construct and presents a perfect, if somewhat circular, correlation between art and artist. If you do the core activity you must be an artist. The obverse holds true as well, for if you are an artist what you do must be art.

This position, as Becker asserts, presents problems if the correlation doesn't occur. If the notion of 'gift' implies spontaneous expression or sublime inspiration then, if critics or audiences perceive the lack of these, the danger is of having the art being seen as illegitimate, thus there is an incongruity for those who perceive artists this way. Craft-like approaches in art, according to Becker, are in danger of not being seen to conform to the characteristics of 'art', that is the activity centred around the notion of art as constructed through the late Middle Ages and carried on since in the Romantic ideal. If the 'work' involved in art is exposed, there is also a risk that the ideology that perceives an artist as a spontaneous genius working free of constraint will also be exposed (Becker 1982, p. 18).

In line with this argument Becker then asks the fundamental and pointed question: what if the person regarded as the artist doesn't do the work an artist must do? In this case can the work be described as art? He concludes that, ironically, this is a matter of degree usually from art to art which then imposes a degree of relativity on to the answer. It is not deemed appropriate, for instance, for a sculptor to send his work to a foundry to be completed, but it is nonetheless appropriate for a composer to employ an orchestra to perform their work. The question thus appears incongruous once you look across various cultural fields.

Becker then raises an important consideration in regard to the idea that an artist's position is dependent on producing art works which embody their special gifts and talents. As a result of the connection between earning capacity, reputation and property rights the participants in art are concerned about authenticity. That is did they really do this work? The artist's reputation is tied to the work and each work presented either adds to or subtracts from their reputation. In short, they reinforce one another. In this case it can be argued that the whole industrial–financial landscape of most culture industries is dependent on maintaining this appearance of the artist as an individual responsible for the work. It is the cornerstone of, for example, the use of intellectual property and as such copyright is dependent on it (McIntyre 2007).

While Becker refutes the notion that the individual is totally responsible for art works, he does concede, importantly, that there is an individual who undertakes the central core work deemed to be artistic. However, in doing so he strongly emphasises that the output is dependent on a network of cooperating individuals. To add weight to this position he suggests, as an example, that there may be aesthetic conflicts between the artist and what has been termed the support individual. Becker asserts that the imposition of support people's reputations can cause a change in the nature of the desired work (1982, p. 25). He suggests that the artist can only do things that the support people are prepared and capable of doing. To put this in larger terms, the artist's ability to make artistic choices, that is their agency as creative individuals, is seen to be bounded by the institutional constraints of the cultural field they work within, which includes, amongst other things, current technology and the techniques needed to utilise that technology. Becker argues in this case that the art is not only bounded by the limits of technique but also by what existing institutions can assimilate (1982, pp. 26–8). If it is financially and technically impossible to mount a major concert piece in the classical music world it may have to be adapted to whatever the performers, venue, promoters or institution promoting it can handle. From this perspective the artist must accept the constraints and work within these limits.

Becker also points out that a further constraint on the artist's agency or their ability to create as they choose is the idea of convention in art (ibid. pp. 28–34). To undertake any cooperative effort the group, artists and support personnel, must agree on the terms on which they will cooperate. Conventions exist that prevent them from having to re-invent the wheel, as it were, so they then can select from a standard set of pre-existing standards, rules or conventions. In music these conventions are embodied in the instruments used and, more subtly, in the available musical language. If, for instance, a musician wished to work completely outside any of the currently accepted systems of music, the instruments necessary for the new music's performance would have to be built afresh and the musicians necessary to perform it would have to be trained and so on. Consequently, given the difficulties of this enterprise, most creators normally abide by the conventions. They work within the institutional constraints and abide by the earlier agreements about these things which have generally become customary. From Becker's point of view this situation does not make unconventional work impossible – just difficult and therefore most often improbable. Change, nonetheless, is possible since the basis for most cultural product's power to bring audiences into its emotional orbit is from the expectation of convention since, as Becker explains (1989, pp. 29–30), playing with expectation creates tension and resolution. If creators step too far outside the convention, they face the danger of their creation not being recognised as such. Unsuccessful innovation is the province of the crank while successful innovation is most often seen as the province of remarkable individuals.

Despite this common perception Becker's account of art worlds doesn't emphasise the impact of the remarkable individual preferring to concentrate on exposing the necessary team effort required to produce cultural artefacts within a recognisable network of activity. On the other hand, he has also been criticised for giving, in line with the Chicago school he emanates from, 'little detailed attention to the overarching macrostructure of society and polity within which these worlds function' (Zolberg 1990, pp. 124–5).

To sum up, Becker's analysis highlights the difficulty of only considering the individual when investigating various creative works. The assumption that only particular individuals can be credited with a work belies the evidence that art is, according to Becker, a collective process. Without the collective activity of support personnel within an art world, the creative works may not come to fruition. Becker thus asserts that creativity and innovation are far more reliant on social activity than is normally admitted to. Agreeing with Becker, Vera Zolberg also asserts that 'introducing new ideas in the face of entrenched interests is likely to require complex strategies' (Zolberg 1990, p. 132). It is with this realisation that we could include here the work of empirical sociologist Pierre Bourdieu (1993) and his notion of the field of cultural production as an arena of social contestation. However, we will come to these ideas shortly. Meanwhile, we can briefly consider the work from Richard Peterson (1982, 1985).

Peterson produces evidence that there are a series of what he calls constraints that have an effect on the form and content of cultural production. These are primarily social in character, and he lists them as law, technology, industry structure, organisation structure, market and occupational careers (Peterson 1985, p. 64). He argues that 'the nature and content of symbolic products are shaped by the social, legal and economic milieu in which they are created, edited, manufactured, marketed, purchased and evaluated' (ibid. p. 46) in an increasingly complex network of influence (ibid. p. 45). While this position can be seen to equate in some senses with notions of art worlds, and possibly encompasses something much broader, identifying these factors as constraints, and not also enablers, leads to some misleading assumptions. However, the idea that they have an effect on the production of culture is an important one, as we shall see.

Meanwhile, given the above, and for our purposes extrapolating out to creativity, the concept of 'artist' can now be broadened far beyond the Romantic ideal, the one which is commonly assumed or traditionally used. Using Becker's notions, and following Arthur Berger, the term artist can now also be understood 'to refer to all those involved with the creation and production of texts that are distributed, spread, broadcast, narrowcast, cablecast, or beamed by satellite through the mass media' (Berger 1995, p. 146). This usage can be broadened again to not only include those traditionally designated as creative individuals – that is those associated with the fine arts – but, following Florida, also scientists, novelists, designers, architects, musicians, dancers, poets, engineers and mathematicians. Given Wolff's and Becker's critiques, this list must also include their support personnel; in other words, any creative individual who deals in some way with ideas, concepts, theories and their implementation. Therefore, it should also be possible to redefine a creative person, and more specifically those concerned with cultural production, as any individual involved with the creation and production of texts. As has been pointed out by Berger, however, in line with what has become known as reception theory, this definition must also include any agent capable of making meaning from the text. The implications of this stance have been explored extensively by poststructuralist writers and have led to assertions that 'the author is dead'. It is to an investigation of this seemingly perplexing standpoint that we will now turn and make an attempt to place it within the broader development of cultural studies.

5
The Cultural View

In locating creative work within a social context we can begin to see the problematic nature of considering only the individual producer's action when investigating creative activity. The evidence, according to both the neo-Marxist views of Wolff and the symbolic interactionist perspective of Becker, amongst many others, supports the idea that creativity can no longer be credited to particular individuals only. Taking the idea that all art is a social product one step further are the poststructuralists (see Harland 1987, Moxey 1994) who have been instrumental in altering the broader focus of cultural studies (Frow & Morris 1993, Real 1996, Sardar & Van Loon 1998). At the time of the appearance of poststructuralist thought, cultural studies were a cluster of approaches to theory that investigated notions of identity, power, meaning, discourse and representation and, for our purposes, not only placed a strong emphasis on the text but also stimulated a reappraisal of cultural consumption. In playing their part within this larger project, the poststructuralists not only put in place what can be called the dissolution of certainty but also helped destabilise the idea that the individual producer is the sole locus of the act of meaning-making. In doing this they helped dismember the meta-narratives of Romanticism for those who were engaged in the cultural studies project.

Deborah Haynes, as only one example of this process at work, saw the artist figure of the late twentieth century as a 'postmodern parodic ex-centric bricoleur'. In order to understand what she means, it is pertinent at this point to mention some of the characteristics of postmodern creation. Irony and satire, she believes, have been replaced by parody and pastiche. While parody at least has some connection to the past, being essentially a dialogue with it, pastiche just simply plunders. For Haynes it is based on 'random imitation, or even cannibalisation, of styles of the past, wherein traditions are treated as products for consumption in the new shopping mall of history' (Haynes 1997, p. 134). She goes on to say that this form, a development of the third stage of multi-national capitalism, 'with its electronic and nuclear-powered technologies, including television and the computer, supports reproduction and consumption rather than older forms of productive creativity' (ibid.). She claims that many artists working in the latter part of the twentieth century used parody rather than pastiche to reconnect themselves to a relationship with artists of the past. They are not, however, central figures, with some exceptions, in the mainstream art worlds and are thus 'ex-centric'. In addition, whether they employ parody or pastiche they are often bricoleurs. This is a term Claude Levi-Strauss used to describe 'the way some cultures recycle and recombine both old and new elements for new uses. Artistic techniques developed in the twentieth century – such as collage, montage in all its varieties, and assemblage – all can be described as forms of bricolage' (Haynes 1997, p. 138). While denying individual genius in the use of these techniques, and the idea that art exists to serve a higher purpose, there has also been a return to what can be called a hyperfocus on personality. This idea is manifest in the notion that 'anyone can be an innovative artist through careful manipulation of publicity or extreme exhibitionism' (ibid., p. 143).

To summarise, bricoleurs cannot invent anything new in the way that Romantics conceive of this process. They simply utilise what has already been done and rearrange it. Therefore, from this perspective the idea of independent creators building something new couldn't possibly be correct. There is only an endless process of recycling. This postmodern conception of creativity, also supported in part by the notion of art worlds or the idea that art is socially produced, cuts at the very core of the idea of artistic greatness. The notion of genius, or more strictly the specific commonly held conception of it, can then quite readily be deconstructed. Therefore, the concept of author as originator and all that it entails has to be, according to this argument, defunct.

This view – that the conception of the artist as it had been previously viewed is not a useful one to use anymore – is partially aided, albeit inadvertently, by the research of both Becker (1982) and Wolff (1981,1993), whose work on collectivist art processes de-emphasised the role of the individual artist as the sole source of creativity. But others, however, simply dismissed the artist altogether, stating that the idea of the author/artist is null, void and therefore totally unimportant. In particular, the essays of Roland Barthes and Michel Foucault have contributed considerably to this position.

Barthes' essay entitled 'Image-Music-Text' (1977) is of particular interest for us. By making the deceptively simple claim that the 'author is
dead' Barthes called into question the idea of the author as genius. His
assertion was that interpretation is the site of meaning-making, and
since this is arguably the case, the author must have little control over
what meaning the text conveys. In this case 'the artist', itself a historically specific construction, conflated with the notion of 'the author
[cannot be] the sole origin and source of authentic meaning of a text'
(Wolff 1981, p. 117) as it is only in the relationship between the text
and the reader that meaning-making takes place. Thus the interpreter
should be seen as the creator, not the producer. Barthes' is a radical
and unsettling argument. It insists 'on the complete removal of the
concept of authorship from analysis' (Wolff 1981, p. 118). This total
de-centering of the author leaves the text privileged over the modernist
conception of 'the selfconscious subjects who project meaning into their
work' (Seidman 1994, p. 266). This move by Barthes, of rejecting the
notion of authorship completely:

> replaces the original modernist couplet – *subject* (author)/*object*
> (work) – with something else which itself has the appearance of
> a couplet – *practices* (writing)/ (intertextual) *field*. But the relation-
> ship of text to its intertextual field is active, creative, and practical.
> (Seidman 1994, p. 266)

In this way the text, the object that was thought to result from the
artist/author's work, ceases to be a fixed object itself but now can be seen
as a locus of an endless process of meaning production. The text, according to Barthes, is not a line of words releasing a 'single "theological"
meaning (the "message" of the Author-God) but a multi-dimensional
space in which a variety of writings, none of them original, blend
and clash' (Barthes 1977, p. 146). For Barthes, 'the text is a tissue of
quotations drawn from the innumerable centres of culture' (ibid.). He
concludes with the statement that:

> ...a text is made up multiple writings, drawn from many cultures
> and entering into mutual relations of dialogue, parody, contestation,
> but there is one place where this multiplicity is focused and that
> place is the reader, not, as was hitherto said, the author. The reader
> is the space on which all the quotations that make up a writing are
> inscribed without any of them being lost; a text's unity lies not in its
> origin but its destination ... the birth of the reader must be at the cost
> of the death of author. (1977, p. 148)

This declaration is, of course, a device on Barthes' part. He acknowledges that there are writers, that is, people who compile words on a page, but what he wants to take to task is the concept of authorship, not the fact that people write. His famous phrase 'the death of the author' (ibid.) can be seen as analogous to the cry that rings out when a monarch dies and is replaced with another; 'the king is dead. Long live the King'. It is a phrase that seems absurd until its rhetorical intent is thought through.

Michel Foucault certainly took the phrase, 'death of the author', seriously. In accepting that the liberal-humanist notion of the fixed subject, exemplified in the genius model, was no longer tenable, Foucault was intrigued as to why the conception of the author-god figure persisted and, since it does, tried to examine what function this concept still serves. Foucault argues in his essay 'What Is an Author?' (1977) that it is not enough to simply 'repeat the empty affirmation that the author has disappeared .... Instead we must locate the space left empty by the author's disappearance' (Foucault 1977, p. 145). Foucault pursues the argument that the author's name does serve a function. As Wolff outlines, the possibility that Foucault's work suggests (1981, p. 121) is to see the author function as a means of classification, in that certain texts or works can be gathered around the name itself. It also characterises the operation of certain discourses, not the least of which is that of proprietorial ownership and its connection to copyright. Additionally, the information about the author that we have in biographies and the like is also important as it can colour the function of the author's name. These functions are summarised by Foucault as follows:

> (1) the author-function is linked to the juridical and institutional system that encompasses, determines, and articulates the universe of discourses; (2) it does not affect all discourses in the same way at all times and in all types of civilisation; (3) it is not defined by the spontaneous attribution of a discourse to its producer, but rather by a series of specific and complex operations; (4) it does not refer purely and simply to a real individual, since it can give rise simultaneously to several selves, to several subjects – positions that can be occupied by different classes of individuals. (1977, p. 153)

After examining in some detail the author-function, a different thing to the 'real' author, Foucault recognises that a work cannot develop 'without passing through something like a necessary or constraining figure' (1977, p. 159). In a manner similar to Barthes' distinction between writers and authors, Foucault insists that the physically identifiable person exists but what we ascribe to the name of that person in relation to the text is open and fluid. As Wolf explains, his task has been to illustrate that 'what is under attack is a concept of "author" as a determinate and fixed source of artistic works and their meanings' (1981, p. 123). What Barthes is trying to do is deprive 'the subject (or its substitute) of its role as originator, and of analyzing the subject as a variable and complex function of discourse' (Foucault 1977, p. 158). In Foucault's final analysis, he insists that the time will come when we will be indifferent to all of these conceptions, even to the author-function itself.

It is possible, given the period both Foucault and Barthes were writing in, that is just after the failures of the Paris Uprising in 1968, as Steven Seidman points out, these critiques of the subject/author may be an 'instance of opposition to all forms of social domination' (Seidman 1994, p. 266). One of the most universalising and overarching forms of seeing the world in deterministic ways, at least from the poststructuralist perspective, is that of structuralism, and it is primarily this perspective these writers fought against. As Randall Johnson indicates:

> the attempt to come to terms, in one way or another, with phenomenology and various forms of objectivist approaches to society, ranging from Marxism to structuralism, informed the work of a whole generation of French intellectuals, including Roland Barthes, Michel Foucault and Jacques Derrida. (Bourdieu 1993, p. 269)

The structuralist position they were reacting against is adequately summarised by De George and De George (1972). They explain that there has been a concern throughout Western thought from ancient times onward with deep organising systems that seem to determine action. The specific roots of the intellectual movement known as structuralism, however, can be traced to the nineteenth century and possibly three significant figures: Karl Marx, Sigmund Freud and Ferdinand de Saussure. Each of them shared:

> a conviction that surface events and phenomena are to be explained by structures, data, and phenomena below the surface. The explicit and obvious is to be explained by and is determined – in some sense of the term – by what is implicit and not obvious. The attempt to uncover deep structures, unconscious motivations, and underlying causes which account for human actions at a more basic and profound level than do individual conscious decisions, and which shape, influence, and structure these decisions, is an enterprise which unites Marx, Saussure, and modern structuralists. (De George & De George 1972, p. xii)

As an example of the effects of this line of reasoning we can take the work of Theodor Adorno, writing in reaction to the success of what he and Horkheimer labelled the 'culture industries'. Adorno was steeped in the ideas of Marx and Freud and after fleeing totalitarian Germany prior to the Second World War, and then arriving in the heart of Western popular culture in the United States, argued that the production, texts and consumption of popular culture, as it took place in the West, was highly problematic. Being a civilised European and a classically trained musician, he took as his specific target the popular music industry and its mass audience.

In general, Adorno (1941) argued that there was a negative dialectic in operation between what was labelled high culture and popular culture, the latter being consumed mainly by the working class. High culture, which Adorno himself was steeped in, was potentially revolutionary through its ideals which he thought embodied universality, complexity and an underlying unity or wholeness. In essence, Adorno 'equated culture in its ideal state with art, with special, exceptional forms of human creativity' (Hesmondhalgh 2002, p. 16), and in the process of making those arguments 'provided a version of a mode of thinking about culture that is still common today' (ibid., p. 16). Low culture, that is, the products of film, television and popular music, was to be seen as debased, trivial and meretricious. Popular culture was only significant for the working class because high culture was absent from their cultural intake; hence the negative dialectic.

Like Bertoldt Brecht, Adorno saw the structures of the culture industry serving particular interests and, for Adorno, the dissemination of popular culture they engaged in was used to lull people into accepting the capitalist way and prevented them from seeing how alienated they actually were in their workplace. Adorno and his compatriot Horkheimer critiqued the culture industries on the grounds of their lack of value and the false propositions many held about them, and also 'argued that the introduction of industrialisation and new technologies into cultural production did indeed lead to increasing commodification' (Hesmondhalgh 2002, p. 16); they missed the fact that 'it also led to exciting new directions and innovations' (ibid.). Adorno's approach to audiences also revealed a problematic set of assumptions. In his opinion the culture industries were about the business of manipulating a childlike audience. These he characterised in one of two less than complementary ways. The audiences for popular culture were either, in Adorno's terms, easily led and malleable or they were obsessive and alienated individuals who were not fully integrated into society. Overall they were passive individuals engaged in 'de-concentrated' listening, which was engendered by the simplicity of the culture they engaged with.

Since behind Adorno's ideas we can see the implicit assumption of a stimulus/response model, characteristic of the structuralists he was relying on, it can be argued that he gives very little agency, that is the ability to make choice, to the predominantly working-class mass audience he was writing about. In essence it is, for Adorno, social practice that ultimately determines what those engaged with low culture can do. It is this allocation of what is essentially an 'acted upon' subject position to the subordinated classes that troubled many poststructuralists and, as stated prior, fed their 'opposition to all forms of social domination' (Seidman 1994, p. 266).

Poststructuralist thought, locked perpetually in its relationship with structuralism, argued with the notion that one can be trapped completely within a totalising and determinist structure whether that structure is an all encompassing social order, a psychic self governed by a set of predetermined conflicts or a system of language that orders experience. As Chris Weedon argues

> like all theories, poststructuralism makes certain assumptions about language, subjectivity, knowledge and truth. Its founding insight, taken from the structuralist linguistics of Ferdinand de Saussure, is that language, far from reflecting an already given social reality, constitutes social reality for us. Neither social reality nor the 'natural' world has fixed intrinsic meanings which language reflects or expresses. Different languages and different discourses within the same language divide up the world and give it meaning in different ways which cannot be reduced to one another through translation or by an appeal to universally shared concepts reflecting a fixed reality. (Weedon in Storey 1994, p. 172)

This primarily idealist position argues instead that 'the mind-set that allows us to think that our pictures of the world are not pictures but the world itself' (Natoli 1997) is entirely open to question. In their endeavours to go beyond the totalising structures they were working against, poststructuralist thinkers tended to argue that one always deals with plural meanings and plural subjectivities which are all working within a multiplicity of communicative discourses, none of which should be considered as more superior than any other.

To elaborate, at the basis of communication is the sign and, for linguists such as de Saussure, there must be two levels to it. These can be termed a signifier (audio/visual/written images) and a signified (the concept the images represent). For poststructuralists, and this is an important difference between this way of thinking and structuralism, as typified by theorists like de Saussure, 'signifiers are always located within a discursive context and the temporary fixing of meaning in a specific reading of a signifier depends on this discursive context' (Weedon in Storey 1994, p. 175). Discursive fields consist of competing discourses or ways of giving meaning to the world, and these discourses organise social institutions and processes. However, within discursive fields not all discourses carry equal weight and they inevitably compete for dominance. Some will reaffirm the status quo and others will challenge it. Some are seen as 'natural' and others must fight for recognition. Since texts not only exist within variable discursive fields they must also be seen as both polysemic and polyvalent. That is, not only do signs carry multiple meanings they, by virtue of the variable subjectivities of the audiences who interact with them, must also have multiple understandings. Once these ideas are then coupled with a conception of the subject, the person who engages with the text, as also fluid and mobile, the possibility of control or domination by supposedly determining structures becomes far less certain than under the humanist conception of the individual.

Humanists 'presuppose an essence at the heart of the individual which is unique, fixed and coherent' (Weedon in Storey 1994, p. 175). It is what makes the person who they are. Furthermore, for the humanist, 'human reason is regarded as the sole and sufficient arbiter of truth, goodness and justice' (West 1996, p. 154). For humanism the cognitive subject is central to the individual, but where it sees the individual as 'a conscious, knowing unified, rational subject, poststructuralism theorises subjectivity as a site of disunity and conflict' (Weedon in Storey 1994, p. 175). John Fiske affirms the pluralist position of the poststructuralists by stating that 'the social histories of people in societies as diverse as Western capitalist democracies are constructed out of such a variety of social experiences and social forces as to provide for almost as much individual difference as any natural gene bank' (Fiske 1990, p. 81). Ien Ang, in her book *Desperately Seeking the Audience* (1991), also highlights the fundamental irreducibility of the audience to a singular subjectivity when she states that 'the social world of actual audiences consists of such a multifarious and intractable, ever expanding myriad of elements that their conversion into moments of a coherent discursive entity can never be complete' (1991, p. 14). Chris Weedon also asserts that against the 'irreducible humanist essence of subjectivity, poststructuralism proposes a subjectivity which is precarious, contradictory and in process, constantly being reconstituted in discourse each time we think or speak' (Weedon in Storey 1994, p. 175).

From these two points, that is the complexity of subject composition of readers/audiences/receivers and an active and multiple reading of the text/message, it can be seen that the text itself becomes a potential of meanings capable of being read with a variety of modes of attention by a variety of readers. These sets of ideas, outlined briefly here, have a significant set of implications for anyone studying creativity; one that cannot be ignored as they have a profound effect on the way creators can be viewed or conceptualised. By deconstructing the liberal-humanist subject, the conception that underpins the author-genius model, and also arguing against the domination of structure, the poststructuralists put in place a multiple faceted and fluid subject, with access to variable truths within competing discourses that help to constitute meanings themselves, which can then be interpreted variably. In this scenario, the producer of messages has very little control. This is *not* the picture normally associated with the all powerful-genius.

Without returning to the individual position of the scholars of aesthetics, and by deconstructing the liberal-humanist subject, both Foucault and Barthes set up a multiple faceted and fluid subject to replace the author-genius figure, one with access to variable truths within competing discourses. But the new subject they put in place constituted meaning through interpretation, not production. Poststructuralism therefore, like structuralism, problematises the very idea of a creator or cultural producer being in charge of, and in absolute control of, the meanings of the work they produce. In valorising reception over production, this work adds the reader or active audience to the list of those responsible for the creation of meaning.

But does this position necessarily recognise the impossibility of a degree of control by a producer in the making of meaning during interpretation? Deborah Haynes makes the observation that 'the birth of the postmodern signals many changes, including new myths and models for the artist' (Haynes 1997, p. 135); with the death of one conception of the author the birth of another takes place. The author is dead; long live the author.

Janet Wolff considers the implications of this poststructuralist position by suggesting that:

In abandoning humanist notions of the author as unconstituted, fixed and originary, we need not at the same time deny the central relevance of the author-artist for a sociology of art. Now I would

argue that there is a middle way between the atheoretical biograph-
ical mode and the absent subject. Recent work in the social history
of art has suggested that we can still focus on the artist as producer,
on the understanding that we reconceptualise subjectivity as provi-
sionally fixed, as fluid and inconsistent, and as itself the product and
effect of discourse, ideology and social relations. In other words the
sociology of the arts still has a place for biography; and creativity,
though located, determined assisted and compromised, operates as a
category within this discourse. (1993, p. 147)

The concern here is with the notion that someone must instigate the
use of sign systems to coalesce them into a communicative message and
in doing so set the possibility of what is being communicated. Wolff is
thus more concerned with those who literally, rather than interpretively,
bring those texts into being. As Vera Zolberg argues, even Becker who, as
we have seen, is an advocate of the de-emphasis of the central role of the
individual artist, more often than not, attributes a corpus of work 'to a
principal author. Despite the fact that creative genius is more often myth
than reality, it cannot be said that art works give birth to themselves by
some parthenogenetic process' (1990, p. 114).

Just because it can be argued that authorial dominance and unity can
be seen as a construction of a particular historical discourse, and the
power to make meaning should reside more aptly with readers or audiences, it does not necessarily follow that the notion of authorship can
simply be replaced by a vacuum. Zolberg argues that even with a much
modified conception of authorship this modification does not necessarily preclude the importance of the author. Citing Giddens, Wolff goes
on to posit the view that 'the de-centring of the subject must not be
made equivalent to its disappearance' (Giddens quoted by Wolff 1981,
p. 136). She contends that:

> The author as fixed, uniform and unconstituted creative source has
> indeed died. The concept of authorial dominance in the text has also
> been thrown open to question. But the author, now understood as
> constituted in language, ideology, and social relations, retains a cen-
> tral relevance... in relation to the meaning of the text (the author
> being the first person to fix meaning, which will of course subse-
> quently be subject to redefinition and fixing by all future readers).
> (Wolff 1981, p. 136)

This position not only has wider implications for the author/artist
as subject, but also for cultural production or creativity in general.

We will pursue this discussion shortly but for now the question still remains as to what constitutes the ground for the reconstitution of the author/producer. Foucault, as we saw earlier, at least attempts to ask the pertinent question of what can possibly fill the space left by the dated conception of the author-genius figure.

It can be posited that Stuart Hall's work on what is called the 'encoding-decoding model' (1980) does begin to provide at least a larger space than that provided by Barthes or Foucault. For Hall the author, constructor, producer or creator maintains a larger modicum of importance in the production of cultural artefacts and certainly in the process of communication itself. In short, the development of Halls' model signals a partial reconstruction or relocation of the conception of the producer. His model admits to the possibility that while interpretation is an important aspect to the creative process, a degree of power to control meaning still may reside with the producer.

Hall (1980), when dealing with sites of creation, or texts, utilised the terms 'preferred', 'oppositional' and 'negotiated' readings to account for the variety of ways an audience may approach a text. Preferred readings are those where the reader's social situation aligned them with the dominant ideology and thus the audience/text relationship would produce what Hall called dominant readings of the text. Oppositional readings are those where the audience opposes the meaning in the text and produces readings opposite to those offered. This corresponds in a way to Umberto Eco's use of the term 'aberrant decoding'. Eco (Corner & Hawthorn 1993) stated simply that whenever there are significant social differences between the encoders and decoders of a text, encoding would be necessarily aberrant. The text would be decoded using a different set of codes and conventions from those operating during its encoding. Some readings may be so oppositional that the text itself may be misinterpreted or indeed entirely rejected in terms of what the producer intended. That is, if the text fails to allow space for meaning to be generated in terms of the subjectivities of social experience of the audience, it is unlikely to be understood. On the other hand, negotiated readings, as described by Hall, are those that accept the dominant interpretation in general but modify it to meet the needs of their situation. As Fiske suggests, Hall suspects that the majority of audience members would belong to this group (Fiske 1987, p. 64), and he argues that negotiating meanings with the text 'allows the socially situated viewer an active, semi-controlling role in' (Fiske 1987, p. 82) the process of creative interpretation, that is, the making of meaning.

The earlier work of Raymond Williams tends to support Hall's conception that there is significant correspondence between production and consumption. Williams notably doesn't eschew the need for a communicative producer but also couches this idea in a socially constituted process where reception is equally important. He argues that:

> Communication is the crux of art, for any adequate description of experience must be more than simple transmission; it must also include reception and response. However successfully an artist may have embodied his experience in a form capable of transmission, it can be received by no other person without the further 'creative activity' of all perception: information transmitted by the work has to be interpreted, described and taken into the organization of the spectator. It is not a question of 'inspired' or 'uninspired' transmission to a passive audience. It is, at every level, an offering of experience, which may then be accepted, rejected or ignored. (Williams 1961, p. 29)

David Morley, who undertook to empirically test Hall's ideas and whose work opened the way to the development of the notion of active audiences, also reinforces the idea that a producer is capable of providing, at least in part, the limits to variable interpretations. He argues that to make an interpreter, or audience, equivalent to a creator in the making of meanings is a difficult enterprise that 'ignores de Certeau's (1984) distinction between the strategies of the powerful and the tactics of the weak' (Morley 1993, p. 15), and discounts 'the difference between having power over a text, and power over the agenda within which that text is constructed and presented' (ibid.). Morley goes on to assert that the power of an audience to reinterpret meanings is often constrained by the discursive power of those who construct the text. Morley contends that 'the problem, as Ang (1990) argues, is that while "audiences may be active, in myriad ways, in using and interpreting media... it would be utterly out of perspective to cheerfully equate "active" with "powerful" " '(Morley 1993, p. 15). Keith Negus and Michael Pickering, arguing from this position, recommend that 'we may then need to bend our thinking about the active audience back towards a notion of conditioned frames of improvised action, though we should not do so at the expense of a creative sense of agency' (2004, p. 154). This position, it seems to me, agrees somewhat with Lawrence Grossberg's assertion that cultural studies endeavour to 'examine the complexities and contradictions not only within culture but in the relations between people, culture and power' (Storey 2006, p. 631).

In the light of the above, I would suggest that what we have seen in the development of this cultural perspective is the operation of a classic Hegelian process. Firstly a thesis was established, via aesthetics and the genius model, that producers of culture controlled its meaning. This position was modified by the structuralists who saw that underlying all action was a set of deep structures that helped determine that action. An antithesis developed out of these ideas. This was the essence of the poststructuralist project, but it swung the pendulum too far in the direction of opposing any control over meaning-making by producers at all. From both the thesis and antithesis a new synthesis can be seen to have developed. This synthesis recognises that *all* of the elements in the creative process, that is the creator, artefact and interpreters, embody certain similar, sometimes contradictory and competing discourses. Not only that, but there is a continual dialogue between them. It may well be that the creative process of meaning-making is the result of a continually changing power relationship between all of the elements that constitute the communication process. These elements include the producer of the artefact, the artefacts themselves and the interpreters of those artefacts. Vera Zolberg's approach essentially agrees with this position. She argues that we need to give:

> some attention to the various aesthetic structures (of art forms) and different forms of social structure of art: production, dissemination, and reception. These are viewed as interdependent forces in setting limits on change or permitting change under certain conditions. (Zolberg 1990, p. 169)

With these ideas in mind the ground for a reconceptualisation of creativity may be seen to be in place – a reconceptualisation that is neither completely agent centred, such as that put forward by the genius model, nor one that is structure centred, where either the bio-psychological structures or the socio-cultural conditions these exist in determine creative work. Most importantly, in accounting for the work of the poststructuralists and consequently those working in cultural studies, this reconceptualisation of creativity must also recognise the interaction of production, texts and reception as interlocking sites of meaning-making and thus sites of creativity.

6
Reconceptualising Creativity

What would a model of creativity that is neither completely agent centred, like the genius model, nor overly privileges the bio-psychological or socio-cultural structures that are seen to determine an individual's action look like? Whereas social theorists of art attempt to de-emphasise the individual and emphasise societal patterns (e.g. Kavolis 1972) or valorise co-operative and collective effort in creativity (e.g. Becker 1982), others with a biological, psychological or psychoanalytic base to their work have attempted to investigate creativity through a focus on individuals (e.g. Galton 1892, Lombroso 1891, Freud 1959, Guildford 1950, 1970). In addition, some theorists concerned with looking beyond the determinisms of an either individualist or structural approach (e.g. Barthes 1977, Foucault 1977) have called for a reconceptualisation of the way the initiators of the creative process are perceived. It is argued here that the most adequate reconceptualisation of creativity may lie not in any one of these single positions but in the confluence of a number of them.

The basis for this position may be found in the fact that, despite the emphasis in psychology on studying creativity as a trait of individuals, a dominant paradigm in Western culture, anthropological research indicates that this conception is not universal (Sawyer 2006, p. 113). Furthermore, 'historical research has discovered that the individualist conception of creativity is relatively recent, and wasn't common 500 years ago' (ibid.) even in the West. In other words this way of thinking about creativity is itself socially, culturally and historically located. In this case there must be other more reliable, and possibly more universal, ways of accounting for creativity; as Mihaly Csikszentmihalyi suggests, 'perhaps more than new research, what we need now is an effort to synthesise the various approaches of the past into an integrated theory' (1988, p. 338).

Sternberg, in the introductory section to his book, *Handbook to Creativity* (1999), suggests that confluence approaches to creativity may be a more useful and fruitful way to think about creativity. This approach hinges on the idea that 'multiple components must converge for creativity to occur' (1999, p. 10). It has been supported more recently by a number of researchers and can be found, for example, in Teresa Amabile's work in social psychology, Howard Gardner's (1993) confirmation of the systems model and Sternberg and Lubart's (1991) investment theory of creativity. In addition, John Dacey and Kathleen Lennon suggest that 'all human capacities have biological, psychological, and social elements' (1998, p. 8), and it is the interplay or confluence of these 'salient factors that collectively make creativity most likely to develop' (Dacey & Lennon 1998, p. 10).

While there are a number of these approaches being suggested, I want to argue here that the systems model of creativity proposed by psychologist Mihaly Csikszentmihalyi (1988, 1997, 1999, 2004), coupled with the recent work on cultural production by empirical sociologist Pierre Bourdieu (1977, 1990, 1993, 1996), could quite readily replace the older Ptolemaic, or person-centred view, with a more Copernican conception, where the individual agent is still seen to engage in creative activity but is now constituted as part of a much larger structured system in operation (Csikszentmihalyi 1988, p. 336). We used to think that the individual was the only locus of creativity. But on the evidence it has to be recognised that, while they are still involved and do what they have continually done, we need to see individuals as part of a much larger process at work. They are only one of a number of active factors that need to coalesce in order for creativity to occur.

Given this view, it now seems that we should be paying attention to the interdependent forces at work in creativity. These forces come from the social and cultural structures involved, including the ones that revolve around the production, dissemination and reception of creative products; the part played by formal and aesthetic structures (Zolberg 1990, p. 169) of the type embedded in bodies of knowledge; as well as the part individuals play when they undertake creative actions in relation to those structural elements. This includes not only production but also the creative action of interpretation that most audiences undertake. As Janet Wolff asserts, 'all action, including creative and innovative action, arises in the complex conjunction of numerous structural determinants and conditions. Any concept of "creativity" which denies this is metaphysical and cannot be sustained' (Wolff 1981, p. 9). Both Mihaly Csikszentmihalyi and Pierre Bourdieu, explicitly and more broadly, attempted to explain creativity and cultural production in just these terms.

Concerning himself with cultural production rather than creativity *per se*, Bourdieu's theory of practice was 'a probing reflection on one of the oldest problems in the Western intellectual tradition, namely, the relationship between the individual and society' (Swartz 1997, p. 96). Bourdieu himself stated that 'all of my thinking started from this point: how can behaviour be regulated without being the product of obedience to rules?' (Bourdieu quoted in Swartz 1997, p. 95). He wanted to reintroduce the concept of agents 'that Levi-Strauss and the structuralists, among them Althusser, tended to abolish, making them into simple epiphenomena of structure' (Bourdieu 1990, p. 9). As Randall Johnson explains, in his writings:

> Bourdieu sought to develop a concept of agent free from the voluntarism and idealism of subjectivist accounts and a concept of social space free from the deterministic and mechanistic causality inherent in many objectivist approaches. (Johnson in Bourdieu 1993, p. 4)

Bourdieu also suggests that rather than these two forces, subjectivism (agency) and objectivism (structure), being diametrically opposed they are in fact interlinked. Bourdieu, attempting to locate agency, an individual's ability to freely make choices, and structure, those objects that are perceived to determine behaviour, as a set of complementary pairs, argues that producing culture is always informed by an ability to understand and control our own actions (agency), but 'the possibilities of agency must be understood in terms of cultural trajectories, literacies and dispositions' (Schirato & Yell 1996, p. 148). From this perspective it is the interplay between agency and structure that actually makes practice possible. As David Swartz asserts, Bourdieu argues against:

> conceptualising human action as a direct, unmediated response to external factors, whether they be identified as micro-structures of interactions or macro-level cultural, social, or economic factors. Nor does Bourdieu see action as the simple outgrowth from internal factors, such as conscious intentions and calculations, as posited by voluntarists and rational-actor models of human action. For Bourdieu, explanations that highlight either the macro or the micro dimension to the exclusion of the other simply perpetuate the classic subjective/objective antimony. Bourdieu wants to transcend this dichotomy by conceptualizing action so that micro and macro,

voluntarist and determinist dimensions of human activity are integrated into a single conceptual movement rather than isolated as
mutually exclusive forms of explanation. He thus proposes a structural theory of practice that connects action to culture, structure and
power. (Swartz 1997, p. 9)

For Bourdieu what connects agency and structure is *habitus*, a concept
which has become one of his theoretical trademarks. However, before
we proceed further with this idea, it is pertinent here to give another
very brief description of the activity a reflective practitioner undertakes
in accumulating usable knowledge in their own production of culture.
Donald Schon in his book, *The Reflective Practitioner: How Professionals
Think in Action* (1983), suggests that 'knowing' for a reflective practitioner can have a number of properties. He suggests that in the process
of learning to adjust their action, while in the process of acting, practitioners are absorbed into 'a kind of reflection on their patterns of action,
on the situations in which they are performing. And on the know-how
implicit in their performance. They are reflecting *on* action and in some
cases, reflecting *in* action' (1983, p. 55). It is the utilization of the above
processes that Schon describes as practitioners 'finding the groove' or
having a 'feel' for their material (ibid.). These ideas correspond quite well
to Bourdieu's concept of the habitus which, using similar terminology,
has been described as:

> a 'feel for the game', a 'practical sense' (*sens practique*) that inclines
> agents to act and react in specific situations in a manner that is
> not always calculated and that is not simply a question of conscious
> obedience to rules. Rather it is a set of dispositions which generates
> practices and perceptions. The habitus is the result of a long pro-
> cess of inculcation, beginning in early childhood, which becomes a
> 'second sense' or a second nature. (Johnson in Bourdieu 1993, p. 5)

Habitus has also been described as an 'acquired system of generative
schemes objectively adjusted to the particular conditions in which it is
constituted' (Grenfell & James 1998, p. 14). Bourdieu himself described
it as a set of 'generative principles of distinct and distinctive practices'
(1998, p. 8). As a term it accounts for the way people like to be, their
preferences and taste, values, desires, ideas and narratives that have
been produced by the social institutions, such as family or religion,
they engage with. It is revealed in the cultural preferences a person possesses. According to this theory, people have long-term ways of seeing

the world that are peculiar to them but also shared by many others. Bourdieu argued that these components of habitus are not produced idiosyncratically but are actually produced in the wider society, and the agents within that society choose from within these sociocultural limits:

> The habitus is the product of the work of inculcation and appropriation necessary in order for those products of collective history, the objective structures (e.g. language, economy, etc.) to succeed in reproducing themselves more or less completely, in the form of durable dispositions. (Bourdieu 1977, p. 85)

In essence, agents make choices out of the available conditions on offer to them, but these conditions, echoing Marx, are made for them. That is, the social and structural conditions both delimit and provide the possible choices seen in action and, as far as we are concerned, this is certainly the case for creative action. Furthermore, agents, while capable of free choice within the realms of what is possible, 'do not act in a vacuum, but rather in concrete social situations governed by a set of objective social relations' (Johnson in Bourdieu 1993, p. 6). These concrete social situations have been labelled 'fields' by Bourdieu.

Fields are characterised by relations between agents, and since these relations are dynamic, a field, according to Randall Johnson, is 'a dynamic concept in that a change in agent's positions necessarily entails a change in the field's structure' (Bourdieu 1993, p. 6). They are thus spaces where struggles for dominance take place. For example, Bourdieu argues in relation to the field of literature or art that this field:

> is at all times the site of a struggle between the two principles of hierarchization: the heteronomous principle, favourable to those who dominate the field economically and politically (e.g. 'bourgeois art'), and the autonomous principle (e.g. 'art for art's sake'), which those of its advocates who are least endowed with specific capital tend to identify with a degree of independence from the economy, seeing temporal failure as a sign of election and success as a sign of compromise. The state of the power relations in this struggle depends on the overall degree of autonomy possessed by the field, that is, the extent to which it manages to impose its own norms and sanctions on the whole set of producers. (Bourdieu 1996, p. 60)

Fields, however, can't also be simply equated to institutions as the boundaries between them can't be sharply drawn. While there has been some comparison of Becker's notion of 'art worlds' and Bourdieu's concept of 'field', it should be noted that Bourdieu has written elsewhere that:

> without entering into a methodological expose of everything that separates this vision of the 'world of art' from the theory of the literary or artistic field, I will merely remark that the latter is not reducible to a *population* [italics in original], that is to say, to the sum of individual agents linked by simple relations of *interaction*, or more precisely, of *cooperation*: what is lacking, among other things, from this purely descriptive and enumerative evocation are the *objective relations* which are constitutive of the structure of the field and which orient the struggles aiming to conserve or transform it. (Bourdieu 1996, p. 205)

Fields are thus structured arenas and they are built around particular types of capital. Bourdieu makes a crucial set of distinctions between the types of capital he recognises. These include:

> Economic capital, which is immediately and directly convertible into money and may be institutionalised in the form of property rights;... cultural capital, which is convertible, on certain conditions, into economic capital and may be institutionalised in the form of educational qualifications; and... social capital, made up of social obligations (connections), which is convertible, in certain conditions, into economic capital and may be institutionalised in the form of title nobility. (Bourdieu 1986, p. 243)

Social capital is important as the ability to maintain social relations within the field is critical for success in that field. Symbolic capital, seen in awards and so on, also contributes to the maintenance of reputations and provides a way of making distinctions between players within the field. Bourdieu suggests that 'a work of art has meaning and interest only for someone who possesses the cultural competence, that is, the code, into which it is encoded' (Johnson in Bourdieu 1993, p. 7). Possession of these various codes results from a long process of immersion where they are acquired or inculcated through 'the pedagogical action of the family or group members (family education), educated members of the social formation (diffuse education) and social institutions (institutionalised education)' (ibid.).

Capital, as used by Bourdieu and like its economic counterpart, has value but only within the context that particular knowledge can be used in, that is, the field appropriate to the knowledge. Within the field of film, for example, cultural capital could be the acquisition of the ability to engage with the audio and visual language of cinema and the knowledge necessary to reproduce this for the screen. Differing fields are, therefore, differentiated by the modes of production and use that they are put to. As Johnson suggests:

> To enter a field (the philosophical field, the scientific field, etc.), to play the game, one must possess the habitus which predisposes one to enter that field, that game, and not another. One must also possess at least the minimum amount of knowledge, or skill, or 'talent' to be accepted as a legitimate player. Entering the game, furthermore, means attempting to use that knowledge, or skill, or 'talent' in the most advantageous way possible. (Bourdieu 1993, p. 8)

Bourdieu adds another component to his view of cultural production by asserting that the possibilities of action are produced in a field of works. The field of works, as distinct from fields themselves, can be conceived of as the accumulated cultural work completed up to this time in a particular field. According to Jason Toynbee (2000) it includes techniques and codes of production. For Bourdieu it is a 'system or schemata of thought' (1996, p. 236). As such, the heritage of collective works built up over time is accessible to each creative agent as 'a space of possibles, that is, as an ensemble of probable *constraints* which are the condition and the counterpart of a set of *possible uses*' [italicised in original] (Bourdieu 1996, p. 235). From this perspective, it is the choice made from what is possible that accounts for action in the creative process.

We can therefore claim that Bourdieu's concern with cultural production, coming about through practice that is both enabled and constrained by the structures that are interacted with, and is manifest in a person's habitus, allows for the conception that creativity can be conceived as an interaction between agents and the structures they engage with. It is this interaction that produces novel products, original ideas and unique processes.

Following Bourdieu, it can also be argued that producers of media content, while having the ability to make creative choices, are not free in the absolute sense in making those creative choices (1996, p. 235) as they do so utilising aspects of the field of works and within particular fields. The field of contemporary Western television production, for example, is occupied by other agents who also have access to the cultural, symbolic, social and economic capital pertinent to this field of cultural production. It is to the field that a producer must take a television series idea in order to have its merits judged as a worthwhile possible series. In this scenario the television producer draws on, via their own habitus and accumulated cultural, social and symbolic capital, the specific sets of knowledges pertinent to the cultural practices of a television producer. These knowledges, conventions and techniques reside within the accumulated works that exist within the traditions of the field of contemporary Western television production, that is, its accumulated field of works. In undertaking this cultural production the television producer and their crew, as agents working within the structures of the television industry, exemplify the notion that practice is always informed by a sense of agency and that the possibilities of agency must always be grounded in 'cultural trajectories, literacies and dispositions' (Schirato & Yell 1996, p. 148). It can therefore be suggested that it is the interplay between the spheres of an individual's habitus, the field they operate in and the accumulated knowledge that exists in the field of works that makes practice possible. This conclusion seems to me to be remarkably similar to the ideas proposed by Mihaly Csikszentmihalyi in his elucidation of the systems model of creativity which, as will be explored more fully immediately below, accepts that, in this example, television producers work within a system that shapes and governs the creativity they engage with while these creative agents contribute to and alter that system.

Although these two authors are dealing in similar territory and may be describing essentially the same phenomenon, Csikszentmihalyi's prime concern is to pinpoint the phenomenon of creativity itself and explain the mechanisms which surround it. Unlike Bourdieu, his concerns are primarily rooted in Darwin rather than Marx. However, the similarities between them occur in the idea that Bourdieu's elucidation of cultural practice, one that attempts to coalesce agency and structure, appears to complement that of Mihaly Csikszentmihalyi, whose conception of creativity also locates a creative agent within a structured system, although it isn't described in these precise terms. Nonetheless, both authors emphasise the location of the agent in a sociocultural context. There are also similarities to be observed in regard to Bourdieu's conception of field and Csikszentmihalyi's use of the same term. The concepts of *field of works*, set out by Bourdieu in his book *Rules of Art* (1996), seem remarkably similar to that of the *domain*, explained more fully in a moment. In addition, the concept of habitus could prove useful in attempting to provide a mechanism for including an individual's personal yet shared background as a factor in the process of creativity. However, before we pursue these comparisons too much further, an elucidation of the systems model is of most immediate concern as it is Csikszentmihalyi who works more directly with the notion of creativity.

Csikszentmihalyi sees creativity resulting from a complex system that is, for him, less Ptolemaic than Copernican in operation (Csikszentmihalyi 1988, p. 336). He doesn't ascribe sole responsibility for creativity to the productive individual but neither does he assert that creativity is beyond the locus of individual producers and located solely within the societies and cultures they inhabit. From this perspective creativity is the result of an interactive process that incorporates a person, a field and a domain in a non-linear system. Csikszentmihalyi asserts that:

> What we call creative is never the result of individual action alone; it is the product of three main shaping forces: a set of social institutions, or *field*, that selects from the variations produced by the individual those that are worth preserving; a stable cultural *domain* that will preserve and transmit the selected new ideas or forms to the following generations; and finally the *individual*, who brings about some change in the domain, a change that the field will consider to be creative. (ibid., p. 325)

Instead of looking at the separate elements in the creative process these are incorporated within an interactive and non-linear system which can be studied by investigating moments within it. Csikszentmihalyi argues that our customary view is that creation takes place firstly with an idea manifesting itself from within the creative person's head as it were – the flash of lightning, the light bulb turning on or the stroke of creative genius within, as Freud characterised it, a quasi-neurotic individual. Csikszentmihalyi then goes to great lengths to state his view that the information that goes 'into the idea existed long before the creative person arrived on the scene. It had been stored in the symbol system of the culture, in the customary practices, the languages the specific notation of the "domain"' (1988, pp. 325–39), in other words the conventions, rules and ideas the person has access to. It is the task of the person working within the creative process to produce some variation in this inherited information or domain.

The person may be an unusual individual in one of many ways predisposed to make those variations. For instance, they may be born with sensitivities to light or sound not possessed by others or have a set of environmental factors operate on them such as sibling position, social class or educational opportunities which incline them to use, for example, information processing strategies in an unusual way. In other words they contribute an idiosyncratic set of skills and predispositions that are peculiar to them but also shared amongst many others. Howard Gardner, who was one of the prime movers, in collaboration with David Feldman and Csikszentmihalyi, in the systems model's inception, states that 'a creative individual is one who regularly solves problems, fashions products, and/or poses new questions in a domain in a way which is initially considered novel but which is ultimately accepted in at least one cultural setting' (Brockman 1993, p. 32). If what this person produces is seen to be creative by the people working within this area, then creativity is said to have taken place. 'It is the task of the "field" to then select promising variations and to incorporate them into the domain' (Csikszentmihalyi 1988, p. 330).

Pursuing these ideas a little further, it can be seen that the *domain* is the symbol system that the person and others working in the area utilise. It is the culture and conventions the person becomes immersed in. It includes all the work done to this point within that particular field and may be held within a person's idiosyncratic knowledge base or accessible from other sources within the field. There are three main ways the domain can contribute to the creative system. These include the clarity of structure of the domain, its centrality within the culture and its accessibility (Csikszentmihalyi 1997, p. 38). The clarity of structure within the domain works to hinder or help creativity, by providing a basis for assessment. The more consistent the internal logic of a domain, that is, the more there is no doubt about what constitutes novelty, the easier it then is to make decisions about creativity within the domain. For example, it is faster to resolve problems of creativity within the domain of maths, a clearly structured domain, than it is to perceive what is a creative contribution within, as a contrast, cultural studies. In terms of the centrality within a culture of particular domains it can be argued that medicine is a central discipline within this society. Therefore, it is easier for those concerned with this domain to access resources to contribute to creative endeavours within it. The third dimension, accessibility, is important for creativity as the speed with which information is processed within the domain correlates directly to the amount of novelty the field is capable of generating since 'no person or work or process can be considered creative unless it is so deemed by relevant social institutions' (Gardner in Brockman 1993, p. 33). This, of course, is where the domain intersects with the field.

For Csikszentmihalyi, 'the easiest way to define a field is to say that it includes all those who can affect the structure of a domain' (Sternberg 1988, p. 330). 'Field' used in this sense not only correlates well with Bourdieu's use of the same term but it also, despite the very strong caveats Bourdieu placed alongside it, has some correspondence with Becker's use of the term 'art world', in that it is related to the social organisation of the world the person operates in. Just as Peterson (1982, 1985) argues that there are societal structures that affect creative output, Csikszentmihalyi asserts that fields can affect creativity in one of three different ways; firstly, by being reactive or proactive. A reactive field, according to this thesis, does not solicit novelty whereas a proactive one does by actively demanding novelty from the creative individuals concerned. As an example, the social organisation that constitutes the field of popular music requires constant novelty in order to maintain its commercial base. Secondly, the field can affect creativity by choosing a broad or narrow filter in the selection of novelty:

> Some fields are conservative and allow only a few new items to enter the domain at any given time. They reject most novelty and select only what they consider best. Others are more liberal in allowing new ideas into their domains, and as a result these change more rapidly. At the extremes, both strategies can be dangerous: It is possible to wreck a domain either by starving it of novelty or by admitting too much unassimilated novelty. (Csikszentmihalyi 1997, p. 44)

Thirdly, the field affects creativity by being 'well connected to the rest of the social system and thus able to channel support' into that particular domain (ibid.). In line with the idea that there are limited resources available in any economy and a set of unlimited wants, each field must engage in negotiations for access to those limited resources. Those fields that are at the centre of, and well regarded within, the political economy they exist in are more likely to channel resources to the activities that the particular field favours.

Csikszentmihalyi gives a compact analogy that explains the interdependence of the three components in this system. He uses the idea that a fire cannot exist without tinder, air or a spark. However it is the spark, or in this analogy the person, that appears to be active in the process and thus is seen as having chief responsibility. Not so according to Csikszentmihalyi; 'the spark is necessary but without air and tinder there would be no flame' (1997, p. 7). Each element is necessary but not sufficient, in and of itself, in the production of the flame. A further analogy also highlights the interdependence of the system at work. Csikszentmihaly argues that:

> to study creativity by focusing on the individual alone is like trying to understand how an apple tree produces fruit by looking only at the tree and ignoring the sun and the soil that support its life.... In other words, if one wants to understand creativity, it does not make any more sense to turn to a study of the individual than it would to a study of the field or of the domain. Real understanding may, however, come from investigating the interaction among all three. (Quoted in McIntyre 2004, p. 6)

This interactive system can therefore provide a holistic view of the way media practitioners bring cultural artefacts into play as it goes beyond thinking of cultural producers as supra-human specially gifted individuals and allows for the recognition of multiple factors that contribute to, influence and shape creativity. It also doesn't deny, importantly, that individuals have a significant role in the creation of any cultural artefact. Instead, it brings them into a systemic relationship that provides a cohesive explanation of creativity which sees each factor in the system as necessary but not sufficient.

While Runco has argued that the systems view is largely process oriented (Runco 2004, p. 661), he also tends to misrepresent the holistic and integrated aspects of the model by laying it out in a strictly linear fashion, echoing the Hegelian dialectic in its action. This may be the result of Csikszentmihalyi using the term 'circular causality' to indicate that the system may start at any point, but the use of this somewhat misleading term misses the essential non-linearity of the model. Runco, seeing the model as a linear one, suggests it is a theory 'in which creative ideas originate with an individual, may then influence a particular field (e.g., experts and curators and others devoted to one interest or area), and may eventually even have an impact on the more general domain' (Runco 2004, p. 661). While this précis provides a convenient and familiar description that falls back into a linear cause-and-effect process, this representation misconstrues how the system actually works, that is, in a non-linear way. As explained above, the process doesn't necessarily start with a person. The evidence for this can be seen, for example, in the idea of a field as a generative force (Csikszentmihalyi 1988, p. 333).

There have been other critiques of the model where some have used a rejection of its basic assumptions, such as value distinction, as a way to defend disciplinary territory. For example, Robert Weisberg, performing an about face from his earlier stance (2006, p. 68), argues that the relativist nature of creative attribution makes it difficult to be absolute and precise in an objectivist and positivist sense when examining creative people. He states:

> Let us say that we want to study the thought processes or personality factors involved in creativity in painting. Whom are we to study? As a start, we could study living painters whose work has been deemed important by the field. Let us say we do that, and we draw some conclusions as to what factors are important in making someone a creative painter. However, let us assume that in 10 years those painters are no longer in favor; that is, their work is no longer valued, which means that, if we use value in our definition, they are no longer creative. Therefore, our conclusions from 10 years ago are no longer relevant to creativity. (2006, p. 66)

Apart from this objection, which itself neatly illustrates the positivist's dilemma when confronted with a relativist argument, one that has occurred a number of times in the history of science, it is not really a sufficient reason for rejecting these ideas. As an example, Weisberg later argues that:

> *creative thinking* occurs when a person *intentionally* produces a *novel* product while working on some task. Sometimes those intentional novel products are valued highly by society, and sometimes they are not, but all of them are creative products. A novel product intentionally produced by a person is a *creative product*, and the person who produces such a product is a *creative person* [italics in original]. (2006, p. 70)

In his efforts to concentrate solely on a psychologically reductionist approach, in ascribing *novelty* to a work, Weisberg overlooks the idea that the basis for ascribing that novelty will always be relative to the position of judgement being used. That is, in order for a judgement to be made as to whether a work is novel or not, even if it is the person themselves deciding this prior to literally taking the work to the field, this person must have initially had access to the criteria of judgement well before ascribing novelty. This criteria has most often become so naturalised for them, a form of habitus, that they forget that it had been originally sourced from the field and domain when they learnt how to manipulate aspects of it themselves. As Csikszentmihalyi argues:

> In order to function well within the creative system, one must internalise the rules of the domain and the opinions of the field, so that one can choose the most promising idea to work on, and do so in a way that will be acceptable to one's peers. (1999, p. 332)

As Foucault and others have demonstrated, there are very few persons working within cultural domains who can escape the conditioned discourses they operate within. It is therefore inescapable that judgements, of the type used to decide whether something is novel or not, are, in fact, relative to the knowledge one has about what is being judged. As Janet Fulton (2010) asserts, one then needs to consider the connection Boden had made between P- and H-creativity in order to provide a way out of what is essentially a constricting ontological debate. Boden argues that 'there can be no *psychological* [P] explanation of this historical [H] category. But all H-creative ideas, by definition, are P-creative too' (1994, p. 77).

Rob Pope (2005, pp. 67–70) does argue more directly that the systems model, or more correctly Csikszentmihalyi himself, who despite his sensitivities to social networks and contexts, 'still privileges the notion of creator as a "person" singular [thus] playing down creativity as an overtly collective or collaborative activity' (Pope 2005, p. 68). However, despite this being the obverse reaction to that of Weisberg above, this criticism downplays the arguments presented in the papers Csikszentmihalyi produced in 1988 and 1999. In his 1988 paper he suggests that:

> What we call creative is never the result of individual action alone; it is the product of three main shaping forces: a set of social institutions, or *field*, that selects from the variations produced by the individual those that are worth preserving; a stable cultural *domain* that will preserve and transmit the selected new ideas or forms to the following generations; and finally the *individual*, who brings about some change in the domain, a change that the field will consider to be creative. (Csikszentmihalyi 1988, p. 325)

In his 1999 paper, 'Implications of a Systems Perspective for the Study of Creativity', Csikszentmihalyi argues that:

The occurrence of creativity is not simply a function of how many gifted individuals there are, but also of how accessible the various symbolic systems are and how responsive the social system is to novel ideas. Instead of focusing exclusively on individuals it will make more sense to focus on communities that may or may not nurture creativity. In the last analysis it is the community and not the individual who makes creativity manifest. (1999, p. 333)

Despite this, as Pope suggests, 'the systems approach as practiced by Csikszentmihalyi' (2005, p. 68), fails to fully explore the nature of collective enterprises. While this criticism may have some validity in terms of Csikszentmihalyi's concentration on 'the person' and his lack of an explanation of multiple and temporally contiguous points of decision making, it does not entirely negate the applicability of the model itself to collective activity. This application can be illustrated by Csikszentmihalyi himself when he uses it to explain the collaborative production of films (2004). Furthermore, Keith Sawyer, who adapts the model for his own research work, has little difficulty in using it to explain the collective activity of, for example, an improvisatory drama group in Chicago or a jazz ensemble in New York. He also has no hesitation in using it in his book *Group Genius: The Creative Power of Collaboration* (2007) as the basis to explore creativity as it occurs within a corporate setting. As a further indicator of the model's applicability to group creativity, the notion of an agent encompasses collective enterprises, for example in the way this term is used in actor network theory (Callon 1987, Latour 2005). By assuming that a creative agent can be either individual or collective, the model's relevance to collaborative activity becomes clearer.

Pope also challenges the model by asserting that it doesn't explain the interaction between domains that leads to what he labels '*hybrid forms*' (Pope 2005, p. 68). Noting that there is opportunity for individuals, who have a personal background partially routed in their idiosyncratic experiences, to bring information from other domains they may be familiar with into the one they are currently working in, it could be said that this criticism seems a little disingenuous. In order to be valid this criticism would require a field that was hermetically sealed from the rest of society. However, as the model indicates, all fields are in fact subcategories of the societies they exist in. Just like individuals, fields do not act in a vacuum. Through this process the cross-fertilisation Pope sees as necessary appears to be built into this dynamic model.

The third criticism Pope suggests is problematic for the systems model is that he claims there is insufficient discussion on Csikszentmihalyi's part of the field not recognising creative acts that are outside its experience (ibid.). In contrast to this proposition Sharon Bailin argues (1988, pp. 96–7) one can never have a case where the symbol system is so radically altered that it is no longer at least partially recognisable to a field of experts. Even if they reject the work because they can't understand it or they feel threatened by the new ideas and a new domain mutates out of the old, as happens periodically, that new domain will still owe some of its characteristics to the old domain. There will be familiarities to deal with in new domains just as much as there will be dissimilarities.

Finally, Pope also suggests that Csikszentmihalyi didn't recognise the poststructuralist implications of the model (2005, p. 69). This is not surprising given the discipline Csikszentmihalyi works in, but this situation doesn't mean, however, that those implications are not there. In many ways the model supports the dissolution of the author-genius model which both Barthes and Foucault had advocated. However, rather than just stopping at the point of deconstruction, what the model does differently is put in place a new and reconceptualised way of seeing creativity. In essence if the model holds true, it will do so regardless of the views the person who developed it has. Without drawing too many parallels this same process can be seen, for example, in Charles Darwin's initial development of the theory of evolution, which then proceeded to have a life of its own well past its developer's initial formulations (Watson 2001).

Despite these caveats Pope still believes that this 'systems based approach offers a powerful corrective to notions of creativity focused exclusively on creators or on creative products' (2005, p. 69). Placed alongside this point of view is the appeal made by Beth Hennessey and Teresa Amabile in their most recent review of the psychological research into creativity (2010). In this review they suggest that:

> The staggering array of disciplinary approaches to understanding creativity can prove to be an advantage, but only if researchers and theorists work together and understand the discoveries that are being made across creative domains and analytical levels. Otherwise, the mysteries may deepen. Only by using multiple lenses simultaneously, looking across levels, and thinking about creativity systematically, will we be able to unlock and use its secrets. What we need now are all encompassing systems theories of creativity designed to tie

together and make sense of the diversity of perspectives found in the literature – from the innermost neurological level to the outermost cultural level. (2010, p. 590)

Working from the point of view of sociology, Bourdieu suggests something similar. In order to understand cultural production we need to reject the direct relation of individual biography to the work of art as well as reject internal analyses of the individual work and even that of intertextual analysis. 'This is because what we have to do is all these things at the same time' (Bourdieu 1990, p. 147).

Finally, drawing all of this together, it can be argued that the systems conception of creativity appears close to what Bourdieu was attempting to do with the concepts of habitus, field, various forms of capital and field of works, that is, provide a way of seeing that recognises the degree of freedom an individual possesses within the constraints and enabling factors of the sociocultural sphere they exist in. As such the systems view of creativity points to the tension that exists between the agency of the individual and both the possible strictures placed upon them by the institutions or structures that govern society and culture and the ground for action afforded by them. It also provides a model that illustrates in many ways Anthony Gidden's concept of structuration (which we will be examining more fully shortly). As a result, it goes a considerable distance in attempting to resolve the tensions that exist between the agency of the individual and the power of the structures they operate within, in as much as both Bourdieu's ideas and the system model are ways of resisting the polarising dichotomies that are thought to exist between the agency of the individual and the determinist positions of structuralist approaches. It is to an exploration of the question of agency and structure and in particular its relationship to free will in creativity that I wish to turn to now examining this question through the lens of radio production.

Part II
Issues for Media Practice

7
Agency and Structure: The Case of Radio

I have argued that the most adequate synthesis of ideas we could use to understand creativity may be found in the systems model of creativity initially proposed by Mihaly Csikszentmihalyi. I have also argued that this model is similar in many ways to the ideas on cultural production developed by Pierre Bourdieu. While they are certainly not identical, both of these views appear to displace the notion of the individual being at the centre of creativity and cultural production but at the same time recognise the individual agent's ability to make choices out of a set of structures that bound their actions. To my mind they are both attempts to redress the questions raised by the supposed antipathy of structure and agency that tend to exist in subjectivist or objectivist accounts relevant to this topic. That is, this reconceptualised way of seeing creativity and cultural production denies that individuals can't help but act in the ways they've been predetermined to do. Nor does it accept that individuals are absolutely free to make their own creative decisions regardless of the structures, discourses and so on that surround them. This resolution of the actions of both agency and structure can be highlighted when we look at an actual case in operation.

The Australian Broadcasting Corporation (ABC), modelled in many ways on the British Broadcasting Corporation (BBC), is a state-funded and regulated institution that has operated since it made its first broadcast in 1932. As a parliamentary-funded organisation it could be expected to be controlled by the state (structure). However, it quite often displays a significant degree of creative freedom for the people (agents) working within it, as does the BBC, on which it was modelled. This creative freedom has had to be protected at various times as the ABC's history indicates a degree of attempting to maintain a measure of independence from governmental interference, whether that is from either the Labour or Liberal governments, both of whom have held power for a number of years in Australia. And yet, the ABC remains a breeding ground of creativity, producing culture that is controversial in both an artistic and a political sense. In the words of Julius Sumner Miller 'Why is this so?', could the answer be in the degree of free will (agency) the creators have within this institution (structure)? Since agency is the ability to make choices and depends on the operation of free will, one can ask a fundamental question: what constitutes the freedom to act and therefore the freedom to create? To answer these questions we need firstly to briefly investigate the nature of freedom itself and what acting freely could possibly mean. Does freedom simply mean the ability to act without constraint? Or is it a case of having relative autonomy? Once we have a workable answer to those questions we can then see how this applies to the case of the ABC.

When one looks for a way of defining freedom, most often common usage sees it as an absence; an absence of control, being free from constraint, the ability to act without restraint or not being subject to control. It may also be described as 'the power of self-determination attributed to the will' (OED 2010b) as in the term 'free will'. Rather than treating freedom in what can be described as a fairly naïve way, Eliott Deutsch, for one, concludes that our actions 'although relatively "free" in virtue of their fundamentally rational character, are nevertheless highly influenced by both individual and social determinants which set up strong *dispositions* to act in certain ways' (Deutsch 1982, p. 104). As ground for this position we can turn to the Scottish philosopher David Hume (1952). Hume attempted to explain the way free will and determinism interact, declaring that free will is entirely compatible with causation. The analogy of the way the bone of an arm moves within its socket explains quite succinctly his position. As Teichmann and Evans show:

assuming you do not suffer from rheumatism or such then your arm bone will be able to 'move freely in the socket' (as we say). Now suppose that someone complains 'It isn't moving freely at all, because it is restrained by the shape of the socket'. Would that be a sensible comment? No, for it suggests that only if your arm was separated from the shoulder socket could its movement be completely free. But that is not the case. An arm floating by itself in space has no power of movement at all. Should we decide that free-will is made possible by causation? We might well agree that choice is made possible by causation. The trouble is that once causation is introduced into the picture we will have to say that choices themselves are not caused. So we end up with choice but not with free choice. Part of the problem might be due to the fact that the terms free-will, liberty and determinism can be understood in different ways. (1991, p. 39)

They go on to conclude that 'our kind of free will does not presuppose a random universe, but neither does it allow the possibility that all choices are themselves forced outside circumstances' (ibid., p. 45). Bouveresse extends these ideas by claiming that the philosophical problem, that is free will, has an underlying ontological problematic where theories that summon social structures and determinisms in an attempt to clarify our supposedly 'most personal and free actions are often understood as being equivalent to a pure and simple negation of the realities that we call freedom and the personality' (Bouveresse in Shusterman 1999, p. 48). However, as Pierre Bourdieu argues, 'those who think in simple alternatives need to be reminded that in these matters absolute freedom, exalted by the defenders of creative spontaneity, belongs only to the naïve and the ignorant' (Bourdieu 1996, p. 235). It is the conception of the *relative* nature of free will that adds another dimension to the nature of the subject and their ability to act freely. To reiterate the various conceptions put forward so far of the subject, it can be seen that:

> liberalism treats the subject as autonomous, rational, often presocial individual, wary of its rights in relation to other individuals; Marxism treats the subject as a collective agent in contest with other collective agents. In both cases the subject is the ground of history. By the late twentieth century both positions have become unconvincing; liberalism's subject as citizen and entrepreneur and Marxism's subject as revolutionary proletariat no longer work as characters in the play of human time. In Germany intellectuals of the Frankfurt School like Adorno acknowledging the bleak situation, retreated to the defence of critical theory. In France structuralists like Althusser theorised history without agents. Starting in the 1970's there has been, in both countries, an effort to reconstruct a theory of the subject as agent of change. (Poster in Caputo & Yount 1993, pp. 71–2)

Working in England Anthony Giddens was one of those theorists who was attempting to conceptualise the subject as an agent of change. Unlike theorists such as Michel Foucault who initially concluded rather pessimistically that 'in the end we are judged, condemned, classified, determined in our undertakings, destined to a certain mode of living or dying, as a function of the true discourses which are the bearers of the specific effects of power' (Foucault quoted in Jordan & Weedon 1995, p. 441), Giddens saw the subject as at least partially responsible for their own actions. In making this argument he provided a way of accounting for an individual's freedom to act within the confines and possibilities of social and cultural dispositions.

In an echo of Bourdieu's intellectual project, Giddens started by attempting to eliminate the oppositions and divisions that permeate the discussion of agency and structure. In trying to explain what he perceived to be the duality of structure, that is the inter-dependence of structure and agency, he coined the term 'structuration'. He used this rather ugly term to refer to the way 'that structures make social action possible, and at the same time social action creates those very structures' (Haralambos & Holbern 1995, p. 904). He went on to suggest that 'human agents, by their actions, can therefore transform as well as reproduce structures' (ibid.). In *Central Problems in Social Theory: Action, Structure and Contradiction in Social Analysis* (1979), Giddens contends that 'the structural properties of social systems are both the medium and the outcomes of the practices that constitute those systems' (1979, p. 69). That is, 'it is you, I and every other individual that create structures' (ibid.). Giddens, unlike Bourdieu, argues that institutions are then simply the sum of the people who exist within them. Following on from this he states, according to Haralambos & Holbern, that a social system is 'simply a pattern of relations that exists over a period of time and space' (1995, p. 905). In this way a social system is mobile and capable of change as a result of the changes in those interactions that occur over time. Institutions such as the state or bureaucracies are then patterns of social relationships and social practices, or behaviours, 'that display some continuity over time, but which may also change as time passes' (ibid.).

Despite the critiques levelled at these ideas, for example by Margaret Archer (2000), what is important about Giddens' propositions, for this discussion at least, is that he, like Bourdieu, moves away from either simple determinism or absolute freedom to explain human actions. In doing so he reconstitutes the subject as autonomous but within limits. By making this observation 'he tries to resolve the dispute between determinists, who believe that human behaviour is entirely determined by outside forces, and voluntarists, who believe that humans possess free will, and can act as they wish' (Haralambos & Holbern 1995, p. 906). Like Bourdieu, Giddens sees both agency and structure as having some validity. Constraints, of the institutional variety, don't just determine actions but place limits on what options are available to agents and those limits provide the ground for possible action. In short they are also, at one the same time, enabling.

Giddens argues that what constrains or enables most agents are the power relationships that exist in most social organisations. Power as used by Giddens has what he calls a 'transformative capacity', and this capacity can be used by agents to enact change either in things or the actions of other people. This capacity can be used to 'exercise power over other people, and so constrain people and reduce their freedom' (Haralambos & Holbern 1995, p. 906). However, as Giddens endeavours to point out, 'power also increases the freedom of action of the agents who possess it. What restricts one person, enables another to do more' (ibid.). In this way Giddens not only perceives the complex and diffuse nature of power, similar in some senses to Foucault who also saw it as productive as well as constricting, but also attempts to account for the way purposeful human action can reproduce and transform structures or social organisations.

One of the major social organisations, or fields, that an agent must interact with is that of the macro-structure of the state. Aristotle, in defining this institution, held that 'every state is a community of some kind, and every community is established with a view to some good; for everyone always acts in order to obtain that which they think good' (Aristotle quoted in Pojman 1998, p. 320). With the development of the modern nation state other theorists have added their views as to what constitutes the state. Max Weber, for one, famously defined the state as a human entity that can successfully claim the legitimate use of physical force within a given geographical region (1946, p. 78). The state in this sense can be said to consist of a law-making government or legislature, a bureaucracy or civil service which implements those decisions, 'the police who are responsible for law enforcement, and the armed forces whose job it is to protect the state from external threats' (Haralambos & Holbern 1995, p. 505). This basic description is often extended to include a wider set of institutional apparatuses such as those that are responsible for welfare, health and education services. Carol Gould argues that even though the institution of the state appears to have an autonomous existence apart from the social relations evident among its citizens, it should be clear that 'such institutions or objectified forms are socially constituted, i.e., they have been brought into being by the decisions and actions of agents and can also be changed by them' (Gould 1988, p. 113). In addition, Owen Kelly, writing in his book *Community, Art and the State* (1984), states that the modern, liberal, democratic state is not 'some kind of all-powerful Leviathan. In fact it is not any kind of object at all.... It is a system of relationships' (Kelly 1984, p. 44). The state is thus:

> A method of patterning and organising social action which is being modified every day...it is a series of active relationships between organisations; and a way of organising those relationships which are rooted in specific assumptions and beliefs. (Kelly 1984, pp. 44–5)

The emphasis that is placed on these assumptions and beliefs is usually a good indicator of 'the dominant values of the state, and of the consensus which it is engaged in fostering' (Kelly 1984, p. 45). The state then, according to Kelly, fulfils four basic functions which include encouraging and propagating consensus around the national interest which it does through a reward and punishment process, 'involving grants, concessions, licences and regulations' (Kelly 1984, p. 44). It therefore 'intervenes in the economy in both positive and negative ways' (ibid.) and allocates, through the political system, limited resources to what can be seen as seemingly unlimited wants.

The political system that Australia, as a modern liberal democratic state, operates with includes some basic institutions or structures borrowed in part from both the United States and the United Kingdom. It certainly has the three loci of power fundamental to most democracies, that is the judiciary, executive and legislative, enacted in its constitutional separation of powers, but like most twenty-first century states the fourth estate, what we now call the media, has also become extremely important in the political process. In this case the media often derives its political power by acting as the *vox populi* or voice of the people. In a book entitled *Outside Interference: The Politics of Australian Broadcasting* (1979), Richard Harding puts the proposition that:

> The essence of democracy is a multiplicity of viewpoints, a recognition by those who at any given moment possess political power that their opinions and actions may be unwise or unpopular or wrong. A wide-ranging and independent press and a vigorous and free broadcasting system are thus both the symbols and the guardians of democracy.... The democrat encourages independent broadcasting, without interference, and his support should not waver if some of the values thereby expressed are antipathetic to his own. (1979, p. vii)

The role of many government broadcasters has been under suspicion in terms of the above ideal since the co-option of them in the service of propaganda, particularly by the Nazis during the Second World War and also the various services provided by authoritarian states in Eastern Europe and Asia during what was termed the Cold War (Thussu 2006). The perception of these latter broadcasters, however, can be contrasted to the supposedly independent stance of national broadcasters such as the BBC in Britain and the case in point here, the government-funded radio network in Australia, the ABC.

Australian radio broadcasting overall has been based primarily on a combination of the American free market model and the British public service model. There are a significant number of commercial operators as well as a government-funded institution that broadcasts a number of differing services under the umbrella of the ABC. Once the Australian Broadcasting Commission Act was passed in 1932, after the initial teething problems of the nascent radio industry warranted it, the government took responsibility for providing a national service 'and ensuring that both the national and the commercial stations operated in the public interest' (Holloway 1975, p. 15).

After a long period that saw it through the so-called golden age of radio (Lane 1994, Hendy 2000) and a later move towards a neo-liberal orthodoxy (Thussu 2000, p. 82), the Commission became a Corporation in 1983. In an ABC position paper in 1985 entitled 'The Role of a National Broadcaster in Contemporary Australia', the Australian Broadcasting Corporation declared that it is essentially 'a public funded institution, insulated from market place pressure in its programming choices but accountable to the public and to Parliament' (ABC 1985, p. 5), and the 'basic functions and duties which Parliament has given to the ABC are set out in the Charter of the Corporation [s.6(1) and (2) of the ABC Act]' (ibid.). Through this charter the ABC is recognised as an institution which complements Parliament, helping inform the electorate 'by providing a forum for debate about community issues – national broadcasting assists in the effective functioning of a democratic society' (ABC 2000). That charter also gives the ABC a duty to provide 'innovative and comprehensive broadcasting and television services of a high standard' (ABC 1987, p. 5). There is also an assertion that 'an appropriate philosophy for a public service broadcaster such as the ABC must not be didactic in ways that unduly restrict the passions, artistic freedom or creativity of its staff' (ABC 1985, p. 14). Despite this adherence to parliamentary regulation, successive governments right throughout the ABC's history have sought to curtail the perceived power, and by extension thus the passions and artistic freedom, of this national institution:

> During the 1930s, the United Australia Party government of J.A. Lyons tolerated very little discussion of politics, international affairs and current intellectual controversies. At the time of the Czechoslovakian crisis in 1938, Lyons even considered taking action to prevent the broadcast of anything which might be 'unduly disturbing to the peace of mind of listeners'. William James Cleary, the chairman of the ABC, on the other hand, believed that Australians should become more interested in talks and commentaries, especially on controversial matters, and that the ABC should help to stimulate this interest through the promotion of more talk sessions. The result of these conflicting outlooks was constant government attempts to influence ABC program content. (Thomas 1992, p. 66)

During the long run of the Commission most of the period after the Second World War was spent in what could be called a comfortable relationship with the Menzies' Liberal government. At this time the commissioners who oversaw the operation of the ABC were appointed by that government, and the life of a commissioner was often seen as a reward for services provided in an earlier incarnation for the incumbent government. During the 1960s, however, the ABC developed programmes such as the weekly investigative programme *Four Corners* and the nightly current affairs programme *This Day Tonight* which tested the boundaries of that relationship with government. When the Labour Party came to power in 1972 they also sought to change the nature of the ABC, perceiving that its ethos at this point was geared towards the prior Liberal government. The underlying philosophy was that if you change the people, you change the nature of the institution.

It was during this period that innovative radio in the shape of 2JJ was first established under the auspices of the ABC and its anti-authoritarian 'credo' put into place. 2JJ was to become 'anti-radio radio', similar in some ways to the United Kingdom's BBC 6. When the Australian Liberal Party, led by Malcolm Fraser, returned to power in 1975, his perception was that the ABC had now become too left-leaning, and consequently the ABC once again found itself under threat. The Fraser government possessed a ready means to gain command of the national broadcaster as the Parliament, controlled by the Liberal government, had power over funding. This government also exercised its right to appoint commissioners (Harding 1979, p. viii). Once it came to power the Liberal government then set about immediately changing the faces within the institution. An enquiry was also hastily set up to give the incumbent government some powers to continue on and attempt to neutralise the perceived powers of the ABC.

When Labour again came to power in Australia in the 1980s, this time with Bob Hawke as Prime Minister, the ABC was once again vetted for supposedly pro-Liberal appointments. Over the ensuing 13 years the Labour Party had as much chance to increase pro-Labour appointments as had the Liberals during the Menzies' period in office in the 1950s. However, during this period a view was entrenched in the mind of the Liberals that a pro-Labour ethos had once again been established at the ABC. This perception was used extensively during the 1996 election campaign to boycott ABC news and current affairs programmes by Liberal politicians seeking re-election. Programmes such as *The 7.30 Report*, hosted by Kerry O'Brien, became particular targets of the Liberals' campaign during this period. After they came to power there was, once again, a downgrading of the ABC's potential to enact its role as the fourth estate with the government implementing extensive funding cuts. As a result, the implementation of a massive staff restructuring programme under the auspices of Jonathan Shier attempted to move the ABC much closer to a corporate model, a process originally begun by Labour appointee David Hill. All of this activity demonstrates the understanding on governments' part that the way to control this institution, this structure, was to change the individual board members with those who have particular political inclinations and let their decisions filter down. An extract from the press in 2000 illustrates the longevity of this process.

John Howard [Liberal] is no worse than Paul Keating [Labour] when it comes to stacking the ABC board. Six of the nine board members have open connections to the Coalition: Liberal power-broker Michael Kroger; former liberal federal MP Ross McLean; former Liberal party member, managing director Jonathan Shier; conservative economist Judith Sloan; and Howard confidants, chairman Donald McDonald and Maurice Newman. Newman replaces the last Labor appointee, businessman Russell Bate. But in 1996, the final year of the Keating government, four members had open Labor connections: former South Australian Labor premier John Bannon; former Australian Workers' Union industrial officer Janine Walker; social worker and former departmental adviser to the Burke government in Western

Australia Wendy Silver; and managing director Brian Johns. Two other appointees to that 1996 board were widely seen to be Labor allies – Text Media Group director Diana Gribble and a long time Howard rival, the former federal Liberal minister Ian McPhee. The remaining three former members had diverse backgrounds. (Harris 2000, p. 2)

It can be seen in this case study that each successive government in Australia has attempted to curtail the activities of this major part of the fourth estate, a source of, in terms of its charter, innovative broadcasting and criticism, and those attempts have always been allegedly in the interest of the incumbent government. By introducing new agents into the institutional framework of the ABC, this action has had the effect of attempting to circumscribe, in an indirect way, the agency of the creators of those more innovative and often controversial programmes. The more recent case of the *The Chaser*, a news comedy programme that was remarkably popular and effective in lampooning the political scene, illustrates this point. However, in trying to curtail freedom of expression in this way, the institutional nature of the broadcasting structure has itself been open to change. It can thus be argued that the principles behind the methods employed by successive governments to curtail the power of the ABC demonstrate the veracity of Giddens' conception of 'structuration', outlined above. That is, institutions are essentially a system of relationships between agents who exercise their ability to make choice within a system and, by doing so, are capable of transforming that social organisation.

However, apart from the ramifications changes in executive positions at the top of the hierarchy may have on the overall way decisions are made at the macro-level of the institution, it would be of direct benefit for the claims being made above to see whether similar assertions can be replicated at the micro-level of daily management of cultural output at the ABC. If cultural output can be seen to be changed at this level and most immediately affected by the gatekeepers or cultural intermediaries (subject of course to executive decision making), who are in place to carry out the necessary functional aspects of daily broadcasts, then some further reinforcement of Giddens' claims can be made. Fortunately, these claims can indeed be readily exemplified at the micro-level by briefly examining the position Arnold Frolows and later Richard Kingsmill have played as Programme and Music Directors (McIntyre 2006) in the recent history of the ABC's national youth network station

Triple J, the station that had developed from the inception of the supposedly rebellious anti-radio radio, 2JJ.

Triple J has, as part of its brief, itself a necessary subset of the overall ABC charter, to play Australian-produced music. In doing this in a way that at times runs counter to the way commercial operators have acted, over its brief history Triple J has been 'applauded and criticised for its radical and sometimes brash approach to broadcasting ... its influence has extended into other sectors of the radio broadcasting industry' (Andrews cited in Moran 1992, p. 95). The impact of the station has at times 'caused commercial broadcasters to rethink their programming strategies, incorporating political policies which ... years ago, no mainstream broadcasters would have touched' (ibid.).

Arnold Frolows occupied the Programme Director's (PD) position at Triple J for a considerable period of this history. This powerful position enabled him to decide, with his team, what was presented to the Triple J audience. In an attempt to explain how individuals work within groups, Marshall Scott Poole proposed what he called adaptive structuration theory, using Giddens' concept to attempt to explain at a less macro-level how group decisions are made. The advantage of this perspective, Poole argues, 'is that it mediates the seeming dichotomy between action and structure that is inherent in much group research. It gives an account of how group members produce and maintain social structures, which acknowledges creativity and self-reflexivity' (1990, p. 240). Using this as a mechanism it can be seen that this is what allowed Frolows to assume the critical role of cultural intermediary at this influential station as the music meetings he chaired at Triple J made decisions about what was played on air. With the recent change in personnel and restructuring of the way airplay decisions are made on Triple J, the role of the cultural intermediary at this influential station has now become centred on Richard Kingsmill and Kirileigh Lynch. Both started in these roles in 2003. Rather than using a team made up of various personnel from within the station for structured music meetings, as Frolows had claimed was occurring earlier, Kingsmill and Lynch trialled a slightly different approach. They:

> liaise with on-air presenters and music experts in the station. Not all on-air presenters will be into music and there are others such as receptionists through to production staff who are really expert in music. We generate emails and talk to everybody to gauge their opinions. We canvas widely in the station and listen to everything. We try to

balance the playlist to make sure we've got what we need for the type of music we play. (Kingsmill, R. 2004 pers. comm., 17 Sept)

This situation was, in essence, similar to Frolows' approach, although much less formalised. Either way the effect was the same in that it allowed decisions to be made about what audiences would be listening to on this station. In order to understand this situation and how the structures Programme Directors (PDs) and Music Directors (MDs) engaged with played a part in those decisions, it is necessary to look at a few specific cases.

From the music industry's perspective 'reps from the record companies hawk new releases to music directors and program directors' (Marlow 1995, p. 14) that suit the format of that station or, increasingly, network. From there the PD and MD meet, often along with other station functionaries, to discuss new tracks and what will be added. Mike Byrne, a PD who has worked within commercial networks for some time in Australia, indicates there is an orderly process to the mechanisms of song selection and replacement. He states that:

Firstly, the Music Research is studied, to see which songs should be slowed down in rotation and which should be increased in rotation. The playlist is shuffled accordingly and that reveals how many spots are available for new songs to enter the playlist. If there are 3 spots for new songs, as the number of songs in each category are tightly controlled by the station format policy to ensure an even rotation of songs. Next the research on the re-currents is checked to see if any of these songs are becoming too tired with the audience and need to be rested. Then either songs that were dropped from the playlist today or in recent weeks are added to the re-currents to make up the numbers, based on their best recent research figures. Finally, a list of songs that have been rested are checked to see if any can enter the appropriate Gold category. (Byrne 1999, p. 4)

However, while this is a good guide to the normally structured nature of decision making, the basis of the decision making may at times be more ad hoc than formal. A number of writers working in the United Kingdom, the United States, New Zealand and Australia (Rohthenbuhler 1985, 1987, Lull 1992, Negus 1992, Marlow 1995) confirm that the list of methods PDs and MDs use to select music for on-air delivery include 'gut instinct', 'vibe', that is, whether people are talking about an artist, how they are performing on the charts, how well the song has done in other international markets, is it selling well in the local record stores and whether or not it rates in the station's own request programmes. Karen Neill's New Zealand study found that in fact 'PDs utilise a wide range of criteria during the selection process' (2000, p. 29). The factors accounted for in her study include playlist balance, staff opinion, commercial imperatives and consultant opinion, and these factors also were entwined with a PD's own understandings of what the song's qualities are, such as how it catches attention through the use of its 'hook' and technical quality, coupled with the artist's track record and familiarity. However, it is often the hook that takes precedence as 'the PD (listening on behalf of the audience) needs to be assured that the audience will be "hooked" instantly' (Neill 2000, p. 32). In this case they will often listen for the first 10 seconds and then skim through to where the hook reappears through the song. However, Neill confirmed that 'a PD's own instinct (or gut feel as it is referred to in the industry) was the most important factor in playlist selection' (ibid.).

A very similar list of factors to those used by their commercial counterparts, which contribute to the decision-making process, is confirmed by Richard Kingsmill from Triple J when he states that:

> We certainly listen to our audience. I do as much field work as I can going to record stores but not as much as I'd like. Once every couple of weeks I'll visit stores and see what's moving and what's not. We use the overseas press as a guide but we need to stay ahead because we have that reputation. Consequently the charts are not that critical to what we do. If there's a vibe on the band, some grass roots activity, people are talking then, this is a really important thing. Gut feeling is also something I use a lot and that comes from years of listening. You develop an instinct for what will work. Not that I'm always right. But it's these last two that we tend to do most. (2004 pers. comm., 17 Sept)

Kingsmill, reflecting the other studies into this decision-making process, places the emphasis amongst this range of factors onto 'grass roots activity' but also, most importantly, onto his own instinct. This process of using a 'gut feeling' about a song can also be described in Pierre Bourdieu's terms as the result of acquiring the right radio-based 'habitus'. To reiterate, habitus has been described as 'a set of dispositions which generates practices and perceptions [and] is the result of a long process of inculcation...which becomes a "second sense" or a second nature' (Johnson in Bourdieu 1993, p. 5). PDs and MDs from both the commercial spheres and their counterparts at the ABC have been socialised or encultured into their professional activity until decision making becomes for them a 'second sense' operating at the level of tacit knowledge or 'gut instinct' (Schon 1983). They have a 'feel' for what will work and what won't. In this way these radio functionaries act and react in ways that are not determined nor are these decisions made in the context of absolute freedom from determining factors (Johnson in Bourdieu 1993, p. 5).

With these examples from both commercial radio and the ABC at our disposal, one focused at the macro-level and the other at the level of daily decision making, it can be seen that no radio station, whether it is a commercial one or a public-funded one, operates outside a system of constraints and enablers. It can also be seen from the above that those constraining and enabling factors range from the apparatus of the state itself with its regulations and broadcasting acts, the political will of the government of the day, the institutional framework that affects executive functioning in an institutional sense, as well as the domains of necessary and often naturalised professional radio knowledge that enables daily decision making inside the activity of producing daily content for the radio station. These claims then serve to reinforce Janet Wolff's contention that:

> Everything we do is located in, and therefore affected by, social structures. It does not follow from this that in order to be free agents we somehow have to liberate ourselves from social structures and act outside them. On the contrary, the existence of these structures and institutions enables any activity on our part, and this applies equally to acts of conformity and acts of rebellion...all action, including creative and innovative action, arise in the complex conjunction of numerous structural determinants and conditions. Any concept of creativity which denies this is metaphysical and cannot be sustained. But the corollary of this line of argument is not that human agents are simply programmed robots, or that we need to take account of their biographical, existential or motivational aspects...practical activity and creativity are in a mutual relation of interdependence with social structures. (Wolff 1981, p. 9)

8
Journalism: Structures and Motivation

A common misconception that accompanies the common-sense view of creativity is that a person, in order to be creative, must have little or no restrictions on their activity. To be free to act and think in any way desirable is seen as the ultimate set of conditions to become creative. No rules, no guidelines, no limits. This however may not necessarily be correct for, as we have seen earlier, creativity may well be the result of the necessary confluence of a set of factors and circumstances that may involve not only a person but also the structures of a field and domain. It can be claimed that the field, or social organisation one works in, which can range from the society itself to large institutional frameworks such as the state or particular industries through to smaller social organisations such as work teams and the nuclear family unit, can both enhance and constrain the creative process. While this can be seen to be true for radio it can also be claimed to be true for journalism.

Journalism is, at heart, a form of writing and most journalists would see themselves as writers. Many journalists are motivated by the desire to become great writers. In fact many journalists have become great writers. Sometimes, however, hard-nosed news journalists caught up in their daily rounds don't see themselves as creative at all, preferring instead to see feature writers or literary authors as the creative ones. But as Roth and Altshuler argue, 'all writing is creating. It starts with a blank sheet of paper and an idea. It ends with creation – as simple as a note to the milkman or as complex as a five-hundred-page novel' (1969, p. 1). From this perspective all journalists, no matter how they are designated, engage in creative activity on a daily basis.

> Journalism is indeed the great game. It is demanding with all its facets: it has boring calms and furious storms; it demands speed, accuracy and integrity; it often involves sacrifice and sometimes danger; it can be a royal road to literature. (Fatchen quoted in Jervis 1987, p. 3)

But the creativity involved on that royal road may not be of the Romantic type that insists on being unconstrained and free from the daily disciplined work-oriented world. This contention doesn't preclude journalists from being described as creative, especially if the phenomenon of creativity is conceived in the way the research literature, set out in the earlier part of this book, indicates and recent empirical evidence suggests is the case (Fulton 2008, pp. 3–6).

While there have been a number of ethnographies of the newsroom produced (for extensive summaries, see Zelizer 2004, Cottle 2007), Janet Fulton's work in investigating journalists as creative entities (2008) moves one step closer to recognising that creative work of this type takes place on a systemic basis. As such it can't be claimed that journalists are, of course, 'free' to write as they please in the absolute sense typified by more watered-down versions of Romanticism. On the contrary, it can be seen that when journalists become inculcated into their profession they become absorbed into a social organisation that has its own culture, its own sets of logics and its own traditions and history. Journalists who exist in this social organisation therefore recognise the conventions under which things are done and usually abide by these sets of circumstances. These circumstances are, as Elizabeth Jacka argues, a 'complex interweaving and contradictory set of histories, expectations, tastes and commentary, which is thereby a site of conflict and contestation' (Cunningham and Turner 1993, p. 228). This arena of contestation, or field, is a site where the production, circulation and appropriation of goods, services, knowledge or status occur. Fields are 'structured spaces that are organised around specific types of capital or combination of capital' (Johnson in Bourdieu 1993, p. 6). Writing in an article entitled 'The Political Field, the Social Science Field and the Journalistic Field' (2005), which was originally delivered as a lecture in November of 1995 in Lyons, France, Bourdieu contends that fields, like the journalistic field, are a:

> site of actions and reactions performed by social agents endowed with permanent dispositions, partly acquired in their experience of these social fields. The agents react to these relations of forces, to these

structures; they construct them, perceive them, form an idea of them, represent them to themselves, and so on. And, while being, therefore, constrained by the forces inscribed in these fields and being determined by these forces as regard their permanent dispositions, they are able to act upon these fields, in ways that are partially preconstrained, but with a margin of freedom. (2005, p. 29)

In a similar way to the field, the domain of journalism, a subset of the culture one works within including the entire symbol system a culture uses, such as language, through to techniques, skills and specific jargon derived from the forms and structures pertinent to journalism, can also govern the creativity of journalists in both positive and negative senses. In this case access to the domain or symbol system of journalism will not only constrain what is possible to do but also enable decision making to take place.

For example, if deadlines are paramount, as they are for most journalists, then the organisational structure that facilitates these deadlines is significant in the construction of the end product. That is, for a journalist to meet deadlines an appropriate set of functional symbol systems need to be accessed by the journalist in order to meet the deadline. In this case the idea of 'news sense' in any radio, television or print newsroom is often the resultant product of an immersion of the journalist in the conventions of news gathering. News sense, the ability to judge when an item that enters the journalist's realm is newsworthy (Sheridan-Burns 2002), is often derived in a process of enculturation and socialisation from the people the journalist works with. As one journalist has stated, ultimately 'one gets ones values from ones mentors and teachers, news directors particularly' (Williams, J 1993, pers. comm., 22 July). In the long term these values become subsumed by the journalist as common-sense and then labelled as 'news sense'. The journalist's actions, their decision-making abilities as agents, like radio programme directors, intersect with the structures they work with (Bourdieu 1998). As a result journalists become predisposed to act in certain ways. Bourdieu calls this process the acquisition of a habitus. To reiterate, habitus has been described as:

a 'feel for the game', a 'practical sense' (*sens pratique*) that inclines agents to act and react in specific situations in a manner that is not always calculated and that is not simply a question of conscious obedience to rules. Rather it is a set of dispositions which generates practices and perceptions. The habitus is the result of a long process of inculcation, beginning in early childhood, which becomes a 'second sense' or a second nature. (Johnson in Bourdieu 1993, p. 5)

The way journalists apply their habitus as journalists, part of which is constituted by their 'news sense', is often dependent on the formal procedures of news gathering and processing. The necessity to produce bulletins on the hour, for example, necessitates access to consistent sources of reliable information. As Denis McQuail (1994) asserts, news gathering then becomes standardised and routinised and news organisations come to prefer events with certain criteria. These can be listed as events that have short time spans; have great scale and intensity; are clear and unambiguous; are unexpected; are culturally close to the intended public; and have continuity, that is events that are already in the news and are consistent with past images and expectations (McQuail 1994, p. 214).

McQuail goes on to outline further factors that influence news selection based on three broad areas: people, place and time (1994, p. 214). He lists a number of news selection factors in relation to these three areas. These include, firstly, powerful people, since journalists have more access to these. This will of course include people like Ministers of the state. Secondly, these factors include personal contacts as journalists tend to go to these sources first. Thirdly, journalists go to places where power is exercised as well. Fourthly, they concentrate on places where events happen which include courts, police stations, parliaments, airports and hospitals. In addition, places where the media are located are included since 'news nets' are established at specific sites around the globe (the Middle East is a useful example here). Next, predictability and routine are important as they are centred on 'beats' and 'rounds' which are located near specific sites (these are also social settings that have networks of social relations between the journalist and the source who frequent those particular places). Proximity is thus also important as is the timeliness of any event. Timeliness is related to the notion of 'scoops', that is, getting the story in print, on air or online prior to others. Finally, timing in relation to the news cycle is important since many events are staged to coincide with the regular times of broadcast (e.g. most politicians and their media liaison officers are well aware that there is no use staging an event at 6.00 pm for television broadcast that night) (McQuail 1994, p. 214).

It is around these sets of typical selection procedures that most news is processed; processing in this case 'refers to the application of work routines which affect the nature of this product as it passes through the chain of decision making' (ibid p. 214). As such processing of news begins at the moment of selection and 'can be considered in terms of a series of decisions and choices directed towards the achievement of a product which fits the goals of the media organisation' (McQuail 1994, p. 225). The processing of information therefore may incorporate a set series of already fixed decisions and often follows a set order dependent on the form of journalism involved; in general though it will follow a four-phase sequence.

This sequence extends, as McQuail indicates (1994, p. 225), from an initial phase where a universe of substantive ideas is considered, through to a second narrowing down phase, according to professional judgements of the industry and from what is presented from sources to the industry. It is this phase where the application of 'news sense' generally occurs. The third phase of decision making occurs where format, design and presentation decisions are taken (ibid.). For example, for broadcast and print journalists the way a story is written follows a well-worn format. For breaking news in print, rather than features or opinion pieces, journalists will follow what has become known as an 'inverted pyramid'. With this structure the most important news is written into the beginning of the story. The reason this has occurred is that historically when a paper is being laid out by the compositors, they know that the ads take precedence in terms of space. The bromides were pasted up and if a story was too long to fit on the page once the ads were in position, then the bottom of the story was simply, and in this case literally, sliced off to make room. Therefore, the journalist would write the story so that the importance of the information would taper off as the story progressed down the page. This situation has changed only in technical terms as compositing moved away from razors and into the digital world. However, the conventions of the inverted pyramid remained.

For the broadcast journalist time allocation becomes an important factor. For example, for a television journalist, as Julie Williams outlines (1993, pers. comm., 22 July), the 'package' also has a standardised format and includes a set time for that story. At the beginning of the news day the position of the story in terms of the running order will be indicated, for example lead story or 'kicker' (colour stories occur at the end of the news broadcast). The allocated length of the story will be indicated on the run-down board. The structure of a 'package' is as follows:

a)   Presenter intros story
b)   Opening par (25 words or less – sums up story)

   c)   Cut to grab
   d)   Next par (25 words max – gives background)
   e)   Stand up
   f)   Closing par (25 words max – conclusion)
   g)   Sign off. (Williams, J 1993, pers. comm., 22 July)

The last phase of decision making for journalists is where technical decisions become paramount (McQuail 1994, p. 228). Without venturing too far into arguments over technological or social determinism, preferring instead Stephen Hill's notion of alignment (1988, pp. 33–4), it can be argued that the journalist will bring their output into line, to some degree, with the news processing technologies available in the newsroom.

As media product, that is 'news', moves through the system of production it flows along these routine channels and encounters 'gate areas'. These are points where decisions are made and these are occupied by decision makers or gate keepers. Quite often the decisions they make are standardised as most gatekeepers apply tried and tested criteria in their decision making, criteria that accord with the news sense they have developed, through absorption into the culture, traditions and logic of the profession. However, as has been argued elsewhere (Negus 1996) the notion of gatekeeping may be oversimplifying this process. It may be more accurate to say that what occurs at these gate areas is a process of cultural mediation since these gate points are significant in the selection and thus systemic creation of the cultural product known as 'news'. However, while gatekeeping is central to Hirsch's filter-flow model of raw materials passing through gate areas, and notwithstanding the critiques of the supposed misunderstanding of the notion of the cultural intermediary as delineated by Bourdieu himself (Hesmondhalgh 2006), it is hard to deny that those who stand at gate points are involved in 'a series of interactions and mediations as people in particular occupations connect together and play an active part in the production, distribution and social consumption of' (Negus 1996, p. 67), in this case, news stories.

The individual journalist, as an equal part of the tripartite model of systemic creativity, is implicated in this interplay in as much as they may be caught between a common-sense desire for 'creative freedom' and a perceived understanding of the professional parameters they work within. In this case the person's idiosyncratic attitude to things such as deadlines will govern whether they are predisposed to make decisions from within the possibilities presented to them or whether they can come up with novel answers to problems which have these supposed limits placed on them. Some journalists will thrive under the professional circumstances they find themselves in, producing innovative and groundbreaking reports, and others will succumb to the pressure of deadlines with their writing suffering as a result. When they produce a news story it may result from an activity where they fit the novel content they have acquired through their actions as news-gathering journalists into a pre-existing form, the news story, in order to produce or create a story that is unique for their audience. Not only must a journalist be motivated to produce quality journalism (Gardner, Csikszentmihalyi and Damon 2001), many journalists are also motivated by the desire to become great writers. As stated, many journalists have become great writers. All too often, though, many of them find the craft restricting and limiting to their creativity; there are deadlines to meet, sub-editors to appease and column inches to fill. In this case the imperatives of news selection may be perceived by differing individuals either as providing a set of guidelines for producing efficient decision making or problem solving or as a set of delimiting conventions to work within. It is common, as Negus and Pickering assert, to most often see convention in negative terms. However, 'conventions are also enabling' (Negus and Pickering 2004, p. 68). If this is the case the sets of structural factors that exist within most news room cultures, outlined briefly above, can be viewed therefore as either motivators or inhibitors to the creative process dependent on the individual journalist involved and the belief system they engage with, which may see these factors as either inhibitors or enablers. Motivation can thus be seen as integral to the creative process.

Teresa Amabile in her book *The Social Psychology of Creativity* (1983) looked at what she called the 'intrinsic motivation principle'. This principle proposes that most people will be creative when they are 'motivated primarily by the interest, enjoyment, satisfaction, and challenge of the work itself (intrinsic motivation), and not by external pressure (extrinsic motivation)' (Amabile and Tighe 1993, p. 16). From this perspective people are most likely to experience creative burnout or, in the parlance of literature and thus journalism, suffer from 'writer's block' when they are overwhelmed by the external pressures and are not enjoying the process itself. These extrinsic constraints which will lead, according to this hypothesis, to a stifling of creativity can be listed as 'external evaluation, surveillance, contracted for reward, competition and restricted choice' (ibid.). These terms are used in very specific ways however. Evaluation in this context becomes a concern with outside approval, and if this process comes to dominate a writer's thoughts, the work will suffer and at the extreme will shut down the necessary concentration required to complete the task. Surveillance is related to this concept and is used to mean the actual presence of a person whom the creator may wish to please either in a personal or a financial sense. Once again this person's concerns will begin to dominate the task and can be inhibiting. Competition, as an external motivator, also becomes a problem when the reaction of another person governs the level of satisfaction with the work. Restricted choice refers not to the formal limits of the craft but more to the available ways of accomplishing the goal. The danger here is that the restrictions will become paramount and the emphasis on the freedoms and options within the possibilities on offer will diminish. Reward is associated with financial remuneration, gaining of kudos or any number of external motivators used to engage the creator in the completion of the task. The argument suggests that once the reward is not present the internal motivation can also cease to operate.

Added to these supposed inhibitors there is also the danger of 'satisficing' occurring. Satisficing, a term coined by Herb Simon and Alan Newell, means completing the task in a way that is just sufficient to meet the demands of that task without fully realising what potential the task might offer. Amabile and Tighe suggest:

> satisficing is more likely when an individual is extrinsically moti-vated....Since the task is viewed merely as a means to an end, attention will be narrowed to only those paths that lead directly out of the maze toward the reward, and cognitive effort will be the minimum necessary to attain the extrinsic incentive. On the other hand, in the absence of salient extrinsic incentives, the problem-solver might explore the pathways and search for the most interesting connections that will lead to an exit (a solution). Achieving a cre-ative response most likely requires this sort of heuristic approach to the task, exploring pathways rather than taking the well-worn, guar-anteed algorithm for getting out of the maze. Individuals will most likely take the more exploratory route when their social environment does not present salient extrinsic demands. (1993, pp. 20–1)

Despite these claims all of the above constraints, or extrinsic motivators, have been found in the working conditions of many highly creative writers. For example, William Shakespeare produced works of inordinate creativity under tight deadlines and the pressures of running a theatre company from week to week. What's more, he did it with no 'safety net', operating in Elizabethan England, where the welfare state was non-existent:

> He was in terms of background and education, no-one very special. Not the scion of some illustrious family. Not a privileged member of Elizabethan society. He was, in fact, a very practical sort of character, a theatrical tradesman almost, running a theatre, dealing with the frustrations and trivia of everyday business matters. What is more he was obliged by the nature of his job to produce at short notice, like today's newsroom scriptwriters, lines that would be easy to deliver by his actors. No doubt the deadline pressures kept him in a highly adrenalised frame of mind. But you would not think that this was the sort of lifestyle conducive to generating a superabundance of plays and verse universally acknowledged to be of supreme power and beauty. (Evans and Deehan 1988, p. 17)

There are many other examples of great creative works being produced in the presence of what appear to be overbearing extrinsic motivators of the type described by Amabile.

Songwriters, Lennon and McCartney, also produced a body of work considered by many to be the defining collection of songs written in the twentieth century. Their ability to produce these remarkably successful tunes was often exhibited, in the early stage of their career, under conditions of extremely tight deadlines (Miles 1997, p. 151) and extensive surveillance, particularly from the world's press. It can also be argued that competition was the chief motivating factor in their prodigious output with writers seeking to both outperform and outdo the other (McIntyre 2006b, 2011).

Virginia Woolf, despite the demotivators she perceived so well, still managed to produce a body of written work which 'put women at the center of a changing world and offered a vocabulary of feminism to women and men alike' (Gray 1998, p. 78). Her essay entitled 'Professions for Women' is an eloquent expose of the restrictions many women have had to contend with in the desire to be creative and professional writers.

As a writer, Ernest Hemingway, the American novelist and short story writer famous for his pared-down style, also took the restrictions placed on him by the spare prose of journalism, narrowed even further by the dictates of being a foreign correspondent using cablegrams to file stories, and refined this style into what has been called an art form (Meyers

1985). He started his writing career as an editor on his high school paper and literary magazine and then became, at an early age, a cub reporter for the Kansas City Star. The newspaper still refers to Hemingway in its style guide, and Hemingway himself saw this guide as 'the best rules I ever learned for the business of writing' (Kansas City Star 2010). These rules he applied assiduously across his career. It admonished the writer to 'Use short sentences. Use short first paragraphs. Use vigorous English. Be positive, not negative.... Eliminate every superfluous word' (ibid.). It was in the use of this restricted choice that Hemingway created a writing style that served his output well, both as a writer of journalism and as a literary writer.

An explanation for these seeming discrepancies in the way extrinsic motivators are perceived to operate for creative individuals may lie a little further afield than simply looking at the dichotomy of extrinsic or intrinsic factors themselves. For example, as Eisenberger and Shanock (2003) argue, the characterisation of extrinsic motivation as a largely negative process can be traced to a quite Romantic view of creativity. They believe that 'philosophical Romanticism provides fundamental insights concerning the contribution of perceived self-determination to intrinsic task interest and creativity' (Eisenberger and Shanock 2003, p. 122) since creativity, from this perspective, is assumed to be about self-determination which is thought to be reduced by a set of 'constraints on autonomy, including reward' (ibid.).

> For romanticists, the non-specific promise of reward or the reward of conventional performance often decreased intrinsic motivation and creativity, leading to the premature conclusion that reward generally reduces intrinsic motivation and creativity. (Eisenberger and Shanock 2003, p. 125)

Despite the emphasis on the importance of intrinsic motivation and what happens if it is not present, Eisenberger and Shanock (2003), contrasting Romantic and behaviourist understandings of reward as a motivational factor, suggest, in part, that 'when individuals believe they can obtain rewards by being creative, they become more creative' (Eisenberger and Shanock 2003, p. 128). It should be noted here that the world of art and writing are not the only creative arenas in which motivation is stimulated 'externally':

> Consider James Watson, the codiscoverer of the molecular mechanism for the transmission of human heredity. Watson's

autobiography indicates extrinsic as well as intrinsic motivation as a source of discovery (Watson, 1968). Watson savored the hunt for the genetic code; at the same time, he greatly enjoyed leisure activities. His desire to win a Nobel prize seems to have been instrumental in returning him to work from extended periods of diversion. Scientists and mathematicians, often identified as paragons of intrinsic motivation, including Einstein, Feynman, von Neumann, and Ramanujan, were strengthened in their resolve to pursue difficult research problems by the acclaim they anticipated from the scientific community or the public (Clark, 1972; Gleick, 1992; Kanigel, 1991; Lanouette, 1992; Macrae, 1992). Personal recognition is an important motivating force for most creative scientists. They are careful to establish priority of discovery and are delighted when their contributions are honored (Mansfield & Busse, 1981). (Eisenberger and Shanock 2003: 121)

Eisenberger and Shanock go on to propose that 'the expectation that creativity will be rewarded causes individuals to define the task as requiring creativity, to become immersed in it, and to search for novel ways of carrying it out' (Eisenberger and Shanock 2003, p. 128). This is an opposite finding to that of Amabile allowing for the conclusion that extrinsic motivators are just as important to creativity as intrinsic ones are. The case can thus be made that, no matter whether one engages intrinsic or extrinsic motivation, 'encouragement of creativity, in the form of tangible and socioemotional rewards, strengthens creative motivational orientation' (ibid.).

Cheek and Stahl take this idea a step further, arguing for a degree of subtlety in assessing motivation. They suggest that the impact of certain extrinsic factors, factors that are not generated internally:

will depend on the individual and the nature of the contingency. Shy individuals, for example, may be especially sensitive to evaluative feedback (Cheek & Stahl 1986). At least as significant is the nature of the extrinsic factor. Feedback that is informative rather than evaluative, for instance, though still extrinsic, does not inhibit creative efforts. (Runco 2007, p. 309)

It could thus be suggested that either intrinsic motivation or extrinsic motivation may be required to set creative activity in motion, dependent on the context, but following this activation, there may be a necessity for the person to become absorbed into the work to finish the task; and despite a wish for it to be otherwise, most creativity involves a fair degree of work. As Evans and Deehan indicate, little that is termed creative simply happens:

> Painters and writers, not surprisingly when you think about it, often report that they get up in the mornings feeling like the rest of us: a bit dull or listless, not really enthusiastic about the thought of work. Because they have fixed working hours – again like most of us – they set to, however, putting words on paper or paint on canvas. There is no scintillating muse jolting their mood or intellect into action, no automatic pilot guiding their hand towards a creative end. Simple, careful, scrupulous, laborious work. Sometimes the creative individual has to fight to concentrate on the task in hand, just as many of us have to struggle to keep our mind on the job and off an impending lunch or dinner date. (1988, p. 26)

Even Tchaikovsky, who wrote some of the most popular pieces of music from the nineteenth century, held similar thoughts stating in a letter to a friend that inspiration 'does not always respond to the first invitation. We must *always* work, and a self-respecting artist must not fold his [*sic*] hands in the pretext that he [*sic*] is not in the mood' (quoted in Evans and Deehan 1988, pp. 25–6).

It is in the use of the term 'mood' that a solution to what may act as a major motivator in the creative process could be found. As Eisenberger and Shanock suggest 'people performing challenging tasks to their maximum ability often experience an engrossing and seemingly unique phenomenological state that prolongs and invigorates performance' (2003, p. 128). It is claimed that it is this experience that acts as a recurring motivator for many people engaged in cultural production because 'its goal is primarily the experience itself' (Csikszentmihalyi in Csikszentmihalyi and Csikszentmihalyi 1988, p. 29). Csikszentmihalyi illuminates his view of the flow experience himself by summarising how others in his study have described it:

> people describe the common characteristics of optimal experience: a sense that one's skills are adequate to cope with the challenges at hand, in a goal directed, rule-bound action system that provides clear clues as to how well one is performing. Concentration is so intense that there is no attention left over to think about anything irrelevant, or to worry about problems. Self-consciousness disappears, and the sense of time becomes distorted. An activity that produces such

experiences is so gratifying that people are willing to do it for its own sake, with little concern for what they will get out of it, even when it is difficult, or dangerous. (1991, p. 71)

This 'flow' experience has been described by Reed Larson in an essay entitled 'Flow and Writing' as an optimal state 'in which the person is absorbed in their activities and when actions follow smoothly from the thoughts' (Larson in Csikszentmihalyi and Csikszentmihalyi 1988, p. 163). While the emotional state is definitely a positive one, sufficient attention is accessible to negotiate other tasks and people feel in control of the situation being engaged fully in the task at hand. In this alert yet relaxed state, 'people feel motivated to be doing what they are doing, and their attention is effective' (ibid.). This circumstance usually occurs when people have clear goals and a reasonable sense of how they will accomplish their goals. Larson goes on to say that in the state of flow people know:

> what they want to accomplish and understand the rules governing how one gets there. In addition, feedback, either explicit or self generated, appears to be important: One has to know when one is doing something right and something wrong. The most central element, however, seems to be the balance between the perceived challenges of the activity and a person's skills. One must experience the activity as presenting opportunities for action that are well meshed with one's talents.... Only when this balance occurs does the opportunity exist for enjoyment and deep involvement. If the challenges of the activity are too great for a person's skills, anxiety takes over.... On the other hand if the challenges of an activity are too few for a person's skill – or if one sees no way to make an activity challenging – boredom takes over. (Larson in Csikszentmihalyi and Csikszentmihalyi 1988, pp. 163–4)

While the flow state has been variously linked to drug-induced experiences, metaphysical states or religious ecstasy, as suggested prior, and has been described occasionally in so-called 'new age' terms, there is, it appears, a necessary, but it must be emphasised not sufficient, neurobiological element to it. In his article *In the Zone: A Biobehavioral Theory of the Flow Experience* (2001), Arthur Marr wrote that:

> In a review of recent findings in neuro-psychology Ashby, Isen, and Turkel (1999) concluded that rapid attentional set shifting between

salient cognitive precepts does indeed correlate to feelings of elation and satisfaction, and that the neurochemical processes that enable this shifting also increase cognitive efficiency and creativity. (Marr 2001)

Marr goes on to suggest that:

The practical implications of a bio-behavioral explanation for flow greatly refine Csikszentmihalyi's own prescriptions for the replication of flow in everyday life, and make those prescriptions much clearer by discarding spurious mental processes such as intrinsic motivation, autotelic personality, and the like. For example, short bursts of absorbing activity (e.g. writing sonnets, creating art) that are paced at separate intervals during the day will elicit a high level of neural arousal, will have enough 'momentum' to span those intervals, and create a state of pleasurable alertness that can be extended all day. (ibid.)

While one can argue with a purely bio-behavioural approach and its own declaration of priority, particularly in terms of what is cause and what is effect, the question needs to be asked: how does all of this apply to writing in general and journalism in particular? Without labouring the point too much, if the individual journalist works with a structure they are familiar with, with time frames that are commensurate with their skills, the topic is stimulating and challenging and neither intrinsic or extrinsic factors detract from the attention paid to the task at hand; task engagement could lead to highly effective and creative news stories. If, as is often the case, all of these conditions are less than perfect then a degree of satisficing will inevitably occur. Should the degree of anxiety or boredom be overwhelming or any of these other factors override attention, then the task engagement will cease and, at the extreme, the writer will be blocked.

So what have the journalists got on their side? Knowledge, for one, of the way the large institutional frameworks they work within operate, as well as an understanding of the hierarchies present in the work teams they inhabit. Their professional inculcation should serve them well in negotiating their creative output through the profession's own sets of logics, conventions and traditions, and enable them to resolve and use the arena of social contestation they work in. Alongside this knowledge, skill and the general structure of news that is both predictive and separate from the content is also on their side. This usually comes in the form of a format and style guide which eases the attention needed to allow the maximum concentration on the development of content and thus enables the journalist's ability to enter the flow experience. The pattern, the blueprint and the form also tells us as an audience what we can expect to see in our nightly news or read in the morning newspapers, and it is essential in guiding the journalist in their writing endeavours. It is the concept of form and its necessary relationship to creativity that we should engage with now.

9
Television: Form, Format and Being Formulaic

It was mentioned in the last chapter that there are some consistent sets of practices media professionals use and perpetuate when they produce content for their particular media form. These practices are absorbed as knowledge and reiterated as skill sets used to understand and reproduce the structures of journalism. The same can be said for the forms of television and the format of the station. This knowledge aids in the development of content that will connect with an audience. In doing so media practitioners often follow what has been termed 'media logic' (McQuail 1994, p. 265).

However, there is a proposition that argues when media industries follow 'media logic', which could also be called a standardised set of routines, they inevitably produce formulaic material. For example, Altheide, according to Denis McQuail, 'sees content as tailored to fit media formats and formats as tailored to fit listener/viewer preferences and assumed capacities' (1994, p. 265), which leads to tightly organised and inevitably conventional material. Further, in his famous study into television production in the United States, *Inside Prime Time* (1994), Todd Gitlin argued that 'all modern organisations aspire to order, regularity, which make for efficiency and control' (1994, p. 56). By extension, this control inhibits creativity to the point that, as David Hesmondhalgh asserts in relation to Gitlins, 'the overwhelming imperative for these networks was to make programmes which were "safe", unlikely to disturb advertisers, lobbyists and domestic audiences, envisaged by TV executives as undisturbable' (2006, p. 221). Bill Ryan, the author of *Making Capital from Culture: The Corporate Form of Capitalist Cultural Production* (1991), also asserts that:

> formats have played a crucial role in consolidating the conditions of creative...work and sedimenting professional cultural practice.

Despite the fact that they are unable to exert total control over cultural workers, since formatting operates as a superstructure over existing structures of creative management and a specialised division of labour, corporations can administer the creative stage in a manner which systematically supplies them with the originals they need to expand in an unpredictable and competitive market. From the perspective of the corporations of culture, however, this limited victory in production has been won at the cost of introducing significant problems of realisation in the sphere of circulation. Cultural goods produced under the formatting system reveal a marked tendency towards typicality and repetition. The problem with this is that ... it can generate objects which are bland and uniform, if not outright uninteresting. (Ryan 1991, p. 184)

These ideas deserve some examination from the point of view of the more recent research into creativity set out earlier in this book. The argument, to state it simply again here, identifies the organisational structure and standardised routines of the media as the cause of conventional material, where that conventional material is then generally seen as uncreative. It should be noted that the word creativity, as it is generally used in these discussions, is often taken to mean, in the main, a form of artistic activity emanating from individuals and the discussion tends to operate from a normative framework placing those individuals, sometimes called symbol creators (Hesmondhalgh 2002, pp. 5–6), within some form of opposition or resistance to other members of the field. While there is certainly a very strong case to be made that the power of corporations to influence creative output on television is very significant (Peterson 1982, 1985), often more so than other players in the system as Ang (1990) and Morley (1993) both argue, this proposition may be only a partial account of creativity within television production; necessary certainly but still only partial. It is also granted that there is substantial evidence that excessive control 'from the top' has produced some material on television that is uninteresting to certain critics and certain viewers, but it can also be claimed that it has also produced material that has been interesting to many others, dependent of course on their level of use, gratification and activity as viewers, fans or aficionados. The judgement in this case is often a subjective one. This contention can definitely be argued over but, more importantly for this present discussion, one can also more precisely make the assertion that simply because a structure exists, whether these are institutional or conventional ones, this existence alone does not mean that they act *only* as constraints on creativity and therefore work produced inside these industrial conventions and traditions can *only* be seen as uncreative output.

In the first instance, one must at least be working from an assumption that the notion of creative freedom is somehow equivalent to an absence of constraint before one can claim that structures only inhibit or constrain creative action. This is a position typical of what could be called a remnant Romantic view of creativity or what can also be seen as an individual-centred or agent-focused view. It can be manifest in a number of ways. As one extreme example, Robert Thompson in his book, *Adventures on Prime Time: The Television Programs of Stehen J. Cannell* (1990), goes far enough along this path to espouse notions of auteurism, itself an outgrowth of a Romantic imperative, in relation to writer-producers of particular television programmes.

Without reiterating the problematic of only seeing freedom as simply the obverse side of the imposition of control, rather than as the ability to make choice, one could claim that at the heart of the arguments that surround the formatting of media content, the central concern I want to deal with here, are those same perennial ones that haunt sociology and cultural studies, and that is the question of the relationship between structure and agency. While there have certainly been deep considerations of the nature of agency in relation to both producers and audiences for television texts (e.g. Tulloch, 1990, pp. 9–18), I will generalise here and say that the relationship between structure and agency is usually implied in the discussions about corporate control as an opposition, that is, as agency *versus* structure. In these cases the question seems to be: how can a free-willed producer of creative works be original and authentic, or more importantly in this case, creative, when they are working within the constraints of a tightly formatted structure imposed by corporate culture? While there have been a number of ethnographies of production that reveal that the making of television is less about confirming 'author/god' models and they expose, among other things, a complex understanding of the nature of multiple authorship (e.g. Alvarado & Buscombe 1978, Moran 1982, Tulloch & Alvarado 1983, Tulloch & Moran 1986), few studies have, as yet, moved into seeing the creative processes apparent in television production as systemic. The critical thing that needs some discussion is that there is a tendency to undervalue, and at times ignore, the *enabling* possibilities that, as Janet Wolff, Anthony Giddens and Pierre Bourdieu have all variously indicated, structures are quite capable of providing.

In the second instance, and this is certainly related directly to the first instance and one I want to concentrate on more fully here, there appears to be little effective consideration of the idea that drawing on convention may also be a central aspect of much of what can be labelled creative. In the rush to perceive and critique structural constraints, unconventional work is generally valorised over conventional material in the West, leading one to assume that only unconventional material can be considered unique, and thus in the terms used in the discussion, creative. This is to ignore the extent to which the perfection of traditional or conventional material embodies creative work and to also ignore how culturally specific certain assumptions about creativity are:

> In some contexts and cultures artists are valued for their virtuosity in exercising conventional skills, with the greatest accolades for performances that approach the ideal realisation of the conventional form; in others, aesthetic norms emphasise innovativeness and individuality, with an implicit expectation of radical innovation as the badge of genius. (Gross 1995, p. 2)

However, as Negus and Pickering contend:

> It is a common misconception to regard innovation and tradition as diametrically opposed to each other. When innovation is valued as a defining characteristic of the creative process, tradition often becomes set up against it as inevitably static and unchanging. In this view, tradition inhibits, and is seen as an impediment to be overcome. We want to challenge this notion of tradition. (Negus & Pickering 2004, p. 91)

Perhaps this latter problematic may be partly illuminated by, firstly, investigating the ordered nature of all cultural forms and then, secondly, differentiating between the notions of form, format and formula.

Aristotle, according to Guthrie, thought that 'although at first sight the world seems to be in constant movement and offer no fixed truths [we can] analyse this continual flux and will find that there are underlying it certain basic principles or elements which do not change' (Guthrie 1967, p. 128). This is not to argue for an idealised set of forms that are thought to exist externally and apart from the manifestation of them, as Plato did, nor is it assuming in any detail that human beings encounter a pre-existing order in the universe they inhabit. The concern is, in line with both Bhaskar (1979) and Sayer (2000), not with whether we are imposing order through our minds or whether we are seeing something that is already there; the essential thing to realise is, as Herbert Read asserts in his book *The Origins of Form in Art* (1965), that the construction of valued aesthetic experiences is humanity's ability 'to separate form from the swirling chaos of his sensations, and to contemplate that form in its uniqueness' (1965, p. 7). It makes sense then to realise that, in order to be comprehensible, culture must be organised in such a way as to enable communication. It also follows that we can, by finding out how things are organised, also expose the underlying structures of the cultural form as it is manifest in the works themselves. This is not to pursue what constitutes meaning, as Roland Barthes had attempted to do in S/Z (1970), since that enterprise, while related, is a slightly different task. Barthes' work on the codes the writer and reader share, while structural in nature, led him to his move into poststructuralism, but even then he did not deny the existence of structures themselves. What we are pursuing in this instance is the constitution of structure and its relationship to the way production is organised.

Furthermore, we can also say that the way things are organised then rapidly becomes a convenient way to classify them and classifying things, as Arthur Berger explains, 'is a way of making sense out of chaos (or seeming chaos)' (1994, p. 45). Berger goes on to take a position in the philosophical debate by asserting that 'every system of classification has a bias in it – the system of classification affects what we see and do not see and shapes the way we see things' (ibid.). In this regard some have speculated that humans may be wired to see patterns and this wiring has worked to our advantage, playing a major part in our rapid evolutionary expansion (Koch and Davis 1994, p. x) which translates for our purposes as pattern-seeing may be the function of a specific part of the brain. However, in contradiction to this last statement, Susan Greenfield (2008) has pointed out that neuroscience is a nested process where factors are seen as interrelated; where consciousness depends as much on genetics as the wiring of the brain depends on the experiences it has in the world it exists in. Evelyn Hartcher adds to these views by asserting that 'much of what is perceived even in this basic physiological sense is subject to selection determined by how one has learned to organize and interpret what he [sic] sees' (1985, p. 86). Hartcher contends that 'a fundamental way that all levels of perception operate has to do with what captures attention – whether what we see or hear says 'Look out!' or 'Relax, no problem' (1985, p. 87). It is at this level that Hartcher locates the experience of form claiming that 'art always involves both tension and harmony, no matter which is emphasised, and without both, and both under control, it is not art' (1985, p. 88). She also asserts that 'the basic human experience of arousal and relaxation, activity and repose, while apparently simple, is applied and elaborated in a quite astonishing variety of formulations' in cultural production (ibid.).

As an example, the formal system or organising principle in films, television and indeed in most narrative, as David Bordwell and Kristin Thompson (1990) argue, are the notions of similarity and difference. They suggest that in order to understand a visual drama of the type seen in film and on television, the audience must become familiar with what is presented to them and be able to recall such things as settings and characters. The repetition of these elements and their similarity to those already encountered by an audience provide a certain set of cross references for the audience to be able to follow and be engaged by the narrative. Throughout a television drama, for example, the audience may note the repetition of types of dialogue, thematic music, camera positions, character's behaviour and actions. Motifs, repeated situations, similar camera angles, comparable lighting schemes and thematic music heighten our sense of expectation (Bordwell & Thompson 1990, p. 47). By seeing similar elements in a television programme we can engage in comparisons of characters, events and ideas. Recognising these increases an audiences' understanding of the dramatic narrative. Dramatic narratives, however, could not be composed only of repeated similarities; 'characters must be distinguished, environments delineated, different times or activities must be established' (ibid). The audience may not always want to identify what comes next. Variety, contrast and change are needed to maintain interest against a stable background of similarity and repetition. Though motifs may be repeated, they are seldom repeated exactly, and the similarities between two characters may be highlighted to emphasise their differences. Differences can in turn lead to oppositions. Similarity and difference are, then, two sides of the same coin. To a certain extent each becomes dependent on the other in creating a pattern of events. This situation leads in turn to a progression through the narrative which we call story development. As Bordwell and Thompson suggest, the simplest way of observing development is to compare the beginning with the ending. In the end, 'the constant interplay between similarity and difference, repetition and variation, leads the viewer to an active, developing awareness' (Bordwell & Thompson 1990, p. 49) of, in this case, television's formal system.

To pursue this idea a little further culture can be identified in the simplest sense as an outgrowth of humanly organised sensory experience while noting that this experience also occurs as a result of social and cultural predilections. Nonetheless, one can see different forms within a culture depending on the way experience is organised and engaged with. The way to recognise these forms is often done through their structures, or to reiterate the point, the way they are organised. All television programmes, for example, have some things in common. They are audio/visual experiences organised around the particular senses that deal with sound and vision. Not all television programmes, however, share the same organising principle in terms of their construction or the way they are put together. Dramas, nonetheless, do. It is the way dramas are structured that makes them dramas.

To give another example, mass communication is often categorised by the various media used. Up until the advent of what have been called new media, itself a contentious term, the media could be split into two basic groups as to whether they were broadcast or recorded. Broadcast media included television and radio. Recorded media included film, novels, music, papers and magazines. Each medium uses a particular cultural form, or a number of cultural forms, as the basis for its communication. Having identified the form we can then concentrate on categorising the subgroups found within those forms. For example, Berger has used four basic types of programme to classify the cultural types found on television. These are actualities, contests, persuasions and dramas. As he explains, 'these four types of programs can, in turn, be subsumed under an even more basic set of concepts – concepts that help us categorize each of the four types of programs in various ways' (1994, p. 6). Actualities contain news and documentaries. Contests contain sport and game shows. Persuasions are the ads. The fourth and the most prevalent are the dramas. Here he lists the genres of soap operas, situation comedies, police shows, action adventure shows, hospital shows and so on. As Berger explains, these categories are not completely isolable. A certain amount of bleeding occurs between categories, but he does emphasise that most television programming tends to be dramatic and 'even genres that are not explicitly dramatic, such as news shows and commercials, often have a great deal of dramatic content to them' (1994, p. 8).

The essential point that can be derived from the above examples of classifying cultural output by type is that the basic organisation or structural components of the cultural form defines the cultural form itself. Since communication via the media is one of the major purveyors of multiple cultural forms it can also be argued that structure itself is a necessary component of the genres found on television. Structure is not, however, for our purposes entirely the same thing as genre. We can make the declaration that structures are the blueprint of a form, but genre is the subsystem of classification we use when we recognise the organisation of the cultural form. Formal narrative conventions are thus not entirely the same thing as generic conventions, although they are certainly related.

From one perspective narratives are ways of organising an experience into a coherent set of events that chart the movement, as Tzvetan Todorov (1977) explains, from order to disorder and back to order again. As Berger points out, what we also 'learn from Propp is that there is a logic to narratives and that they are constructed according to rules that have not varied greatly over the centuries' (Berger 1994, p. 30). Roman Jakobson's assertion that narratives can be split into two basic components, story and discourse, is also apposite (Chatman 1978). For Jakobson the story is the unchangeable aspects of the narrative. On the other hand, the discourse is the way we tell the story. We could choose to tell a story which has the same basic elements in the form of a novel, or in song, a poem or a joke, or we could make it into a television drama or a dramatic film. The dramatic form, obviously borrowed from forms common to theatre, is outlined succinctly in Syd Field's book *Screenplay: The Foundations of Screenwriting* (1988). Field explains that the form for a good screenplay is a model, a pattern or a conceptual scheme that follows a basic linear structure. It has a beginning, middle and end that correspond to acts one, two and three. Act one contains the set-up. Act two is where confrontation occurs and act three involves the resolution of the conflict. This is its basic structure. Within that structure we could follow a set of further conventions if we wanted to tell the story as part of a particular genre such as a Western or thriller or, for television, a hospital drama.

From the above it can be seen that the experience of television, as with all cultural products, is patterned and structured. We can now go one step further and claim, which is where we partially fall into line with Barthes' structuralist work, that it is the audiences' expectation of following this system that draws them into actively participating in the ongoing process of the creative work. In the narratives encountered on television audiences will ask 'what will happen next?' and adjust their expectations accordingly. We, as a television audience, therefore actively participate in and engage with the form of, in this case, television drama, proposing developments as the story unfolds while busily re-adjusting our expectations about the form the narrative is taking as the televisual experience develops. Genre consciously works with these formal expectations. For example, television comedy is often the result of the formal expectations being presented not being met. TV thrillers also follow well-worn forms that the audience delights in following. Suspense is, in this sense, no more than the delayed fulfilment of an expectation. It can be seen that television genres are in essence traditional forms that share a dominant style and common traits, which are themselves called generic conventions. Sitcoms, action adventures and soap operas all follow dramatic televisual form but they rely on differing generic conventions.

Following on from this, Berger argues that 'modern popular culture genres can be thought of as variations, modifications, camouflaged versions, and so forth' (1994, p. 22) of the form and structure of the stories Vladimir Propp investigated in his groundbreaking study *Morphology of the Folktale* (1968) since 'a large number of the functions that Propp found in his Russian fairy tales can also be found in contemporary spy stories, science fiction stories, soap operas westerns, and the like' (Berger 1994, p. 22).

Berger then goes on to assert that genre is a more comprehensive term than formula. Formulas, as distinct from form, exist within genres and may even be named subgenres, but these may not, in themselves, be indicative of formularised cultural production. Before we pursue these ideas further though, we can sum up the discussion so far by asserting that all culture has to be structured in order to communicate. To be a film, novel, short story or a television programme cultural production must be patterned or organised in a particular way. Genres are forms that have become conventional ones we recognise. To put it another way, genres are simply traditional forms. So forms are necessary things as far as creativity is concerned since, as Berger reiterates when he refers to Russian semiotician and literary analyst Yuri Lotman, 'one can never have a text that breaks all the rules that people can understand. You can avoid a given system (or conventions in a text) but you must have *some* system' (1994, p. 53). Lotman suggests that we have had 'repetitive texts, for a long time; they are not something new, spawned by the mass media' (quotedin Berger 1994, p. 53). Those repetitive texts, what we are calling genres, appear to have, nonetheless, become a characteristic of this form of communication. As Keith Negus and Michael Pickering suggest:

> Genre is an important concept because creativity is about working within, across and out from the codes and conventions of genres, in whatever media they are manifest. Our understanding of creative practice cannot then be confined to what is taken as inspirational

and radically new. Even where this occurs, creativity still involves working with recognisable codes, conventions and the expectations they generate. Indeed, for much of the time it entails putting together various words, sounds, shapes, colours and gestures in a recognisably familiar and only slightly different way. Most of the time it is that element of difference which provokes a critical response, rather than any sudden dramatic change. (Negus & Pickering 2004, p. 70)

As Sharon Bailin further argues, often 'innovation is meaningful only because the innovator continues to operate within the context of rules which are substantially unchanged' (1988, p. 89). Bailin also proposes, quite persuasively, that 'one difference between creative and uncreative performances relates to having a real understanding of the discipline in which one is engaged' (1988, pp. 97). As a corollary to Bailin's conclusion, Negus & Pickering (2004) argue:

Creativity doesn't emerge out of a vacuum, but builds on one or more existing cultural traditions. This is true of poetry, architecture, film-making, styles of singing and any number of other examples. In this sense creative talent requires a tradition so that it can learn how to go further within it or beyond it. Innovation should be understood by rejecting those approaches which set it squarely against tradition and established cultural practice. (Negus & Pickering 2004, p. 91)

In this case the domain of television, as explained by the systems model, must be seen as part of an open-ended system, especially if the space is provided within the domain for the bending and extension of the rules and conventions of television as well as the adherence to, and importantly for creativity, striving towards the perfection of, conventional televisual forms.

In order for a cultural producer to engage with this process of cultural change, they must understand the conventions and traditions, that is, the rules, forms and structures of the domain they work in, and understand them extremely well. On the other hand, when the creative agent in television production, while sticking rigidly to the forms and conventions of the genre they use, also makes the content far too familiar to the extent that the audience for television recognises that nothing new or interesting is occurring, it is here that the programme ceases to swing between the poles of similarity and difference. If it stays firmly fixed on the pole of similarity and familiarity, no excitement will match the ensuing boredom. Without this movement between the poles of similarity and difference occurring, the televisual work becomes too predictable and ceases to resonate with the audience who will then look for that resonance elsewhere. After all genres 'function as "horizons of expectation" for readers and "models of writing" for authors' (Negus & Pickering 2004, p. 71) which operate within a sociocultural context. Programme can thus, as Jason Mittell argues, 'be situated within larger systems of cultural hierarchies and power relations' (2004, p. 178) and can therefore be understood within wider cultural practices (ibid., pp. 171–81).

It can be argued at this point that there has been some conflation between, firstly, an understanding of formal and generic conventions, secondly, the format of a particular station, thirdly, what constitutes the systematising or routining of television production and, lastly, what is identified as formulaic production. As one example of these conflations in operation, David McQueen suggests that, for the television industry, 'gradual shifts in the conventions of the various genres allows for creativity within the boundaries of tried and tested formulas' (1998, p. 28).

One can also say that the term 'format' is, in one sense, a way of describing the overall content of a television station's output. The same word can be used to describe the overall content of a particular programme. However, the way the term formatting is used in a production sense is slightly different again. Unlike the overall system used to delineate the structure of a single programme, that is its form, formatting can be used as a term to describe a mode of procedure, a way of acting or scheme that systematises production and enables the rapid production of television programmes. As Moran and Hill (2004) state, a format package for television, sometimes called a programme bible, is a way of recording and passing on to other producers, directors, camera people and so on 'the precise production elements and their organisation, including the steps of production' of a particular television programme (Moran & Hill 2004, p. 259). It acts as a guide for production.

Without this structured approach to making television or a method of working that is efficient and fast, it is arguable as to whether television would have as much content to broadcast as it does. *The Simpsons, Beverly Hills 90210, Six Feet Under, The Sopranos, Four Corners, West Wing, Studio 60 on the Sunset Strip, Sylvania Waters, South Park, Top Gear* or *Dr Who*, all seen at various points as creative and innovative television programmes, would not have been easily made as series that were aired weekly if they weren't able to be efficiently and quickly produced in a systematised and routinised way. Television programmes that are formulaic are a different matter again.

If a television show is seen to be formulaic, it may be that the conventions, traditions, rules and structures of the form or format are so readily apparent and so rigidly used that an audience could readily discern too much similarity. They would, therefore, derive no interest from it through the element of difference, as they would perceive no difference to be apparent. In this case a television programme, which may be fresh and exciting in its first few seasons, would risk becoming overly familiar through constant exposure and at some point 'jump the shark', that is, write in an unbelievable event that goes beyond the conventions of the form, in an effort to maintain interest, just as the creators of the sitcom *Happy Days* did in the latter stages of that series production.

Just as form and genre are necessary but slightly different *structural* categories for television, we should also be able to see that formats and formatting are also not *solely* constraining and inhibiting. In many ways they allow or enable the television programme to be made by providing the space for the possibility of action, that is, they provide 'an ensemble of probable *constraints* which are the condition and the counterpart of a set of *possible uses*' (Bourdieu 1996, p. 235). Quoting Kaminsky and Mahan, Berger recognises that 'the work of popular art is two things at the same time: it is like many other things that have preceded it; yet it is also unique, not a precise duplication of anything that has been presented before' (1994, p. 46). Berger explains that most audiences, as elaborated on above, have a desire for the ordered stability of repetition of the sort held in structures and conventions. Balanced against this they also have a need for novelty, a longing for variation and innovation, which in most cases is generally found in the unique content within the form, in the detail, as it were, of the programme. Berger goes on to suggest that all art, and for our discussion here this includes television production, forms a continuum. At one end is absolute originality and uniqueness, if such a thing was indeed possible and still be recognised as a communicative event. Anything that swings too far in this direction would be seen as problematic because, as judgement is applied to it, it could only be read as bizarre, that is, not understood. There is, in this particular case, no similarity or shared convention in existence. At the other end of the scale is rigid adherence to, and slavish repetition of, forms and formats. It is at this end of the continuum, I would claim, that a television show becomes formulaic. If people 'encounter something totally unlike anything they have encountered before, they are confused and mystified. If they encounter something totally familiar, they can be bored very easily' (Berger 1994, pp. 46–7). Therefore, one could claim that there is a constant tension between the two poles that television production must negotiate. Inevitably the producers of culture, especially those who deal in making programmes within culture industries like television, and this includes the makers of outsourced material that is bought in by the corporations, walk a constant tight rope between these two poles when they adhere to 'media logic'. But while becoming formulaic is problematic, one still needs to be aware that structures, of the type seen in forms and formats, aren't just constraining; they also enable the making of television.

Furthermore, as Vera Zolberg suggests, all 'forms have structural properties some of which are chiefly social or external in their implications, and others mainly formal/aesthetic or intrinsic' (Zolberg 1990, p. 169). Having looked at formal structures we could also turn our attention, briefly, to the social structures of industrial production that television uses (Ellis 2004, pp. 275–92). These also provide the possibilities of choice creative agents, and these are not always singular individuals, working within the field and domain of television use:

> Some programs appear to bear the imprint of a single individual, but more than likely that person's apparent 'authorship' of the program or series derives much more from his or her visibility in front of the camera than from any determinative role he or she played behind it. As Ellis notes, television production adapted a particular mode of organisation from the making of feature films, which, in turn, is based upon the factory system of manufacturing: a division of labor among workers, separation of design functions from execution (the lighting director is not involved in the writing of the script and need not even know what the narrative is about), and a clear hierarchy of responsibilities and authority. The economics of commercial television around the world favour the production of multiple episodes of a given program, across which some elements remain constant (in the case of dramatic programs: the central cast members, recurrent settings, duration, etc.). These continuing elements create a framework within which each episode's narrative can differ from week to week. (Allen & Hill 2004, p. 269)

The case of *The West Wing* (Sorkin 2002, Rollins & O'Connor 2003) may be pertinent here. This programme is credited at the beginning of each episode as being 'created' by Aaron Sorkin, but Thomas Schlamme and John Wells also deserve credit for the innovations the series was noted for as do the editors, set and sound designers and camerapeople who contributed from their own fields and domains of expertise. *The West Wing* has been lauded for its scripts and dialogue, but has also achieved recognition, in a cultural capital sense, for its ensemble features, the introduction and execution of the 'walk and talk' expository piece, its use of music, its set design, editing and its filmic features. It won three Golden Globe awards and twenty-seven Emmys which were awarded to the show overall, to writers, directors, actors, music composers and various members of the crew in recognition of their creative contribution. It's also highly demonstrable that the programme draws on pre-existing work from the formal domain of both film and television, such as Frank Capra's *Mr Smith Goes to Washington* and in particular Sorkin's prior work on the movie *The American President*, and it has generated further work in the domain by providing the basis for political comedies like *The Hollowmen*. In this case we can say that *The West Wing* has been dependent for its existence on many of the conventions of the domain of television but has also provided enough difference to run to seven series. Furthermore, without the $6m budget allocated to each episode it's doubtful the series could have been as successful both artistically and commercially as it was, the field deciding it was worth continuing funding the series into its seventh season. Its idealistic salutation to public service has reached beyond the field of television where it has raised the profile of political speech writing (Glover 2011), taken the idea of everyday politics into the domestic realm (Wodak 2009), endorsed the U.S. presidency as a seemingly noble office (Holbert et al. 2003) and provided a rich source of tools for pedagogical activity in the educational sphere (Beavers 2002).

Taking this particular case one step further, just as David Hesmondhalgh argues that texts would not exist without symbol creators (2002, p. 5), it can also be readily seen that *The West Wing*, as well as television texts of all types, would not exist without the continuation of the symbol system itself, found in part in televisual form, as well as the ongoing existence of the field of television, found most often in corporate or large institutional settings as well as in the existence of critics and audiences for those texts. In other words, what we are looking at is a field and domain in operation which both form a significant part of 'a whole matrix of conditions of cultural production and consumption' (Hesmondhalgh 2002, p. 256) where it is critically important, as Hesmondhalgh himself argues, to think of cultural industries like television as producers of texts (2002, p. 264). The only difference here is that if one follows the systems approach to creativity, instead of relying on a predominantly individual-centred conception of creativity, which is then often conflated down to a form of artistic activity, none of these three components of the system of television production, the creative agent, the field or the domain, are more, or less, central than the other in creating television. The structures of the field and domain and the way creative agents are provided with possibilities of action through them are each absolutely necessary but not entirely sufficient by and of themselves to produce television. Each both constrains and enables television production to varying degrees at both one and the same time.

10
Film: Auteur Theory, Collaboration, Systems

Before we venture into an investigation of the movement of thought that has been applied to creativity in the film world I'd like to, firstly, become a little anecdotal.

I've been watching films since I was four years old and was placed in the back seat of the cinema when my mother went shopping on Saturday mornings. She herself was a theatre usherette and trusted her colleagues. Thousands upon thousands of flickering images have skimmed past me in hundreds of darkened cinemas since then. It wasn't until many years later that I started to list my favourite films. I discovered that they shared a few things in common, one of which was the names of John Ford, David Lean and Steven Spielberg. Of course there were many others, but these names seemed to be fairly regular in my listings. So were these names trying to tell me something? Did they all have common themes in the work they produced? Then another thought occurred to me. Could I tell, without knowing, whether I was watching a David Lean movie or a Steven Spielberg movie? If so, how was this possible? Was there something in their movies that marked each of them with their authority? Was it in the visual style they used, their sense of timing in editing, the recurring motifs they used, or simply their thematic preoccupations? Did these filmic authors tell the same stories over and over again? The ultimate question was, were these directors the ones I could hold responsible for my fascination? Many years later I discovered a few academics who had attempted to answer these very same questions. They themselves had names such as Francois Truffaut, Andrew Sarris, Peter Wollen and more recently David Bordwell and Kristin Thompson.

Bordwell and Thompson in the book *Film Art: An Introduction* (1997) outline three ways that a director can be seen as an author of a film. It is possible to add to these Duncan Petrie's (1991) description of Peter

Wollen's structuralist approach. These four ways of seeing the director as an author then correspond in many ways to some of the views of creativity we have been discussing up to this point. Firstly, we can look at the author as a personality. Secondly, we can examine the deep structures of a film to perceive the author's intended meanings. Thirdly, we can observe a group of films as a text or critical construct and, lastly, we can see the author as a production worker in a collaborative enterprise. A similar set of categories are set up by Susan Hayward in her book *Key Concepts in Cinema Studies* (1996), but it can also be argued that these categorisations correspond somewhat to the creator as individual genius sitting within an inspirational or Romantic view of creativity; the structuralist conceptions of sociology; the poststructuralist reconceptualisation of the author-function; and finally, the positions put forward by Howard Becker in terms of art worlds and the idea that films come about as a result of a system in operation. I want to explore briefly each one of these conceptions.

Firstly, it was the early auteurists' views that most correspond to Bordwell and Thompson's category of authorship as personality. These auteurists hinged their arguments on the centrality of personalities to the creative process. Film, like many of the newer forms of cultural production, has sought in many ways to legitimate itself as a 'true art form'. These attempts parallel the move of the novel from being a popular and thus denigrated practice to its being seen as a fundamental and universal expression of the human condition. Like the novel, film was also initially dismissed as a popular form and therefore not worthy of attention as a credible cultural medium. Consequently, given the Romantic conceptions embedded in certain cultural hierarchies, filmmakers could not lay claim to being engaged with a critically worthwhile art form. One way to overcome this designation of low cultural status, as film became more self-conscious of its own stature, was to ascribe the making of a film to an identifiable individual artist or 'genius' figure. The logic underpinning this attempt was that if art is what artists do then, if directors are artists, it follows that film must be art. This argument is reiterated by Ian Jarvie in his book *Philosophy of the Film: Epistemology, Ontology, Aesthetics* (1987):

> An imperative of the romantic view of art is that art must be created by an artist. There must be a person, perhaps a rather special person, who is inspired, through whom the muse speaks. This Artist, or Creator, or Genius or whatever he [sic] is called, is essential to the

romantic view since that view believes that what makes something art is that it is created by an Artist. (1987, pp. 199–200)

Edward Buscombe (1981) points out that one of the earlier examples of this line of reasoning was in the French film magazine *Cahiers du Cinéma*. The writers in this magazine began to speak of *la politique des auteurs*. Their argument was in effect a polemic device arguing for the status of film as an art of personal expression and, according to Duncan Petrie, was the 'first systematic commitment to the film-maker as author' (1991, p. 14).

> While the spiritual guru of the *Cahiers* group was the theorist Andre Bazin, the major voices, who formed *la politique des auteurs* were Francois Truffaut, Eric Rohmer, Jean-Luc Goddard, Claude Chabrol and Jacques Rivette, all subsequently to become 'New Wave' film-makers in the sixties. As Edward Buscombe points out, the (loosely) collective *Cahiers* position was never proposed in terms of coherent *theory* as such. (Petrie 1991, p. 14)

It is important to repeat Buscombe's point that the central idea of this group wasn't, in their terms, to propose a concrete and fully realised theory but simply supply a means of defining a course of action to raise the critical debate around cinema. They were merely seeking to 'advance the claim of the cinema to be an art form like painting or poetry' (Buscombe 1981, p. 23). It was, however, Andrew Sarris, an American, who coined the term 'auteur theory' in an effort to abbreviate what was, to him, the clumsiness of the French term *la politique des auteurs* for his English-speaking readers.

According to Buscombe the ideas expressed by the writers in *Cahiers du Cinéma* simply followed on from the Romantic notion of the author as genius. From the Romantic perspective these genius figures, seen in most cases to be the director, have a 'divine spark' which serves to separate the artist from ordinary mortals and which also can separate the mere journeymen filmmaker from the true genius. Thus, for the auteur theorist, there is an identifiable individual genius figure responsible for certain films where the unity of a work was produced by this individual and thus reflected the personality of the auteur:

> *Cahiers* achievement in inaugurating the *politique* was to shift the locus of the authorial signature in cinema from the writer and, in

the case of Hollywood, the producer, to the director. However, not all directors qualified as auteurs. An important distinction was drawn between the true *'auteur'* – a film artist who works on material in such a way as to transform it into his or her own personal vision, and a *'metteur en scene'* – a craftsman who, no matter how skilled, can only adapt the concepts of others. (Petrie 1991, p. 14)

The auteur critic, in Sarris's view, was 'obsessed with the wholeness of art and the artist. He looks at a film as a whole, a director as a whole' (in Buscombe 1981, p. 23). From the auteurist's perspective, some films can be seen as simply aggregations without a unifying and identifiable trace of a particular director's personality endowing it with an organic unity. Hence the division between the *auteurs* or *metteur en scène*. *Metteur en scène* directors were condemned to have their works described as being less than the sum of their parts (Buscombe 1981, p. 23).

Francois Truffaut, writing in the *Cahiers du Cinéma* magazine, defined a true film auteur as a person who provides something authentically personal to the subject. 'Instead of transferring someone else's material faithfully and self-effacingly, the auteur transforms the material into an expression of his own personality' (Buscombe 1981, p. 23). As an example, the distinction is made between Alfred Hitchcock and John Huston. According to this view, Huston has no personal style as he merely adapts 'though often very skilfully, the material given him, instead of transforming it into something genuinely his own' (ibid.). Andrew Sarris formalised this distinction a little more when he wrote in the 1960s:

the three premises of the auteur theory may be visualised as three concentric circles: the outer circle as technique; the middle circle personal style; and the inner circle, interior meaning. The corresponding role of the director may be designated as those of a technician, (having the ability to put a film together with some clarity and coherence) a stylist and an auteur. There is no prescribed course by which a director passes through the three circles. (Sarris in Mast & Cohen 1979, p. 663)

Mast and Cohen describe the auteur theory as a reaction to the notion that film was, and remains, a collective practice. Truffaut's *politiques des auteurs*, according to them, defended Hollywood studio films by upholding the idea, even though it might be unappreciated or unnoticed, 'the work of an author, an auteur, could be seen in many Hollywood films' (Mast & Cohen 1979, p. 668). In this case the notion of auteur wasn't applied to 'the film's script writer, as many French film critics believed at the time, but the film's director, whose "signature" could be discerned by the sensitive critic who bothered to look for it' (ibid.).

The auteur theory, as interpreted by critics such as Sarris, comes down firmly on the side of agency in the struggle perceived between agency and structure. Andrew Sarris claimed that if 'directors and other artists cannot be wrenched from their historical environments, aesthetics is reduced to a subordinate branch of ethnography' (Sarris in Mast & Cohen 1979, p. 663). Despite these reactions, while the auteur theory has been a useful tool for mapping the terrain of film, some claim that the mark of individuality simply becomes a means of determining value. Andrew Sarris, for one, made the claim that an auteur leaves their mark, and simply by leaving it, increases a film's value. That is, if a film exhibits signs of bearing the stamp of its author, then it must be good. The danger of course being that marks of personality do not automatically guarantee that a film will be 'good'.

The auteurists were arguing not just that an artist's personality would be manifest 'in his [*sic*] work (but) they were seeking to establish that there was, indeed, an artist at work where many had never seen one' (Mast & Cohen 1979, p. 639). As Peter Wollen explains, the auteur theory was not limited to 'acclaiming the director as the main author of a film. It implies an operation of decipherment; it reveals authors where none had been seen before' (Wollen in Mast & Cohen 1979, p. 639).

However, given the variability in methods of production, and as a reaction to the cult of personality displayed by many extreme auteur theorists, some theorists began to look primarily at the text itself instead of concentrating all of their efforts on the personality. The text then in auteur criticism, as Arthur Berger makes clear, is not an individual film but the body of work of a screenwriter, actor, producer or director, and so on. As Berger explains, the critic using this approach looks for the underlying principle that generates the themes that also might produce variations of them (Berger 1995, pp. 93). In this case the 'the auteur critic looks for the structure underneath a corpus of films' (ibid.). With this information in hand the critic can use it to analyse certain films in relation to this structure which is composed of 'the codes or aesthetic and stylistic principles underlying the body of films' (ibid.). What then will concern the auteur critic 'would be such matters as visual style, tempo, recurring motifs, and thematic preoccupations' (Berger 1995, p. 94). Berger's appraisal of auteur theory describes in part some of the ideas that Peter Wollen outlined much earlier in his landmark work *Signs and Meaning in the Cinema* (1969). Wollen pursued an approach that was quite different from Sarris:

> This structured school of auteur criticism is where Wollen places him-self, and is what he attempts to exemplify by his comparison of Ford and Hawks. His approach has only minimal resemblance to the orig-inal French auteur criticism, and to the work of Sarris or the British auteurists of *Movie* magazine. It derives instead from a study of the kind of structural anthropology initiated by Claude Levi-Strauss and the semiology developed by Pierce and de Saussure, an approach which has seen a great deal of controversial attention since Wollen first wrote this chapter in 1969. (Nichols 1976, pp. 529–30)

Geoffrey Newell-Smith sums up, for Wollen, this indispensable struc-turalist approach:

> the defining characteristics of an authors work are not necessarily those which are most readily apparent. The purpose of criticism thus becomes to uncover behind the superficial contrasts of subject and treatment a hard core of basic and often recondite motifs. The pattern formed by these motifs... is what gives an author's work its particular structure, both defining it internally and distinguishing one body of work from another. (Newell-Smith quoted in Nichols 1976, p. 532)

This description is reinforced by Duncan Petrie who points out that Christian Metz was one of the pioneers of this approach. Metz applied the ideas behind structural linguistics to his work on film, demonstrat-ing in the process that it was similar structurally to a language (Petrie 1991, p. 16). Metz was attempting to 'transcend the subjectivity of auteur theory and to construct an objectivist film theory. However, it also led to the development of "auteur structuralism"' (ibid.), which was 'an attempt to transcend the problems generated by the Roman-tic conception of auteurism' (ibid.). While Peter Wollen was one of the central theorists working with these conceptions, there was still a tendency towards reductionism, that is, the tendency to explain the 'concrete (that is, many sided) objects by reducing them wholly to (or reading them off from) just one of their abstract (that is, one sided) constituents' (Sayer 2000, p. 89). This tactic appears to have neatly sidestepped the reconceptualisation necessary to consider more fully 'the process of initiation and development' (ibid.) not fully accounted for by the Romantic conception of Sarris's auteur theory.

However, some critics have taken these ideas one step further and have suggested, in line with Michel Foucault's poststructuralist notion of the author/function (1977), that the author is simply a critical construct thus dispensing with personality, except as a useful categorising tool to aid in analysis. As Bordwell and Thompson (1997) propose, the critic operating with this idea would simply group films by signature of director, producer, screenwriter or other creative individual involved in the making of films. They could then speak about the group of films bearing the name of the director, or the group of films that had the hallmarks of the screenwriter's style or the characteristics of the cinematographer's art. Thus, single films could be grouped in a number of ways. For example, 'this would mean that certain aspects of *Citizen Kane* interact with aspects of other films directed by Welles, or of other films written by Mankiewicz, or of other films photographed by Toland' (Bordwell & Thompson 1997, p. 39). What this situation implies is that the 'author' can no longer be seen as a person, but in terms of analysis, must be seen as 'a system of relations among several films bearing the same signature' (ibid.). This position is similar in intent to Foucault's poststructuralist concept of the author/function. This idea, coupled with Barthes' notions on the 'death of the author', takes creativity beyond the individualist notion of personality as the centre of creativity. In the process it de-centers the idea of personal authorship implicit in the original conception of the auteur theory. For some theorists it does so to the extent that authorship *per se* is no longer important at all, with reading or reception of films now seen as the most important centre of meaning-making.

This shift in the way authorship is attributed in film-making also brings into contention the variability of the methods with which a number of Hollywood directors worked. Some directors were, as claimed by some critics, 'mere hacks', albeit with a discernible style, despite having little control over the final product. Others, however, had greater freedom enjoying a measure of individual 'control over scripts, shooting, and cutting' (Wollen in Mast & Cohen 1979, p. 639). This distinction raises questions about the degree of agency various directors have had while working on the projects they were involved in. It also points to the grounding of the director's role in a series of creative relationships. The director must, by the nature of the work practices of the film industry, negotiate with the other creative workers on the film, a position highlighted by the work of Howard Becker within his conception of 'art worlds' (1982). From this perspective the director must accommodate themselves to the exigencies of everyone else's professional and artistic concerns but manage as best they can to fulfil their own initial vision. It is the relationships a director has with the cinematographer, the producer, the screen writer, the sound designer and so on that determine the effectiveness of the director's vision. Importantly, as stressed above, the idea of negotiation in these relationships leaves space to recognise that the auteur may not necessarily be the director. As Mast and Cohen argue:

> if a director's signature can be discovered by a careful examination of all his works, this is equally true of certain screen writers, cinematographers, and stars. Often the mark they leave on a film will be greater than that of its director.... For every *Modern Times*, which is obviously the work of a single artistic vision, there is a *Casablanca*, whose success may be the result of its director, of the men who conceived the original script, of the writer who amended that original script and wrote much of the dialogue, of its male star, of the particular chemistry between its male and female stars, or of some mysterious compound of all those elements. (1979, pp. 640–41)

The notion of giving precedence, and thus value, to a single author, as argued, denies the very obvious creative constraints placed on the director of a film by the work of all the others involved in the project. It also negates the enabling creative factors the collaborative process puts in place. For example, consider this description from Otis Ferguson where he asserts that the film invariably 'starts at the beginning, which is (1) a writer's idea, (2) a successful book or play if you can buy it, (3) in some other studio' (Ferguson in Mast & Cohen 1979, p. 646). The hardest situation for a writer and possibly the public, according to Ferguson, 'is when the idea comes from a producer and is therefore not an idea – such not being his business – but an impulse' (ibid.). Consider also the comment from John Ford that films are made via a series of committees now and the director may never know who has read the script: 'You can't get an O.K. here in Hollywood for a script – it's got to go back to New York, and through a president and a board of directors and backers and everybody else' (Ford quoted in Sinclair 1979, p. 203). In line with Ford's lament, Ian Jarvie proposes, in opposition to the auteur theory, his so-called committee theory which embodies the idea that:

> the author of a film is a committee; that a film is like a committee report signed by all its members; even if drafted by the

secretary, it will have been overseen and rewritten by the chairman and anyone on the committee powerful or assertive enough. Inside knowledge tells us of some reports that they were actually written largely by *x* or *y*; others are well known to be agonizingly forged/cobbled together compromises between conflicting opinions and forces within the committee. (1987, p. 202)

In support of this claim Jarvie cites ever-accumulating empirical evidence where 'more studio files, out-takes, and personal papers of film makers are open to scholarly inspection' (1987, p. 203). This situation has now been compounded by the extra features available on most films released as DVDs. These indicate that some studios may have loose boundary-maintenance between tasks and roles and, on the other hand, some directors could impose their ideas and will on all stages of the film production. This case, according to Jarvie (1987), is similar to a strong individual committee member or secretary writing the report as in the first example above of *x* or *y*. He also asserts that it can be seen that certain salaried directors have little input to certain films and were only brought into production once all the pre-production decisions were made and then were moved off the set and had no further input into the necessary post-production work. As Jarvie contends, in this case, 'scripting, casting, editing, sound, music, inserts, special effects and second unit work were all out of their hands' (1987, p. 203).

Being aware of these matters, Bordwell and Thompson supply their appraisal of authorship as a form of production work and set it in opposition to, firstly, the emphasis on Romantic personality that was predominant in Sarris's auteur theory, or secondly, the 'personality who leaves a signature' in the structuralist accounts of Wollen, or thirdly, the substitution of personality with a series of critical constructs attempted by the poststructuralists. Bordwell and Thompson point out that there are those who insist pragmatically that a director cannot be the author unless they perform every major role themselves. While this does sometimes occur, it is often a very rare case where it would. The opposing view is 'that although the director cannot perform all of those tasks, he or she must at least have overt veto control at every stage of production' (Bordwell & Thompson 1997, p. 39).

Yet another view, the 'director as orchestrator' model elaborated on by V.F. Perkins in the book *Film as Film* (1972), sees the director's role as a synthetic one where they combine all of the contributions into a whole. In line with these ideas, it is notable that English film critic Peter Wollen did in some stages of his work also recognise the contribution of all the workers who add their expertise to a film. When he first visited Hollywood in the late 1930s:

> he was amazed by the number of workers who contributed to the final product – the producer, the writer, the director, the researchers, the costume designers, the musicians, the cinematographer, the cutters, and special effects men. The question necessarily arises for anyone confronting the collective work practices of a Hollywood set: How can a work of art result from such varied intentions and collective labor? (Wollen in Mast & Cohen 1979, p. 639)

Both Howard Becker (1982) and Janet Wolff (1981) working in the late twentieth century would have no trouble answering this question as, for them, *all* art is the result of a social, collective or collaborative process. As Shekhar Kapur, the director of *Elizabeth: The Golden Age*, asserted, 'we don't create – we are the instruments through which creation occurs' (2007).

Despite these various attempts to go beyond the Romantic view of film-making, few theorists working in this area have, as yet, seen film-making in its broadest sense as a form of systemic creativity as suggested more recently by Mihaly Csikszentmihalyi (1988, 1997, 1999, 2004). There have been exceptions in terms of documentary film (Kerrigan 2006, 2008, 2011), but in order to see this a little more clearly we can take the case of Steven Spielberg, deliberately chosen here as he is often cast as the antithesis of a 'true auteur'. Firstly, we can see that film-making as an independent domain pre-existed filmmakers like Steven Spielberg:

> [It]did not spring from the brow of Jupiter, complete and ready to go. [It] is related to other artistic domains that existed for a long time, such as the theatre, literature, and photography. These already existing domains were combined to make the first movies. Any culture is made up of thousands and thousands of domains like these. (Csikszentmihalyi 2004)

In this case we can also see that Spielberg, as a creative agent, was presented with 'a domain from which one can learn a cultural tradition' (ibid.), by not only his family's entertainment habits but their encouragement of his predilection to make short films. If, as Csikszentmihalyi argues, a creative agent has an abiding and motivated interest in movies, such as Spielberg did, he may want to become a cinematographer, an actor or a director, screenwriter, film editor, or possibly a producer. This agent will immerse themselves in this pre-existing domain of cinematography 'and bring to it something new that may change that domain... and tries to produce a novelty in it' (ibid.). Spielberg took his cues from an excessive amount of television and films like John Ford's *The Searchers* and Frank Capra's *It's a Wonderful Life* which, as John Baxter asserts, became his 'educational medium' (1996, p. 17):

> Broadcast media permeated Spielberg's childhood... 'There are certain young directors, like Steven Spielberg,' says film editor Ralph Rosenblum, 'who were raised in the age of television and seem to have an intuitive sense of film rhythm and film possibilities'. (Baxter 1996, p. 17)

Having developed the early habitus of a film-maker, and supported wholeheartedly in that process by his family, Spielberg learnt through his later socialisation into the field that there was a group of people who could very quickly make decisions about whether or not a newly presented film or a new editing technique was or wasn't a worthy inclusion into the domain of film-making (Csikszentmihalyi 2004). One could have a number of very interesting and novel ideas about making movies, but unless those ideas are selected by the field, and this includes in Spielberg's case not only the corporate structures of Hollywood but his film school colleagues, the agents, critics and audiences he engaged with, that is, all those who could 'affect the structure of the domain', there is little chance that a creative agent will continue to be absorbed into the structures of making movies. Here Spielberg had a benefit which he was initially unaware of:

> If only Spielberg had known it, he already possessed an advantage that would give him the inside track in Hollywood. Being Jewish meant he was born into the culture and ethos prevailing in sixties Hollywood. Had he been part of an industry family, he would have found work instantly. Instead, he was forced to prowl Universal, looking for a connection, a sponsor, a patron. (Baxter 1996, p. 48)

He found this figure in a number of places at various times in his career. Through his short films he was noticed by Chuck Sliver and then Universal executive Sidney Jay Sheinberg helped him move into television production. After he had clawed his way into feature films, Spielberg also performed the same mentoring function himself for a number of younger aspiring film-makers. Once he had made *Duel* its 'virtuosity impressed friends who had been underwhelmed by [his] previous TV work' (ibid.), among them George Lucas. His stock of cultural and social capital was increased as he impressed a number of influential colleagues and many of them, as well as film critics who undertook various intellectual games with the film, began to recognise, encourage and support a fellow traveller. As if to confirm his sense that film-making could only be a collaborative and consensual process, Spielberg learnt early 'how to play the game' (Baxter 1996, p. 51) and laboured continuously with other professionals who would become a predominantly stable group of collaborators:

> Working relationships include Allen Daviau, a childhood friend and cinematographer who shot the early Spielberg film *Amblin'* and most of his films up to *Empire of the Sun*; Janusz Kaminski who has shot every Spielberg film since *Schindler's List*; and the film editor Michael Kahn who has edited every single film directed by Spielberg from *Close Encounters* to *Munich* (except *E.T. the Extra-Terrestrial*). A famous example of Spielberg working with the same professionals is his long time collaboration with John Williams and the use of his musical scores in all of his films since *The Sugarland Express* (except *The Color Purple* and *Twilight Zone: The Movie*). (Wikipedia n.d.)

Having achieved some sort of consensus in his film-making, Spielberg had also realised that the 'art' of film-making was just as much in its financing, promotion and distribution as it was on set or in the edit suite. In this way:

> if the gatekeepers accept the new idea and add it to the domain, then it will become part of the culture. Then another cycle will start, and so on and on. (Csikszentmihalyi 2004)

Once he had made a number of commercially successful movies (Brode 1995), Spielberg sought the critical attention he thought the movies his name was appended to deserved, but 'when Steven Spielberg made the movie version of *Empire of the Sun*, the majority of the critics said that the director was trying to enter "David Lean territory" '(Silverman 1992, p. 192). Whether this qualified him as an *auteur* or a *métier en scène* or a mere hack is irrelevant for our purposes in seeing film as a systemic process. What this does highlight though is the idea that the individual creative agent is also an important part of the system bringing their own particular set of circumstances to bear on the work they are involved in. This action is no more, nor is it any less, important than the structures of the domain or field. The person's contribution can still be seen in what they bring to the collaborative act, as all the other participants in that act do. Apart from the leverage and power commercial success has brought Spielberg, this work has also allowed him to accumulate significant cultural and social capital within the arena of social contestation – that is the field of film. Spielberg's marks of individuality can be seen not only in the tendency towards action techniques and a technical fascination with what he calls 'the god light', but also in the few common themes that are manifest in the films he has been active on. He has been continually concerned with a rather anachronistic sense of chivalry that is to some somewhat medieval in its manifestation, with the almost solipsistic isolation of his protagonists, and the sense that control is power (Baxter 1996, pp. 81–2). Most importantly:

> Spielberg refuses to surrender to *nada*, will not give in to the encroaching darkness, clings to a positive vision despite mounting evidence to the contrary. Perhaps that helps explain why Spielberg has over the years become the world's most popular filmmaker; in addition to remarkable talents for providing entertainment, he more importantly reassures his audience, again and again, that there is hope.... Without optimism, civilized life as we know it would cease to be. People – good decent people – have to believe in something, or they cannot go on. *Schindler's List*, like *E.T.* and a dozen and a half other Spielberg movies, provides an audience with a convincing illustration of such guarded optimism. The film insists that, however horrific things may be, there are straws we can grasp at if only we search long and hard enough to find them. While some may scoff at the very act of grasping for straws in the middle of an all-encompassing storm, Spielberg would probably answer that, however fragile, they are sometimes all we have. (Silverman 1992, p. 192)

However, Spielberg never claimed, nor was he accorded, the title of an auteur in the sense espoused by the early auteur critics such as Truffaut or Sarris, since:

> As a consensus film-maker, he couldn't accept *Cahiers du Cinema's politique des auteurs*, which designated one single person on a film as its driving intellectual force. 'Those directors who believe in the *auteur* theory will have coronaries at an early age,' he told his Cannes

press conference. 'You can't play all the instruments at once'. (Baxter 1996, p. 83)

The interesting aspect of the systems approach, apart from its refutation of the romantically inclined auteur theory, is that it works for all the subfields within film-making. There is a domain and field of editing, of directing, of sound designing, of art direction and so on, all of which have what one could call their own sub-system in play that interlinks with the larger system of film-making. In this way the complexity of the model not only reveals itself as an intricate account of cultural production, but it also goes some way to providing an analytical tool to account for the collaborative process of film-making. This could easily be coupled with other conceptions of the group collaborative process, such as that suggested by Paulus and Nijstad in their book *Group Creativity: Innovation through Collaboration* (2003), which highlights how an individual's skills, knowledge and abilities are manifest in collaborative group work. It can be seen in the way that their conception is set out on how 'the movement of ideas, knowledge sharing and critical feedback on processes and products' (Kerrigan & McIntyre 2010, p. 225) works for Paulus and Nijstad in a group-based process. Importantly, their thinking is 'comparable to the system's model in that the group creativity model also identifies individual, field and domain interactions necessary to produce artefacts' (ibid.). From this perspective the way has been opened for film to be seen as the product of a system in operation of which the individual director, editor, sound designer, cinematographer and so on are each one still necessary but not completely sufficient component part. As Csikszentmihalyi argues, creativity is an open and dynamic system which is motivated by all components of the system where individuals, immersed in a domain, make changes to this symbolic knowledge and the social organisation, who understand the knowledge system, contribute their recognition of unique and novel contributions as valuable inputs into that system. It is only when the whole system has been operating dynamically that creativity can be said to have occurred.

The older and now somewhat dated versions of authorship, seen in both auteur theory and the reaction to it manifest in poststructuralist accounts, can be replaced by this reconceptualisation of creativity represented by Csikszentmihalyi in the systems model. It does not fully negate any of these conceptions but draws them together in a useful confluence of them all. In Hegelian terms the thesis of Romanticism implicit in the original auteur theory, which was called into question by the antithetical view of poststructuralism, has realised a new synthesis in the systems model of creativity as it is applied to film-making. This movement of thought can be exemplified in the way film-making has been conceptualised and reconceptualised since the advent of the auteur theory and seen in this brief overview outlined above. By reconstituting production as an integral though less powerful component of creativity without returning to the agent centred and Romantic approaches of the auteur theory, and of course the reaction to it, that is, the dismissal of authorship inherent in reception theory, the systems model thus provides a critique of the critiques of the auteur theory and moves the idea of creativity in film-making towards a more confluence-based approach.

11
Photography: Art, Craft and Their Symbiosis

In Chapter 10 we discussed the nature of film-making and the authorship of films. The auteur theory was one attempt to account for the way this particular form of cultural production attempted to view itself as an art form. The creative process of the director in particular was seen to be vital to this theory. In many ways this theory was, for film, an attempt to move away from the view that film-making was a collective enterprise based on the craftsmanship of many technicians and move film itself into the realm of high art. If film could prove that it had artists at work, then film-making must be taken seriously as art. Implicit in this process was the use of a hierarchical view of what it means to be an artist as opposed to what it means to be a craftsperson. In the Western cultural world this question of the value of art over craft has been writ large for photography. For example, photography has been historically looked down upon by the established art world in the West. In 1895 Baudelaire declared photography to be a 'hand maid to the arts and science, but their very humble handmaid' (in Wells 2004, p. 13). As recently as 1982 this argument was still causing consternation within the photographic community as the following case illustrates. Allan Bowness, the then director of the prestigious Tate gallery in London, had declared that 'you have to be an artist and not only a photographer to have your work in the Tate' (quoted in Campany 2003, p. 228). Keith Arnatt, in reply to the interview in which Bowness made his declaration, wrote:

> He also says that they collect artists rather than photographs though they would not collect an artist if he or she was an artist purely in the photographic media. It might appear then, as though the Tate collects artists who are photographers but not photographers who are artists. If this is so it is not terribly clear what distinction is

being drawn between artist/photographer and photographer/artist. Does acceptance by the Tate mean, for example, that you must not have worked or work exclusively in the medium of photography, that you must gain your laurels in some other medium before your photographic work is considered worthy? Further...being 'only a photographer' would seem to exclude the very possibility of being an artist. Bill Brandt though, who is described as substantial artist, is not collected 'because he is exclusively a photographer'. It becomes increasingly difficult therefore, to understand the claim made by Elizabeth Underhill, also of the Tate, that what the Tate collects 'is a matter of the substance of the artist himself, not what he works in'. Surely there is something odd about all this though it is by no means easy to say exactly what. (Arnatt in Campany 2003, p. 228)

As Keith Arnatt goes on to suggest there is:

more than a faint suggestion that they believe an artist to be something more than a photographer – that an artist does something that a photographer doesn't, or cannot do. What this could possibly be is difficult to see. If I'm right and there is such a value-judgement at work it is unfortunate, for it should extend the terminal illness of that moribund question 'Can photography be art? (Arnatt in Campany 2003, p. 229)

This case neatly encapsulates one of the central issues in the practice of photography. Some in the world of fine art, when they look at photography, tend to look at it through the lens they have used for works and mediums that have preceded photography and judge it from this perspective. On the other hand, when popular magazines concentrate on photography, they do so with an eye fixed firmly on the techniques and technologies of photography. They will occasionally give awards for 'good' photography, with a work's 'goodness' related to how well it is lit, focused, posed, captured or cropped; in other words what are seen as the craft aspects of the photographer's art.

Since there are distinctions made between art and craft even within the field itself, as the above brief example indicates, and it also has to be said that there are a number of similarities, one can ask – what is the basis for these distinctions and similarities? A further question that is particularly pertinent to our study is that of the bearing the distinction between art and craft may have on the nature of creativity itself. Is either art or craft, as is supposed by common sense, more creative, and thus more valuable, than the other? Finally, is it necessary to make these distinctions at all?

If one simply investigates the dictionary definitions of each of these terms, it would appear that each has far more in common than at first realised. For example, consider the following two extracts from the *Concise Oxford Dictionary*:

> **art** *n* **1.** skill, esp. human skill as opposed to nature; (ability in) skil-ful execution as an object in itself; cunning; imitative or imaginative skill applied to design, as in paintings, architecture, etc. (work*s of art*); (*attrib.*) Pertaining to use of such skill (*art music; art needlework*); (in *pl.*) = Fine *arts*. **2.** thing in which skill may be exercised . . . **3.** prac-tical application of any science; industrial pursuit, craft. **4.** Knack, stratagem . . . ~**form**, established form of composition (e.g. novel, sonata, sonnet), medium of artistic expression; . . . ~**work**, illustrative matter in printed text.[ME f. OF, f. L *ars artis*]. (Sykes 1983, p. 48)

> **craft** (-ah-) *n.*, & *v.t.* **1.** *n.* skill; cunning, deceit; art, trade, (esp. in comb., as *handicraft, priestcraft, statecraft*) **2.** members of a craft; **the** C~ , brotherhood of Freemasons. **3.** (*pl.* same). Boat, vessel; aircraft or spacecraft **4.** ~ -**brother, -guild**, workman, guild of workmen, of same trade. **5.** *V.t.* *make in skilful manner (*handicrafted jewelry; a superbly crafted novel*). [OE *craeft*, = OS, OHG *kraft*, ON *kraptr* strength]. (Sykes 1983, p. 221)

The similarities are obvious at this level with the major emphasis in both falling heavily on the notion of skill. I would suggest, however, that the distinctions run deeper than simple dictionary definitions. For instance, one of the major distinctions made between art and craft can be found in the purposes supposedly set for each. The usage of the term craft generally has been coupled with the assumption that the object created will be utilitarian in function. Art however is primarily valued for its aesthetic appeal. This comparison juxtaposes technical compe-tence with a notion of transcendent beauty. As Harold Osborne points out in *Aesthetics and Art Theory: An Historical Introduction* (1968):

> the making of aesthetic objects has been almost universal through human history. From the emergence of modern man during the upper Paleolithic age, and the fine efflorescence of cave art in the Aurignacian and Magdalenian periods, there have been

comparatively few peoples at any time who did not produce artefacts which we can now enjoy aesthetically as things of beauty. (Osborne 1968, p. 13)

Even though their original utilitarian function has been lost to us, as have the values of the society in which they were made, these earlier aesthetic objects were both transcendentally beautiful and utilitarian. Osborne contends that throughout history works of art were made to serve a purpose and were not made to merely be 'works of art'. The motive for making temples was to honour the gods, for example, a statue was used to perpetuate a person's memory and in the case of the pyramids to ensure immortality. Epic poems were used to preserve an oral society's traditions (ibid.). In this way art works have historically been utilitarian. Conversely, the aesthetic drive has also been part of the craft world of ancient peoples. Aesthetic embellishments have been incorporated into many utensils and artefacts that go far beyond the practical requirements of the object. But this 'aesthetic function seldom if ever stood alone and autonomous' (ibid.).

It has been argued that for most of history the very concept of art as the West has come to know it, or more correctly 'fine art', has been non-existent. For example, Ellen Dissanayake, in *Homo Aestheticus: Where Art Comes From and Why* (1995), asserts that the word art, as used before the late eighteenth century, meant what we would today call ' "craft" or "skill" or "well-madedness", and could characterise any object or activity made or performed by human (rather than natural or divine) agency' (1995, p. 40). Most aesthetic artefacts were judged with the criteria of craft, that is, for their workmanship and how effectively they did what they were designed to do. What is more, these objects and skills were deeply connected to the everyday, being wound into the daily lives of the community. The idea that art is disconnected from daily life and is to be observed and placed on a cultural pedestal, as Osborne asserts, was non-existent. For example the:

> distinction between the aesthetic qualities and the total effect of a work of art do not come readily to the Greek mind at all...no difference of category was recognised such as is nowadays assumed between a creative artist and an artisan who is skilled in the techniques of his craft. The idea of creativity (in the modern, Romantic sense) in connection with the arts was absent from Greek philosophy. Equally foreign to their mentality was the idea of art as an 'expression' of the artist's personality. (Osborne 1968, pp. 13–14)

The Greeks based their idea of art on their theory of manufacture, itself based on the ideas of function and technique. All artisans in the manufacture of their goods produced a use function whether that be literally or socially. The Greek word *techne*, from which we derive the word 'technique', also simply translates as skill or craft. But *techne*, for the Greeks, was a branch of knowledge or more pertinently a form of practical science. It was, however, distinct to the theoretical knowledges of mathematics and philosophy which could exist purely for their own sakes. In other words, the Greeks valued knowledge whether it be theoretical or practical and art, if indeed it existed as we in the West conceive of it for the Greeks, was simply a branch of practical knowledge. But, it must be noted, there was a distinction made in terms of the status of these divisions. Since Greek society was based on citizens who depended on foreign artisans and merchants as well as a slave population to perform the manual work of their city states, it was deemed inappropriate for a free-born citizen to undertake manual labour. Therefore, their attitude to craftsmen, artisans and manufacturers of practical things was one of superiority. Those people who engaged in the practical arts, and the work they produced, were not highly regarded in the Greek social scale. Since the free citizen could, and did, engage in philosophy it eventually became a norm that 'the theoretical arts are good and honourable; the practical arts are only praiseworthy' (Osborne 1968, p. 21).

In *An Introduction to the Arts in Western Civilisation* (1987) Dennis Sporre asserts that during the Renaissance, in a period when there was a revived interest in antiquity, 'men and women found a kindred spirit in the Greeks and Romans' (1990, p. 247). Exploring Greek and Roman conceptions of the world inevitably led to an assumption of some of their values during the Renaissance and, in line with this, there were attempts during this period to prove that painting was a theoretical art. This occurred at the same time that the notion of the individual 'artist as genius' started to become a prominent and socially worthwhile construct. The written transcripts left by Leonardo da Vinci (these notes can be found on the Project Gutenberg website at http://www.gutenberg. org/wiki/Main_Page) were, for example, an attempt to prove the philosophical and theoretical content of his work, and thus elevate its stature, in line with the classical tradition. The corollary of course was that if the object produced had little use value but was based on deeply philosophical ideas, then, ergo, a claim could be made that painting, in particular, was not utilitarian and thus a worthy occupation. The necessary linkage had to be made between what it was possible for a person to engage in and their status. Craft was thus for tradespeople and, in order to increase the status of certain professions, the collective enterprise of the guilds had to give way to the art of the individual genius, which included poetry, sculpture and painting. Thus the vocation of the artist came into being at this time, and the work of art as an object in and of itself began to be held in some esteem. It is at this time in Western history that we first perceive the suggestion that there may be value in the cultivation of experience, including aesthetic experience, for its own sake. Painting was becoming an end in and of itself and the idea of 'art for arts sake' started to become entrenched. In summary of this point, the French critic Andre Malraux writing in 1951 stated, according to Osborne, that:

> the middle ages had no more idea of what we mean by the word art than had Greece or Egypt, which lacked the word to express it. In order that this idea could be born it was necessary for works of art to be separated from their function.... The most profound metamorphosis began when art had no other end than itself. (Osborne 1968, p. 21)

Since 'Art', the conception that came to dominate in the West, is seen as an end in itself, autonomous from its function, then it also can be seen as having little use value. The question then arises of how to deal with art, or to describe it another way, works of transcendent beauty. The development of aesthetics from the Romantic period onward was an attempt to do just this.

The aesthetic principle, the philosophy of the beautiful, initially held that there were fundamental and universal truths embedded in great works of art which had invaluable lessons for all humanity at their core. Great works could be identified by how closely they revealed these truths and contained the essence of them. In later periods it can be seen that the aesthetic impulse of the artist began to concentrate on the formal qualities of the artistic experience, itself divorcing totally any connection to a utilitarian value. Ellen Dissanayake asserts that as Western aesthetics extended, works were allotted to the class of authentic art if it was 'deemed capable of providing and sustaining genuine aesthetic experience. Genuine aesthetic experience was defined as something one experienced when contemplating genuine art' (1995, p. 40). Dissanayake rightly points out the circular logic that underpins this position, and she also notes the futility of attempting to establish criteria for defining the essential elements of this mysterious thing called 'Art'. As 'Art' moved into the twentieth century it became progressively more divorced from any idea of embodying or reflecting social or religious values and concentrated on the formal elements of its own construction. It became an object – the 'work of art'. Eventually, scholars of aesthetics abandoned the hope that 'Art' could demonstrate the essence of itself, the very thing that supposedly made it 'Art' in the first place. 'Art', as conceptualised by the West, has therefore become a peculiar notion 'dependent on and intertwined with ideas of commerce, commodity, ownership, history, progress, specialisation and individuality' (Dissanayake 1995, p. 40). One could also add to this list, status (Gross 1995, pp. 1–2). The list of activities that have been classified with the honorific 'Art' have come to be collectively known as the 'fine arts'. These include from the Greeks, poetry, sculpture, dance and tragedy with relatively recent inclusions, courtesy of the Romantics, being painting and architecture. As Larry Gross notes, 'more recently the practitioners of new media – photography, film, video – have aspired to be included in this honoured group' (1995, p. 1). In essence the exclusions are focused on the 'performers and products whose appeal may be too broad – the *popular*, or *low*, arts – or too utilitarian, such as crafts' (ibid.). In this case art is assumed to spring from 'the extraordinary technical abilities and personal qualities of its makers, unhampered by pragmatic considerations of utility (Gross 1995, p. 2).

In another, more eloquent, summation, John Passmore in *Serious Art: A Study of the Concept in All the Major Arts* (1991) put forward the idea that there must be some connection, what he calls:

> overlapping excellencies, to other recognised arts before a new medium will be accepted into the charmed circle of the accepted canon. Starting with poetry and music, linked as song. Paintings were admitted because they were poetic. Drama was close to poetry in its poetic drama form and this allowed the admission of prose drama which then made way for the novel. Architecture has a dubious linkage for many until it is realised that the close relationship between painting, sculpture and architecture is thought through. All three share a concern for formal spatial relationships. Architecture though was encumbered by the idea that architects were master masons at best and engineers at worst. (Passmore 1991, p. 22)

Passmore goes on to observe that the more recent attempts at admission by photography and film to the charmed circle of what may be called Art have been 'bitterly contested, and sometimes not even sought by their practitioners' (ibid.). As was the case for the novel, the thinking appeared to be that photography and film were 'so largely committed to entertainment that it was ridiculous to take them seriously; in part the objection was that they were both of them methods of mechanical recording' (ibid.).

This idea that a medium could not only record but reproduce the work *ad infinitum* by certain methods of recording brought into sharp relief the bridge that supposedly existed between art and craft. If craft is indeed predominantly utilitarian and art is an object in and of itself, then it becomes highly important that the work the artist does is *not* seen to be reproducible. On the contrary, a craftsperson is only too delighted to see their objects of manufacture reproduced. As Howard Becker notes, uniqueness of an object is highly prized in Art since Artists and the people who admire them think that no two works created by an Artist should be too much alike. However, as Becker points out, 'for good craftsmen that is not a consideration; on the contrary the artist craftsman's control shows in his ability to make things as much alike as he does.... No one wants to buy a copy from an artist, only from a craftsman' (1982, p. 279). John Walker in *Art in the Age of the Mass Media* (1983) adds to this position by stating that:

> Artists face a choice; either they can decide to produce a few original works of art per year which then possess the values of rarity and handwork, or they can decide to produce works of art in editions for the benefit of large numbers of people. Those who take the second option are likely to be treated with disdain by the artworld because mass production is antithetical to that world – it is concerned with the rare and the exceptional, not the commonplace. Artists whose aim is to reach beyond the artworld will probably not care. There is a third option which is acceptable to the art market: a print is conceived in terms of a *limited* edition. Once approved by the artist each print is numbered and signed. The metal plate or lithographic stone is then destroyed to prevent further, unauthorised prints being made. Ostensibly, the reason for small editions is to preserve a high standard of reproduction, but economic factors are also crucial, as is the necessity to preserve a distinction between fine art and outright industrial manufacture. (1983, p. 73)

Walter Benjamin's landmark essay 'The Work of Art in the Age of Mechanical Reproduction' (1970) took the then new phenomena of reproducibility as a sign that Art was about to be transformed and it was photography that was doing it. With the loss of contact with an original's *aura* the ability to technically reproduce an object entailed the possibility that 'Art' was in danger of losing its supposed authenticity, its uniqueness and its existence in a singular geographical locale. For Benjamin this situation was capable of producing a democratisation of culture and artistic reproduction. Interestingly, this merging of the technical and the artistic also had the potential to merge the world of craft with that of art, the world of the mundane with that of the sublime. Photography, in particular, as Margot Lovejoy asserts in her essay 'Art, Technology, and Postmodernism: Paradigms, Parallels, and Paradoxes' (1990), had become the major vehicle for:

> rendering out-of-date many mythical and mystical notions about art: originality as it refers to the aura of the one and only (as related to the copy); 'authorship' and 'genius' – emphasis on the value of the original – as being more important than the social value of art. (Lovejoy 1990, p. 261)

Lovejoy goes on to say that 'parallel to photography, new electronic media are forcing change in the role of the artist, in our concepts of what is art and what its function should be' (ibid.). John Passmore, however, poses a solution that is wonderful in its simplicity. He poses the question 'why not say, more simply, that there is a kind of excellence peculiar to the arts and that any form of activity which can achieve this kind of excellence is an art?' (Passmore 1991, p. 21).

But, in order to protect the mysterious quality of art it has often been proposed that art and craft are thoroughly different and must be kept separate. One of the major treatises that elaborated on this idea and attempted to formularise and maintain a strict distinction between art and craft belongs to the work of R.G. Collingwood in his book *The Principles of Art* (1963). In it he proposes that the craftsperson has to plan the work out precisely before it is carried out, 'that the end was thought out first, most commonly by someone else, that the raw material is available before the work is done, that the maker is dependent on the skills of someone else' (Passmore 1991, p. 23). If an activity *didn't* follow these prescriptions, then it could be described as art. As Sharon Bailin explains:

> for Collingwood, the essence of art lies in the fact that the end does not really exist until the work is completed. It involves, essentially, the expression of emotions and this is achieved only in the course of the execution of the work. If this is the case then the essence of art cannot lie in the perfection of technique. Making something purely technically is a feature of craft and implies a preconceived

end...this sort of claim about the impossibility of foreknowledge is made frequently in art theory and has something in common with the divine inspiration view. (Bailin 1988, p. 90)

Creativity for Collingwood is enacted via spontaneity, imagination and the generation of novelty and as such retains elements of the unexpected, the unforeseen and therefore mysterious. While this view reinforces the notions of the author as genius, this approach represents a paradox in as much as it makes it difficult to explain how an artist exercises control in creating their works of art. Without the application of skill, technical knowledge and a little forethought the artist loses the necessary control to execute the work of art. It is demonstrable that works of art start at many points, one of which is a preconceived idea of what the finished work will be like. If this is indeed the case, art shares more similarities with craft than it does differences.

It follows then that once the distinction between art as unique hand-work and craft as technological prowess is eradicated, the aesthetic problematic posed by the dissolution of the aura in mechanical and now electronic reproduction becomes far less problematic. But, and this is a fairly large 'but', this still leaves the problem of accounting for individual greatness within any of these processes of representation. It may be that to answer this question one has to turn to the acquisition of skill, the mastering of that skill and from there the ability to see beyond the paradigms of the rules, forms and structures the artisan works within in order to explain greatness. The level of skill required for most aesthetic activities could be said to move from the amateur through to the tradesman-like work of the journeyman artisan, to the consummate skills of the master. In this regard, Sharon Bailin argues that there are certain aspects of essential skills that will improve with practice and 'and one can reach the stage where one can accomplish them with speed, accuracy, finesse – and seeming effortlessness' (1988, p. 96). It is this absorption of skill to the point that it becomes almost transparent in operation that one sees in much expert work. Bailin argues that it is this proficiency that enables certain practitioners to go beyond what others have done and this knowledge to see what needs to occur is primarily based on a 'repertoire of acquired and assimilated skills in the discipline' (ibid.). She asserts that there is enough evidence to claim that:

there is not a real discontinuity between achieving highly within the rules of a discipline and achieving highly when it entails going beyond or changing some rules. The latter is, rather, an extension of the former. It would be incorrect to view any discipline or creative activity as taking place within rigid boundaries and being totally delimited and defined by rules. Instead, the possibilities for what can be achieved are really open-ended. Furthermore, one never breaks down all the rules, since to do so would be to abandon the discipline.... It seems, then, that one difference between creative and uncreative performances relates to having a real understanding of the discipline in which one is engaged. (1988, pp. 96–7)

The skills base would, then, encompass not only technical expertise but also critical judgement. In order to shift the creative paradigms of a discipline the artist or creator must be highly skilled, possibly at the cutting edge of the discipline and possess a real understanding of that discipline. In this way craft and art must be seen as part and parcel of the same skills continuum. This recognition opens the way for small c-creativity to proceed along the same continuum towards big C-creativity. Rather than being seen as distinct operations, they can be seen as being intimately connected. In fact, it could also be proposed that they are symbiotic or deeply interrelated as Margaret Boden does when she asserts that H- or historical creativity is an extension of P- or personal creativity.

From this brief summation it can be concluded, as Bailin does, that there can be little support for a view that excludes craft from art or indeed for even maintaining the distinction. As Smith also argues, it seems:

absurd and anachronistic to insist that those who paint or sculpt or engage in the production of graphic art be called artists while those who work creatively in ceramics, weaving, wood, metal and so forth, be called crafts(people).... And it is equally anachronistic, apart from being elitist, to argue that the useless things be called art, and the useful, craft. These distinctions are reflections in the art world of older, more hieratic, class societies, and have no place in a modern democratic society. (Smith 1988, p. 53)

Ellen Dissanayake however has the final word on this matter when she states that:

in a postindustrial, postmodern society, an art world (or 'artworld') determines what 'Art' is and what is 'Art'. It exists, if at all, only as a socially and historically conditioned label. The reader must recognise, however, that this position arises from contemporary postmodern

Western society, which despite our natural ethnocentrism is not, of course, the apogee of humankind's enterprise and wisdom nor its ultimate destiny. We must not forget that although 'Art' as a concept seems to have been born of and continues to be sustained by a commercial society, is therefore only roughly two centuries old, and hence is relative, even discardable, *the arts* have always been with us. And so have ideas of beauty, sublimity, and transcendence, along with the verities of the human condition: love, death, memory, suffering, power, fear, loss, desire, hope. (Dissanayake 1995, p. 41)

12
Popular Music: Creativity and Authenticity

While film and photography have struggled with their attempts to be recognised as 'Art', we also should be able to see that the concept of 'Art' itself is a culturally specific and somewhat anachronistic one. When we also shine the light of enquiry onto Western popular music we can see that this conception of 'Art', as a foundational and often unquestioned assumption linked to notions of creativity by those working within popular music, has led to a set of beliefs, norms and value systems that themselves seem antiquated in the face of current research into creativity. In support of this contention I will argue that, once we reconceptualise creativity based on the research that has been conducted for a number of years now, it also becomes necessary to rethink what may constitute authenticity since, for the popular music art world, one conception may be deeply connected to the other.

To begin that task we can agree that a common scenario posited for the contemporary Western popular music industry is that it is often characterised as 'a ruthless corporate machine that continually attempts to control creativity, compromise aesthetic practices and offers audiences little real choice' (Negus 1996, p. 36). This industry could never, therefore, lay claim to being a producer of truly great 'Art'. Keith Negus asserts that, in this scenario, there are two sides. On one side are 'the heroes – the musicians, producers and performers (the creative artists); opposing them are the villains – record companies and entertainment corporations (the commercial corrupters and manipulators)' (ibid. p. 46). He outlines the fact that these characterisations, oppositions and distinctions have been employed for many years 'to define the good and bad and to distinguish between the true and false in a range of musics' (ibid.). They are there in the declaration that a musician, songwriter or performer has 'sold out' to commercial interests and thus lost their 'creative edge'. It appears that a band's 'credibility' also suffers once they enter what has been called 'the mainstream'. It is claimed that at this point 'the mass' appropriates them and we, who are of course never 'the mass', lose part of what makes us complete as individuals. These musicians thus lose our trust and in our eyes they cease to be 'authentic'.

The issues surrounding the notion of authenticity in contemporary Western popular music are certainly complex ones. They have become part of the very idea of what popular music is in the West and the question of what and who is authentic arouses intense debate. One need only look at the antipathies that occur between what is currently called mainstream music and so-called alternative music (McIntyre 2009, pp. 142–51), to understand that authenticity within popular music, as an issue, is a deeply felt one. Consider this appraisal from Russell Hopkinson, the drummer from the band You Am I:

> You've only got to look at what's at the top of the alternative charts at the moment. It's like, the soundtrack to *Romeo and Juliet* is in the alternative charts. What's alternative about that? It's got a couple of quirky pop songs by Swedish groups on there. Is that alternative? I don't know what it means anymore.... Like call a band 'alternative' and it gives them this slight quirkiness when most of the stuff that's out there that's supposedly alternative is pretty damn staid. It just sounds like another take on pop music to me. (Hopkinson, R 1997, pers. comm., 20 July)

Deciding what is authentically 'alternative' or not is obviously fraught with definitional problems, not the least of which is that authenticity, in the specific case of rock music, is seen to be achieved through supposed artistic freedom and uniqueness where rock performers have to be 'original', most often taken to mean 'devoid of discernible influences'. However, in line with Howard Becker's broader arguments (1982) about the differences between art worlds, in the world of folk music an adherence to the traditions of the past and the forms designated as folk and how closely these can be approximated or replicated is seen to be the hallmark of true authenticity. One form of popular music, that is rock music, supposedly valorises radical and unfettered innovation with this as the mark of authenticity and the other, folk music, is seen to value an adherence to a long and supposedly continuous tradition with this as the mark of authenticity. These disparities not only exist with popular music art worlds, but they also have wider cross-cultural implications since, as we have seen, some cultures value the 'ideal realisation of the conventional form' (Gross 1995, p. 2) and others expect 'innovativeness and individuality' (ibid.) as the prime marker of creativity.

From these examples we can discern that the markers of what is seen to be creative, and thus authentic, are culturally specific. Do these seeming disparities and contradictions exist elsewhere in popular music? The title of Richard Peterson's book *Creating Country Music: Fabricating Authenticity* (1997) would suggest so. In another summary, Graeme Smith (2002) claims that authenticity in country music can be seen in a number of ways. These markers of authenticity may include a faithfulness to style or sound (e.g. personal heritage) and an adherence to the truth of the authentic expression of a person seen in the use of a 'country voice'. Country musicians tell of a collective or shared experience in their songwriting and image building, but there is a certain fabrication or politics involved in this process. The question can be asked as to whose experience is seen as real? Which group/subculture/regional/ethnic/class identity is being put forward in these 'authentic' songs and images? Country music is also characterised by a certain sense of national authenticity. In terms of country music this means two things. Firstly, the authentic nation is seen as a rural place and, secondly, this geographically bound nation that is lauded in country music has a mythologised 'folk' at its centre. The spirit of this nation is found in the folk closest to the land. 'Americanness', for example, is therefore important. Smith argues that the adoption of this position has a particular political, historical or social background and is thus open to negotiation. This situation also leaves open the possibility that authenticity is a negotiated construct. It is not an absolute position but is relative to the norms of the particular musical world one operates in (Smith 2002).

As can be seen from the above examples, this issue of authenticity, in a broader sense, encompasses a number of complexities and imperatives not the least of which is to unearth what is generally held tacitly about the term 'authenticity' itself. In order to understand the term it can be claimed that when we describe something as authentic we usually mean that it is reliable and trustworthy or is genuine and of undisputed origin. The word is derived from the Greek word *authentikos* which itself means principal or genuine. Not much has therefore been lost in the translation. When we 'authenticate' something we attempt to 'establish the truth or authorship or validity or genuineness of [it]' (Sykes 1983, p. 59). Regina Bendix provides a slightly different etymology to Sykes, explaining that the word derives from the Greek '*authentes*' which carries the dual meaning of 'one who acts with authority' and 'made by one's own hand'. Bendix points out that one definition of authenticity 'refers to the clear identifiability of the maker or authorship and uniqueness of an artefact' (1997, p. 15). There is obviously then a concern with authorship. Can the object, idea or process be trusted and can an author exhibit a sense that there is humanity in evidence in what they do? These questions lead inevitably to a further question. Why would we be so deeply and personally concerned with the idea of authenticity? This question can be answered in part by the way 'authenticity' came to be used by many philosophers and their concern with 'being oneself', that is, who one truly is or who we are most genuinely and principally.

Since the Renaissance and the rise of liberal humanist notions of the individual, there has been a concentration on the constitution of the self and consequently a concern with individual self-discovery. These ideas can be seen explicitly in the writings of Jean Jacque Rousseau, the Swissborn French philosopher from the eighteenth century, and its traces can be seen in the later development of the sociological project itself. Importantly for this discussion the idea of authenticity is at the heart of the didactic appraisals of popular music put forward by the neo-Marxists of the Frankfurt school and in particular by Theodor Adorno. The work of Walter Benjamin and Roland Barthes has also been deeply concerned with the expression of what has been called authenticity.

Underpinning these few examples we can see that the Enlightenment project, from its nebulous inception, led in two contradictory directions. It had at its core a belief in a rational progression towards order and at the same time a desire for the freedom of the self. Paradoxically this project inevitably created the very society that led to the anomie and alienation of individuals and at the same time was deeply concerned with the valorisation of that individual. The Industrial Revolution and the dislocation of populations led to a deep concern with society being perceived as being machinelike. Miles Orvell (1989) argues:

> on the one hand the machine was the source of the anomie, the distancing from 'reality' that was so pervasively sensed; yet on the other hand ... the machine could even be envisioned as the foundation for a more egalitarian society. Distinguishing between these two aspects of the machine civilisation – its deleterious effects vs. its exciting aesthetic and utopian possibilities – was precisely the problem for many artists and intellectuals in the early decades of the twentieth century. (1989, p. 154)

Recognising this contradiction much earlier, Rousseau held the opinion that progress, contrary to most scientific thought at the time, did not increase man's [*sic*] happiness. He indicated the obsession with private property and the rise of the political state itself as the causes of inequality and oppression. Marshall Berman, writing in a book called *The Politics of Authenticity: Radical Individualism and the Emergence of Modern Society* (1970), states that Rousseau's later work, *The Confessions*, was a personal search for his own individual self, who he truly was, what he termed his own authenticity. Berman asserts that Rousseau was one of the first to differentiate between what he called 'the tree' and 'the machine', and it can be argued that it is this dichotomy that has served to define the essential polarities that are at the core of most aspects of modern life, especially the views held about and within contemporary Western popular music.

The machine, according to Berman, 'is understood to symbolize everything that is rigid, compulsive, externally determined or imposed, deadening or dead; the Tree represents man's capacity for life, freedom, spontaneity, expressiveness, growth, self-development – in our terms authenticity' (1970, p. 165). Used in this way the machine is seen as a determining structure that is an 'invisible prison'. As Jacques Bouveresse also argues:

> what irks is the idea that we might be, even in the actions we think of as the most free, totally manipulated by invisible agents, who, as Dennett says 'vie with us for control of our bodies [or worse still our souls], who compete against us, who have interests antithetical to or at least independent of our own' (ibid., p. 7). We take if for granted, for example, that the sort of liberty that we need, and the only sort worth having, is the sort of freedom that implies that 'we could just as have easily have done something else instead'. But as Dennett remarks, it is precisely this supposition itself, and not the description one might attempt to give of the conditions necessary and sufficient for us to effectively have this sort of power, which demands to be examined seriously. (Shusterman 1999, p. 49)

In exploring these ideas Rousseau saw that there was a complex and ambiguous relationship that existed between the two seemingly polar opposites of 'the tree' and 'the machine'. Instead of simply rejecting 'the machine for the tree', as man was essentially a 'tree' or part of nature, he saw that the 'machine' itself was an outgrowth of what humanity had accomplished. Instead of rejecting the machine, or the system created by humanity itself, humanity must learn to come to grips with that system. For Rousseau the whirlpool that is the system forces humanity to develop a deep and delicate sensitivity to the forces that swirl around them. He suggests that rather than be destroyed by the unnatural forces they have helped to unleash, humanity must learn to deal with the threat it poses to the individual. From this position Berman suggests that Rousseau was highly insightful in as much as he 'understood how profoundly political the problem of personal authenticity was, how deeply interwoven were the destinies of the self, society and the state in the modern age' (1970, p. 324).

These ideas are buried deep within the structures of the modern world, as witnessed by the repercussions of the French Revolution, the declaration of the rights of man [*sic*], the establishment of the American Constitution, the struggles over the ideals of democracy that have rebounded throughout the twentieth century, and on into the twenty-first. For instance, the dualities expressed by Rousseau, or more importantly, the philosophical concern with identity and authenticity, were of central concern for many figures in sociology.

Theodor Adorno, writing in the middle of the twentieth century, took one part of 'the machine' as his target. Adorno's work itself discloses a systematic approach which uses 'contradiction and exaggeration as method – the revealing of a fundamental contradiction, and the formulation of its opposite poles by means of exaggeration' (Paddison 1982, p. 203). Adorno, like many other theorists writing close to the influence of the Industrial Revolution, perceived the older more agrarian or village-based way of doing things as more 'natural' and these were seen to be closer in origin to the true spirit of humanity and thus perceived as more authentic. In his essay 'On Popular Music', originally published in the journal *Studies in Philosophy and Social Science* in 1941 (and reproduced in a number of readers since e.g. Easthope & McGowan, 1992), Adorno railed against the standardisation induced by the machinery of the 'culture industry'. He used the self-help books for songwriters common at the time as a basis for arguing that popular music, for him a central part of the culture industry, was formulaic. For him the writing of a song was involved in a process of structural standardisation that aimed at a standard reaction. The popular song always functions as surface event 'behind which the scheme can always be perceived' (Adorno in Easthope & McGowan 1992, p. 215). He argued that the various elements in a popular song, especially the so-called standard, 'could be substituted for each other, just like the cogs in a machine' (Negus 1996, p. 37). Adorno was also highly critical of what he termed 'pseudo-individuality'. By this he meant that this process 'endowed cultural mass production with the halo of free choice' (in Easthope & McGowan 1992, p. 217), especially in regard to what was termed free jazz. He argued that when jazz musicians engaged in improvisations they were far from 'free'. They were in fact only making an appearance at spontaneity, and he asserted that 'passages where spontaneous action of individuals is permitted – ("Swing it boys") – are confined within the walls of the harmonic and metric scheme' (Adorno in Easthope & McGowan 1992, p. 217). What's more they were really carefully planning out their improvisations 'in advance with machine like precision' (Negus 1996, p. 38). These products of the culture industry could only lay claim to originality, not truly possess it. Once jazz, like other forms of music, had left its origins in the community and 'been subject to the culture industry it had lost any authentic link to non-commodified forms of expression' (ibid.).

Walter Benjamin, a fellow traveller of Adorno, also believed in an intrinsic quality that could be identified in all art, not just music. He argued this 'aura', this indefinable quality, can be recognised as authenticity. For Benjamin the aura, like Barthes' notion of the 'grain of the voice' (1990, pp. 293–300), is an essence which can be felt. He argued that with the transformation of art into mechanical reproduction the aura, the thing that made it original and thus authentic in the first place, becomes lost. When this essential element is lost the criteria of authenticity ceases to be applicable:

> Authenticity is interfered with whereas no natural object is vulnerable on that score. The authenticity of a thing is the essence of all that is transmissible from its beginning, ranging from its substantive duration to its testimony to the history which it has experienced. Since the historical testimony rest on the authenticity, the former too, is jeopardised by reproduction when substantive duration ceases to matter. And what is really jeopardised when the historical testimony is affected is the authority of the object. (Benjamin 1970, p. 222)

However, by exposing the discrepancy between the original and the recorded work Benjamin unintentionally provided the link necessary for many poststructuralist critics to proclaim the death of the author, or at the very least the death of authenticity (Goodwin in Frith & Goodwin 1990, p. 258). And yet, many of these ideas on authenticity are still proposed and discussed as part of the general discourse of contemporary

Western popular music itself. They have nonetheless been more recently queried within the scholarly world of popular music studies. Martin Stokes, for example, in his book about ethnicity, identity and music proposes that the use of the term authenticity is quite simply a convenient way of marking boundaries and delimiting the self. Boundaries 'define and maintain social identities, which can only exist in a context of opposition and relativities' (Stokes 1994, p. 6). Once these ideas are recognised we can see that, despite music having some solid basis in the physics of sound and the cultural world of its expression, it can't be easily argued that music itself has inherently 'authentic' properties since it is used by 'social actors in specific local situations to erect boundaries, to maintain distinctions between us and them, and how terms such as authenticity are used to justify these boundaries' (ibid.). Stokes goes on to say that:

> clearly notions of authenticity and identity are closely interlinked. What one is (or wants to be) cannot be 'inauthentic', whatever else it is. Authenticity is definitely not a property of music, musicians and their relations to an audience. It is not even a Benjaminesque 'aura' of uniqueness that surrounds a live situation as opposed to mechanically reproduced music, even though one frequently hears the term used in this way .... Instead we should see 'authenticity' as a discursive trope of great persuasive power. It focuses a way of talking about music, a way of saying to outsiders and insiders alike 'this is what is really significant about this music', 'this is the music that makes us different from other people'. (Stokes 1994, p. 6)

In support of this position, that is the linking of authenticity to identity, Joshua Gamson's (1994) investigation of the construction of the 'youth music' category lends some evidence. He states that the structuring and differentiation of 'youth culture', seen to be necessary for ongoing market segmentation, worked principally through the production of stylistic differentiation in consumption and leisure. The performing styles seen as acceptable to this newly created, that is newly created from the 1950s onward, market segment of teenagers were based on this category being different to preceding generations with one of the major differences being the advent of the conflation of the performer and the songwriter. The new youth market gradually moved away from the formal split that existed on Tin Pan Alley between composer and performer and moved instead towards valorising performers who wrote their own material. In this way new artists appeared to control their own destiny,

an important consideration if one assumes the Romantic position of creativity as many did at this time. As a result the entire recording industry
came to be reshaped and began to value, above others, this particular
set of attributes. An artist who sang their own songs could be trusted
to be 'one of us', that is, youth culture at the time. By writing their
own songs performers could display their personal authorship, genuineness and thus authenticity. Under these criteria obviously the Beatles
were more authentic than Frank Sinatra for the generation that accepted
them (Gamson 1994, pp. 161–2).

In the very late 1960s rock performers in particular started to construct
their authenticity around naturalness and the rejection of particular
performance codes too closely identified with their parent's preferred
performance styles. 'Cabaret' was out and only a natural undisciplined
stage craft was acceptably 'real'. As Gamson (1994) points out, young
bands like the Rolling Stones built their authenticity on their musical
and lyrical roots drawing heavily on early rhythm and blues, the music
of Muddy Waters, Jimmy Rogers and Little Walter, which gave them
the cachet of having a deep connection to supposedly authentic or genuine folk origins. In addition, many of the musicians and performers
in these successful English rock bands from this period were products
of the British art school system. As Peter Wicke suggests in his book
Rock Music: Culture, Aesthetics and Sociology (1990), they borrowed heavily from the Romantic philosophy espoused in these art schools. This
philosophy emphasised autonomy and creativity, in the Platonic sense,
on the part of the individual. Wicke, using the work of Simon Frith and
Howard Horne, contends that part of the ideology of the rock musician was to reassert, in the face of their 'commercial' counterparts, not
only proletarian street credibility, but also the bourgeois myth of the
Romantic artist (Wicke 1990, p. 98). Wicke contends that this reclama-
tion forced the notion of individualism in artistic expression into the
centre stage of popular music. Creativity, postulated as the Romantic
ideal, then legitimised the individualism of a bohemian artist's world
which:

> ...bound art to personality, individuality and lifestyle, but at the
> same time made it possible to see in art the liberation of man by
> reminding him of his own inner potential. Being creative meant
> removing the barriers which imprison man from within, meant self-
> realisation and freedom...the individualistic artistic consciousness
> which the British art schools gave to rock music was not consistent
> with the commercial standardisation of music into a mass product

based on the demands of the music market . . . . Behind the criticism of commerce, which was seen as the opposite of creativity and communication, lay the Romantic appeal to the autonomy of the artist, an ideal of honesty, upright behaviour and directness. (Wicke 1990, pp. 98–9)

In a similar way, Bob Dylan's authenticity depended on 'an assumption of the literary aesthetic code of the genius creator' (Gamson 1994, p. 161). Dylan, when he famously swapped one style for another, from folk to rock, was vehemently rejected by his former folk audience on the grounds he wasn't credible or authentically 'folk' anymore. He had to virtually reinvent his authenticity in line with the values of his new rock audience. No longer could he extol the virtues of a purist folk tradition and win favour by attempting to approximate or replicate the conventions held by this art world, courtesy of his imitations of Woody Guthrie, but he now had to valorise radical and unfettered innovation for his new rock audience. Making this sort of stylistic shift is often a risky business in popular music but for Dylan and his new found audience it marked 'a reassertion by the performer of his or her own authenticity' (Gamson 1994, p. 162). Through an assertion of autonomous decision making Dylan stubbornly pursued this shift in artistic orientation.

This necessity to have supposed mastery of the self, to be a free agent, can be evidenced further by the increased authenticity assumed by Stevie Wonder when he renegotiated his contract with Motown in the 1970s and started to write and perform material that he chose himself rather than performing material allocated to him by the Motown A&R department. The same story is applicable to his label-mate Marvin Gaye. In line with the discursive framework surrounding Romantic individuality that had become increasingly popular within the field of rock music, the dominant form at the time, they both overturned what they perceived as control by the machine and became more autonomous and, in the eyes of their potential rock audience, thus far more credible and authentic. On the other hand, even those Motown artists who did not make a claim for the type of authenticity favoured by rock audiences, and thus declare an individual freedom from the machine, so highly evident in Berry Gordy's factory system, have still in a later period become genuinely authentic musical heroes. Just the very mention of the term 'Motown artist' brings with it a certain prestige that gives the associated artist an aura connected to an embodiment of human exuberance and the expression of a genuine human community. I will return to the case of Motown shortly.

Another method of establishing authenticity, according to Gamson (1994), is through a commitment to a close and intimate relationship with an audience. This intimacy supposedly demonstrates the musician's ability to represent and speak for the audience itself. Many a rock band who is seen to stray too far from this relationship has been accused of 'selling out', of losing their authentic nature, of becoming false and lacking credibility. It was the difficulty of moving from the Romantic norms of a tightly organised subculture and an inability to commit to a mainstream audience that Kurt Cobain grappled with right throughout the period of his commercial success and eventual death (Barker & Taylor 2007). How was it possible to remain true to an authentic punk ethos, and still be selling millions of records? Wasn't commercial music manufactured by the machine, therefore not genuine and thus not authentic? If Cobain remained committed to the punk ethos, how could he reconcile his commercial success with the core of his own self-identity? This desire to identify as an artist, defined primarily in terms of Romanticism, can also be seen in the case of Neil Young, a performer who lamented the death of Kurt Cobain, and how he approached his own songwriting:

> Songwriting, for me, is like a *release*. It's not a craft. Crafts usually involve a little bit of training and expertise and you draw on your experiences – but if you're thinking about that while you're writing, don't! If I can do it without thinking about it, I'm doing it great... *I'm* waiting to see what I'm gonna do next. That should give you some indication of how much planning goes into it... *it doesn't have to make sense*, just give you a feeling. You get a feeling from something that doesn't make any sense... To start second-guessing yourself as it's coming out of you, you're gonna jam it up and it's not gonna come out. Thinking in songs – that's where it gets lost. Either playing it or writing it. (Quoted in Barker & Taylor 2007, p. 212)

As Barker and Taylor, authors of *Faking It: The Quest for Authenticity in Popular Music* (2007) emphatically assert, 'of course, this is an old Romantic notion' (2007, p. 212). As they contend, Coleridge drew on this notion in his preface to 'Kubla Khan' and, as evidence shows, embellished it somewhat (Sawyer 2006, pp. 304–5). However, most of the Romantic poets valorised these ideas:

> Shelley wrote of the skylark's 'profuse strains of unpremeditated art,' Keats cried, '0 for a Life of Sensations rather than of Thoughts!' Keats,

especially, was taken with the inherent authenticity of the imagination, with what he called 'negative capability,' or the ability of the poet to let the poem write itself 'without any irritable reaching after fact & reason.' 'If Poetry comes not as naturally as the Leaves to a tree,' he wrote, 'it had better not come at all'. (Barker & Taylor 2007, p. 212)

As Barker and Taylor contend, these Romantic notions have been manifest in terms of the idea of authorship in *lyric* poetry over and over again:

Baudelaire adopted it; so did the surrealists; so did the existentialists; so did Walt Whitman and, much later, the beats. Even prior to the Romantics, inspiration was considered to come from the gods or the muses; now it came from a part of oneself – called at one point the imagination and later the unconscious – that was difficult to know. (2007, pp. 212–3)

And yet the problem remains that all of these authors have been deeply immersed in the structures of the domain of poetry that have guided them in their efforts. Keat's poetry is 'damn clever stuff, involving regular meter and rhyme, which is why it's so effective' (Barker & Taylor 2007, p. 213). His success is just as dependent on his immersion in the structures of poetry as it is in his ability to play with words. As Barker and Taylor argue, 'thoughts, reason, facts – these are as essential to good poetry and good songwriting as inspiration' (ibid.). When Neil Young describes his songwriting in the terms described above he clearly echoes Keats and the other Romantics but, as Barker and Taylor question, how is it possible for someone like Young to compose a significant body of work as he has 'without thinking about it? Young is acting as if he were Lightning Hopkins, just making up lyrics as they come to him. But he's not. His songs are clearly well thought-out' (2007, p. 213).

These seemingly complex conundrums, based as they are on the way the relationship between agency and structure is conceptualised in a Romantic way, become even more complicated when the postmodern lack of concern with originality and authenticity comes into play. What happens when Kraftwerk, the forerunners to much electronic dance music of the 1980s and 1990s, throw away the search for authenticity and create music 'simply by pressing buttons, music that didn't address any personal, human concerns' (Barker & Taylor 2007, p. 242)? Kraftwerk had managed to 'make machine noise into a thing of beauty rather than using it as a metaphor for dehumanisation or dystopian menace' (ibid. p. 249). It was also music that expressed 'almost nothing about the people who created it' (ibid. p. 242). Taking up these ideas many electronic artists rejected the rock musician's notion of authenticity based for them on what they began to see as a false set of values. For example, they rejected the insistence on composing your own songs 'from the heart', as it were, a foundational marker of authenticity in rock music, as a quaint and obsolete myth. Instead, they would build a library of sounds from pre-recorded material, choose from what is possible in this library of sounds and blend them in ways they had not previously heard. In doing this they also blurred the older hieratic distinctions between composer, musician and audio-engineer and paid no heed, unless it was legally required, to notions of copying, plagiarism or theft (Sawyer 2006, p. 228). Electronic musicians like Moby are seemingly confounded by older ideas of authenticity; 'what's stranger at this point in time, given the technology and all, than a band where everybody plays one instrument, and you get one kind of music, song after song, album after album' (quoted in Sawyer 2006, p. 228). Instead of searching for authenticity, postmodern forms, of which electronica is a typical example, simply stepped around the question.

However, from within the sphere of most contemporary Western popular music, it's still the case that if one uses social mechanisms and determinisms in an attempt to explain what are apparently the most private and free actions, these attempts at explanation are most often seen in the polar opposite as a complete negation of freedom (Bouveresse in Shusterman 1999, p. 48). In this case it is just as well to repeat and remember, as Pierre Bourdieu does, that the idea of freedom as the complete absence of constraint, 'exalted by the defenders of creative spontaneity, belongs only to the naïve and the ignorant' (Bourdieu 1996, p. 235). As Regina Bendix has also asserted:

> the search for authenticity is fundamentally an emotional and moral quest. But this experiential dimension does not provide lasting satisfaction, and authenticity needs to be augmented with pragmatic and evaluative dimensions. Declaring something authentic legitimated the subject that was declared authentic, and the declaration in turn can legitimate the authenticator.... Processes of authentication bring about material representations by elevating the authenticated into the category of the noteworthy.... The question of internalised authenticity – the authentic human experience, the exuberant search for the 'soul of the people,' as Herder called it – is a much more

complex temptation, an attractive, troubling series of attempts to pinpoint the ineffable. (Bendix 1997, p. 7)

Despite various valiant attempts in the face of contrary forces and evidence to hang on to the notion of authenticity as the search for the expression of individual identity, Benjamin and Barthes come immediately to mind, there is also, as Lars Eckstein points out, a troubling and:

> unmistakeable divide between the aesthetics of production and the aesthetics of reception. On the one hand, the process of aesthetic production could be labelled 'postmodern' in its appeal to a Jamesonian (1991) understanding of the cultural logic of late capitalism, invariably with regard to notions of multiple authorship, the primacy of economic concerns, and the fabrication of simulacrous media identities. On the other hand, the aesthetics of reception clearly continues to move along 'romantic' lines. As if in a willing suspension of disbelief, audiences of popular music seem to take the subjective depth and integrity of the artist for granted, whose lyrics and music are expected to transport a genuine message relating to genuine feelings or biographical experience. The products of the mainstream popular music industry are, one could argue on these grounds, to a large extent carefully calculated postmodern simulations of the romantic authenticity which the market demands. (Eckstein 2006, p. 242)

But, if the task of reconciling these two disparate worlds and pinpointing authenticity as linked to modes of creativity with any surety is too large there is still no need to simply abandon the search as there does appear to be a way out of the loops, contradictions and paradoxes evident in the quest for the self, the quest for the heart of 'the tree' set in opposition to 'the machine', or as is being argued here, the quest for the individual creative agent within the system of contemporary Western popular music.

There have been other ways suggested to think of creativity and popular music (e.g. Peterson 1982, 1997, Toynbee 2000, Tschmuck 2006). For example, Toynbee placed the creative individual at the centre of a radius of creativity where they use the 'possibles' presented to them in creative activity. On the other hand, Peterson argued that the 'nature and content of symbolic products, are shaped by the social, legal and economic milieu in which they are produced' (Peterson 1982, p. 143). As may be gathered from my prior arguments, I believe Csikszentmihalyi's proposition that creativity comes about as a result of a system in operation comprised of domain, field and individual operating in a non-linear mode (1988, 1997, 1999) provides the necessary reconstructive perspective to reincorporate a modified form of individual agency into the creative activity of musicianship. Individuality as expressed in this model becomes a function of the system, just as the system is a function of the individual; tree and machine operating as an outgrowth of each other. Not in a static or evenly balanced way in terms of power relationships but full of, as Bourdieu (1993) would argue, arenas of contestation where struggles for dominance provide the dynamic life of the system itself. Those dynamic creative efforts can be seen in one of the most notable cases of the music industry acting as a creative system, that is, the case of Motown:

> The early recordings on the Motown and Tamla labels lacked a distinctive unifying sound other than of contemporary rhythm and blues, but as the market indicated its preference for certain types of Motown product, the company's core of songwriters and producers gained more self-confidence in their own personal sound and a house-style began to emerge. By 1962 those artist whose potential was proven, or was considered promising, started to receive the most attention while acts of questionable commercial viability were eased out. And around such talents as the Miracles, Mary Wells, Marvin Gaye, the Marvelettes, Little Stevie Wonder, the Temptations and the Supremes, Berry Gordy's creative team forged the unique Motown sound. (White in Brown 1982, p. 714)

In the process of developing the sound of Motown, Berry Gordy had relied upon:

> a strategy, a theory, of how to run a record company, and he imposed this on as talented a group of singers, musicians, producers and writers as has ever worked together in popular music.... Motown output was rigorously vetted... he kept the new talent acquired on as tight a rein as he could, encouraging what often became cut-throat competition between artists, producers and songwriters to come up with one of the few tracks chosen for release. (Brown 1982, p. 701)

Given this competition, this arena of contestation, it needs to be noted here that all 'parts', or individuals, are not equivalent. Some individuals within these institutions wield more influence and decision-making power. But as Foucault argues, the application of power 'needs to be considered as a productive network which runs through the whole social body, much more than as a negative instance whose function is repression' (quoted in Jordan & Weedon 1995, p. 479). In the case of Berry Gordy who relied extensively on his creative team, it can be seen that he was but one agent, although a very powerful agent, working within a collaborative system. Despite the many claims made about the deleterious effect corporate control, the 'man' and 'the machine', could have on popular music, and Motown's control was strict, it can be argued that 'the music produced was astounding' (Brown 1982, p. 701). This use of creative individuals in the service of a larger endeavour to produce creative products can be accounted for by simply seeing it as a system at work where agency and structure are not opposed but are highly interdependent (for further examples see McIntyre 2006b, 2008).

In this case structure, or what is called in terms of the argument being presented here the machine or the system, particularly within rock music circles, is 'not to be equated with constraint but is always both constraining and enabling' (Giddens 1984, p. 25). This realisation should help to dissolve some of the tensions thought to exist between the supposed subjective intentionality of the musical agent and the objective structuring of the domains and field of popular music. As such it should also help dissolve some of the tensions thought to exist between so-called creative artists, the musicians and the performers, and the economic structures of the industry they engage with. As Paul Levinson further argues:

> The separation of the psychological from the economic, the exaltation of the first and the denigration of the second, only begs the question of how creators can be expected to labour over long periods of time absent adequate compensation. The error here is to assume that the psychological aspects of creation can be separated from the economic at all, to be used as a *de facto* compensation in lieu of money. Once we recognise the way these two impulses necessarily operate hand in hand, we discover something new about the digital revolution. (2006, p. 65)

13
The Digital Revolution: Copyright and Creativity

Before we explore the relationship between the so-called digital revolution and creativity, we should take just a brief pause to remember Thomas's dictum. This dictum states that the way people perceive a situation predisposes them to behave in ways that are in line with those perceptions even if the perception is problematic. Furthermore, once a belief takes hold, such as a Romantic or inspirational view of creativity, 'gradually a whole life-policy and the personality of the individual himself' (Thomas 1967, p. 42) becomes premised on the belief system and they act according to that belief system. This state of affairs has been seen in the way many contemporary Western popular musicians and their audiences have responded to the beliefs they hold about authenticity and its manifestation in the creative action many of these people then take. But what if the belief system has no solid basis in research? What if our cultural assumptions have very little evidence to support them other than our ongoing faith? As Keith Sawyer asserts, a rational explanation of creativity 'requires us to look critically at our own cultural assumptions about how creativity works' (2006, p. 33), and the problem is that research studies 'fail to support our most cherished beliefs about creativity' (ibid.).

This situation has not only become extremely important for the music industry as it confronts shifting ideas about what constitutes authorship, who should be designated as an author and most importantly for this industry, who has the right to exploit those rights, but it is also increasingly the case that most other media industries are now grappling with these issues as well. This includes not only popular music but increasingly film, television, publishing, radio, news organisations, journalists and photographers. What is common to all of their struggles is the centrality of copyright and the increasing pressure this legal structure has come under in the marketplace with the advent of the digitisation of large amounts of media content; as Edward Samuels argues, 'with the transnational technologies of radio, television and the internet, copyright has become a truly international challenge' (2000, p. 248). In this regard, Dayan Thussu (2000) points out that:

> In the 1980s and 1990s fundamental ideological changes in the global political arena led to the creation of pro-market international trade regimes which had a huge impact on international commu-nication. The processes of deregulation and privatization in the communication and media industries combined with new digital information and communication technologies to enable a quantum leap in international communication, illustrated most vividly in the satellite industry. The resulting globalization of telecommunications has revolutionized international communication, as the convergence of the telecommunications, computer and media industries have ensured that much information passes through a digitally linked globe today more than ever before in human history. (2000, p. 82)

From 1969, when the first nodes of the Internet (Green 2010, p. 3) were created in a Pentagon plan to establish a decentralised communica-tion system that could withstand nuclear attack, and academics began to see its potential in information exchange for research, the focus of global communication has been moving towards a system where per-sonal computers are connected to the Internet via satellite and the use of cable is fast becoming an anachronism. In mobile telephony the existing global cellular environment currently consists of a mix of analogue and digital systems that can connect people very rapidly across the globe. Email and now Skype have provided an immediacy rarely experienced over vast distances since the introduction of the telegraph. The Internet, which was once seen as the conduit of a free flow of information, has been evolving into a system that allegedly engenders the free flow of commerce. Global capital can now take immediate advantage of various national stock exchange developments with many national economies at the mercy of international money traders, and large corporations are realising that there are many avenues for both profit and loss they could not conceive of prior to a digitised world. Consequently, there is increas-ing debate over many of the issues the advent of digitised media has raised (Hayward 1991, Castells 1996, Flew 2008, Green 2010).

With a growing number of traditional media firms moving their oper-ations online, all of these delivery systems and the digital consumers they service are eager for content of all types. These traditional producers of media are also having their conventional roles being supplemented, supplanted and competed with by untrained bloggers, supposedly naïve film, television and video makers and musicians who can do as much as anyone else with a few software applications and an ear for what sounds good. It is little wonder then that there has been an increasing concern over the fundamental basis of the so-called culture industries' ability to buy, sell, trade, lease and hire forms of intellectual property. The speed and ease with which content material can be replicated without going to the original producer to obtain either the content itself, or indeed the permission to do so, in an effort to replicate it, reorganise it and reconstitute it, has caused a deep rethinking of what is being reproduced and sold, who could or should own the results of that and therefore, of course, the merits of the methods to do this with.

Following the legal battle between Napster and the RIAA in the United States, piracy concerns in Asia, the dispute over the ownership of content on social media sites and the realisation by so-called Internet prod/users that they have a powerful cultural tool at their disposal, the protection of rights has become of fundamental concern to those billion-dollar culture industries that depend for their existence on the maintenance of intellectual property in the form of copyright. This is especially the case for music, film and book publishing, industries that contribute significantly to many Western GDPs. This significance was highlighted a little while ago in a report entitled 'Copyright Industries in the US Economy: The 2000 Report'. This report asserts that U.S. copyright industries 'contribute more to the U.S. economy and employ more workers than any single manufacturing sector and grow at a higher rate than the U.S. economy as a whole' (RIAA 2003). One of these copyright industries, the recording industry, is seen as:

> one of the great global industries of today. It brings pleasure and fulfilment to people of all ages, cultures and creeds; it is one of the leading creative industries that increasingly drive the development of modern economies; and it is pioneering in the era of digital technologies and electronic commerce. The recording industry's success – world retail sales from US$27 billion to $38 billion during the 1990s – is primarily as an investor in human creativity. Record producers worldwide, independent and multi-national, invest billions of dollars in local cultures. They underpin the livelihoods of a diverse array of artists across the world. (IFPI 2003)

Apart from considering the imbalance in the distribution of profits in these industries, there has been some debate as to how industries like this should be classified. As Patrik Wikstrom (2009) points out, the use of the term cultural industries is an appealing one with a number of obvious strengths, not the least of which is its scholarly heritage and its connection to the critical theorists' initiation of the term culture industry. This latter term, however, still carries a number of negative connotations often used in its initial development as a pejorative. Some also argue that it is an outdated characterisation of the industries that are now largely digitally based, as it is often 'linked to analogue media, nationalistic cultural policies, neoclassical economics applied to the arts etc.' (Wikstrom 2009, p. 14). A number of other terms have been suggested. These include the notion of 'creative industries' (Hartley 2005) which has become especially welcomed in policy circles across a number of countries. Its substitution for the term 'culture industry' has enabled a positive connotation to be appended to those industries that had formerly been seen to negatively dominate and control political and cultural agendas and its use also broadens the base of what may be included in funding opportunities (Pratt 2008, pp. 113–4). What may be included under its umbrella, apart from the traditional media, are 'industries or activities such as architecture, design, fashion, performing arts, crafts and sometimes even tourism, sport and restaurants' (Wikstrom 2009, p. 14). Of course, the use of the term 'creative' as an adjective for these industries appears, as we have seen, to itself imply a relatively narrow understanding of what constitutes creativity and generally conflates the notion of creativity with artistic activity. However, Wikstrom goes on to argue that the term copyright industry is a more accurate description and certainly a more useful term 'than either *culture industry* or *creative industry* since copyright legislation is what makes it possible to commodify a cultural work such as a film, a song, a photograph, a book etc' [italics in original] (2009, p. 10). He argues that those industries that have transferred, or have been forced to transfer, large parts of their business to an online situation have at their heart the development of 'content and personalities and, to be able to license the use of that content and those personalities to consumers and businesses, they need to be protected by copyright legislation' (2009, p. 17). By looking at these industries as copyright industries rather than cultural or creative industries, this terminology emphasises 'the nature of the products that are created and traded within that industry' (Wikstrom 2009, p. 17), and it also emphasises their deep connection to the international system of copyright law. As Terry Flew argues, copyright and the legal framework of intellectual property law has become 'the site upon which so many of the issues and challenges presented by the development of new media' (2005, p. 209) are still being worked through. The central issues raised can be listed as:

> the balance between public and private, individual rights of owner-ship and social use for collective benefit, the nature of knowledge as a commodity and as a public good, and the best ways in which to promote and equitably share the benefits of creativity in an age of digital networks. (ibid.)

With the sorts of financial imperatives at play it's not surprising then that copyright has become a major issue for most of these copyright industries. The digitisation of all forms of data, text, audio and video, words sounds and pictures (Thussu 2000, p. 224), made available across the Internet on various sites and blogs, relayed via satellite over mobile telephony networks and disseminated on various CD, DVD and mp3 formats, has not only caused problems for those with economic con-cerns but it also raises, which is the point of this discussion, some fundamental questions about the nature of creativity and its relation-ship to multi/digital/new media. The use of digital technology to put together a communicative presentation (Tannenbaum 1998, pp. 3–4) enables the developer to copy, sometimes in seemingly perfect and orig-inal form, text, images and sound that have been produced in other realms and, at times, for other purposes. In fact, this can be done with such ease that it, at times, raises the ire of many of those who practice the making of media content. One small case will serve as illustration.

In a recent report in *Time* (2009) magazine on the future of journal-ism, Walter Isaacson argued that the seemingly effortless money to be made from Internet advertising in the late 1990s encouraged newspa-pers and magazine managers to place their content onto their company websites for free. The problem for news organisations occurred when the majority of advertising dollars flowed to groups that weren't involved in actually creating content but provided the conduits on which it was dis-seminated, that is, search engines and a few aggregators. Isaacson saw this as reprehensible and went on to suggest that another cluster of undeserving businesses also stood to benefit from what was fast becom-ing free journalism. The reporters collect the news data, analyse it and synthesise it for consumption and others profit from this costly effort. Internet service providers (ISPs) were a particular target for Isaacson's indignation:

They get to charge customers $20 to $30 a month for access to the Web's trove of free content and services. As a result, it is not in their interest to facilitate easy ways for media creators to charge for their content. Thus we have a world in which phone companies have accustomed kids to paying up to 20c when they send a text message but it seems technologically and psychologically impossible to get people to pay 10c for a magazine, newspaper or newscast. (Isaacson 2009, p. 30)

There appears to be in these sometimes heartfelt and volatile arguments a set of oppositions at work dependent on whether the concern is with consumption or production. On the one hand, consumers, of course, want what they consume to be as free as it can possibly be. Those who argue this case usually employ in their defence an often unquestioned faith in the Romantic notion of 'the artist' whose concern, they believe, is not with worldly goods but their own artistic expression and how an audience will hear, see or interact with this and recognise their talent or at least identify their self-expressive humanity, supposedly unmediated through constraining structures of any kind. The art versus commerce debate is often invoked here. Ironically, the poststructuralist position which abandons all concern with authorship is also employed in defence of this cause. As an example, annoyance flares, especially where the supposed right to access music is concerned:

Perhaps no area of human creativity relies more heavily upon appropriation and allusion, borrowing and imitation, sampling and intertextual commentary than music, nor any area where the mythic figure of the creative genius composing in the absence of all external influence is more absurd. Contemporary technologies have greatly multiplied and democratised opportunities for musical creativity and self-expression, while also providing means for the musically enthusiastic to share music with others and to accelerate the processes of collaboration on which musical innovation relies. Have we reached a crossroads? Will the ever more aggressive legal tactics of corporate intellectual property holders put an end to sharing and collaboration, or is there a 'will to music' that will continue to energetically evade attempts to restrict such practices? (Coombes in Demers 2006, p. ix)

On the other hand, those whose primary concern is not with consumption but largely with production take a slightly different approach. Just as ironically, their arguments are often dependent on whether their belief system is grounded in Romanticism or their livelihood and ability to continue doing what they do is grounded in a more postmodern conception of their own cultural output. Either way they believe they have the right to be paid for the use of what they see as their intellectual property; property acquired through the rights they have to the legitimate pursuit of their daily activity:

> There's a saying on the Internet that 'information wants to be free.' I doubt that information really cares what happens to it, but if by the saying we mean that *we* want information to be free, then that may be true most of the time. That's even true under copyright, which provides that facts are not the proper subject of copyright protection. However, creativity is a different matter. Under the principles of copyright, *we* want creative works to be compensated; that's how we pay the creators for creating their works. So, I assert, 'Creativity wants to be paid'. (Samuels 2000, p. 249)

To be paid one needs to possess property. The question then immediately arises: where did this fundamental idea come from? Paul Levinson argues that territoriality and thus property has been a feature of life for aeons since 'modes of demarcating possession, seem to be everywhere there is life' (2006, p. 55). Simon Roberts (quoted by Maddock 1990, pp. 14–15) argues that while members of hunter-gatherer societies are continually mobile, significant effort is needed if enough food is to be hunted, caught or collected. In adapting to the circumstances of the nomad, groups of hunter-gatherers tend to be small, tend to vary in numbers that can be supported and are mostly made up of kin. Since these are often intimate communities there is little necessity for complex, written customs to clarify what is right or wrong. Since 'large surpluses of food cannot be accumulated and personal belongings are limited to the few that can be carried, hardly any rules about property are required' (Maddock 1990, p. 14). But they are, nonetheless, there. The point is that the concept of property itself has been linked to the prevailing patterns of living and thinking that are common to particular periods.

At the time of the Renaissance and Reformation a struggle was waged in the West between the old theocentric view of the world with that of an anthropocentric one. The first, according to Elizabeth Mensch, assumed that it was legitimate, under a securely and highly 'structured and paternalistic political, economic and ecclesiastical hierarchy' (Mensch 1990, p. 918), that property relations be premised on 'divinely ordained inequality' (ibid.). The second view challenged this. It proclaimed 'equality and freedom as the only possible foundation for a true republican community and also by regarding actual settlement and use of land as the only legitimate source of title' (ibid.).

John Locke in an effort to reconcile these views, and at the same time legitimise the tenure of English government, argued in *The Second Treatise of Government* (1956) that government and social order derived from nature rather than divine will. This placed the origins of government outside the framework of any religious doctrine and placed it firmly in a secular one. The important point as far as we are concerned was that Locke underpinned his ideas on government with those of property. For Enlightenment thinkers like Locke a right to property originated in a person's labour on nature and was a realm of activity that preceded the state. Property according to this formulation included not just land that was brought under cultivation but the things people appropriated from its natural state (Sewell 1990, p. 120). This thinking lay at the foundation of the assumption that property was not only manifest in the physical but could also be extended to include abstract or intellectual entities. It extended the notion of property to include the realm of thought and ideas that could be embedded in plays, books and music:

> Copyright law as we know it began in England in 1710 when the British Parliament enacted the Statute of Anne. The Statute of Anne contained, for the first time in copyright law, legal protection for consumers of copyrighted works by curtailing the term of a copyright thus, preventing a monopoly on the part of the booksellers.... The statute also provided for an author's copyright – although the benefit to authors was minimal because in order to be paid for a work an author had to assign the work to a bookseller or publisher. Since the Statute of Anne almost three hundred years ago, copyright law has been revised to broaden the scope of what is covered by a copyright, to change the term of a copyright, and to incorporate new technologies. (Brennan n.d.)

As such the laws governing copyright, which it must be noted have been largely reactive rather than proactive, have remained flexible to allow new cultural forms to be accounted for and to ensure, as new technologies and forms develop, the rights of property to develop alongside them. As Brennan argues (2001), the most important and far-reaching legal development in terms of international copyright protection was the Berne Convention for the Protection of Literary and Artistic Works that was signed into existence by a number of countries in 1886. The Berne Convention guarantees that the copyright owner should be allowed to exercise control over how the work they own is used as well as collect a fee, called a royalty, for this usage. It operates on the principle of reciprocity. Reciprocity means that all countries who signed the convention guarantee the same rights to writers and artists in other countries as they do for their own writers and artists. The aim of the Berne Convention was to 'provide the basis for mutual recognition of copyright between sovereign nations in foreign works and promote development of international norms with regard to copyright protection' (Brennan 2001). There have been five revisions to the convention. For example in 1908, the Berlin Act fixed the period of the applicability of copyright to the life of the author plus 50 years and it 'expanded the scope of the act to include newer technologies, and prohibited formalities as a prerequisite of copyright protection' (ibid.). Then again in 1928, the Rome Act became the first to recognise moral rights of authors and artists. The United States became a signatory to the Berne Convention in 1988 (ibid.). Various countries around the world had already adopted the Convention. For example, the Australian Colonial Government became automatic signatories to the Berne Convention when it was signed by the British Parliament in 1886.

Accepting that this legal structure governing intellectual property is now firmly in place, it would be pertinent to assert that copyright, in essence, means precisely what its name implies. It is concerned with the right to make copies of an original and the allocation of the right to sell those copies and thus make a profit. The case of Napster versus RIAA, which involved at one point rock bands such as Metallica, was essentially fought over this point.

Metallica argued that they sued Napster, thus placing themselves in opposition to the belief that the record industry, in the form of the RIAA, represented one of the most detested and maligned structures in existence, because 'we wanted to create an open discussion about the value of music before it was too late. We felt that Napster was taking it out of the artists' hands' (Metallica n.d.). Metallica claimed they were:

> using our legal right to go to court to determine whether or not the Napster system is engaging in the act of copyright infringement.... The Napster decision will have a dramatic impact on how artists continue to record and produce music; and as artists, we felt the need to declare our beliefs in the hopes that others will see the severity of the issue. We have no issue with the MP3 format. Rather, it is how the

format is being used, and who controls it. Whether Metallica is heard on MP3, CD, cassette, vinyl, or by any other format is of no concern to us, as long as it is being obtained by legal means. (Metallica n.d.)

Their critics, mostly concerned with both the continuing flow of freely obtainable recorded music and the associated desire to keep the Internet commerce free, pointed to the benefits of free downloads to the music industry itself, asserting that 'industry representatives have failed to point to any data that shows the extent to which MP3s and CD burners, by making copying music so easy, have hurt industry revenues' (Erickson n.d.). These critics cited the increase in revenue to the music industry, generally to the publishing and performance sectors of the industry, as being attributed to Napster and sites like it, which contradicted claims by other sectors of the industry, particularly the recording sector, who argued that file swapping and downloading affected their CD sales.

To get some idea of the value of what is at stake, McIntyre and Morey (2010) recently presented some of the figures involved. For example, for the 2009–10 period the Australasian Performing Rights Association (APRA/AMCOS 2010) claimed total revenues of A$222.1m, which was up from the tax year prior. This revenue, mainly destined for the publishing sector of the music industry, represented a year-on-year growth over the last ten years almost doubling 1999–2000 revenues which stood at A$110.5m. By comparison, the Performing Rights Society (PRS/MCPS) in Britain 'declared revenues for 2008 of £491m (Page & Carey 2009). The estimated publisher's direct revenues for that year from PRS stood at £90m' (McIntyre & Morey 2010, p. 5). While these figures seem healthy overall it should also be noted that this is only part of the picture as a publisher's income will also include, for example, sync fees. Other sources (Wikstrom 2009, pp. 93–5) also indicate that there has been an exponential growth in licensing revenues for the publishing sector, including performance and sync fees, from approximately US$75m in 1995 to a steadily increasing figure that stood at approximately US$195m in the United States and US$180m in the United Kingdom in 2008. Furthermore, while there was a declared £608.2m being made by the music industry in Britain (an 8 per cent growth on 2007), there was a 14 per cent growth in performing revenue (£466.6m) with a negative 7 per cent decline in recorded media revenue of £141.6m. So, reading through the figures, McIntyre and Morey claim that 'the structural situation of the overall industry, comprised of three sectors, recording, publishing and live performance, is changing' (2010, p. 5).

As McIntyre and Morey (2010) go on to show, the International Federation of Phonographic Industries (IFPI) reported in 2008 that recorded music, important of course for the recording sector, had a global trade value of US$18,415.2m. Of this figure, US$13,829.3m represented a fall in physical sales of recorded music of 15.4 per cent while US$3,783.8m represented a growth of 24.1 per cent in digital sales. According to the IFPI (2009) physical sales include audio formats such as singles, LPs, cassettes, CDs and MiniDisc, and music video formats include DVD, VHS and VCD. On the other hand, digital sales refer to sales via online, mobile channels and subscriptions. Income from ad-supported services, ringtone income and bundled subscriptions was included in the digital sales figures in 2008. The IFPI (2009) has revised 2007 digital sales for the major markets to include these new digital categories. Online sales here also include single-track and album downloads, music video downloads, streams, bundles and kiosk sales. Mobile music sales include master ringtones, single-track downloads to mobile, ring back tones, music video downloads to mobile, streams, ringtone income, preloaded music on mobile phones, mobile bundles, greetings and dedications income. Performance rights figures reflect monies received by record companies from collection societies for licenses granted to third parties for the use of sound recordings in music videos in broadcasting (radio and TV), public performance (nightclubs, bars, restaurants, hotels) and certain Internet uses (IFPI 2009). Of the gross figure in 2008, US$802m represented the payment of performance royalties from record companies to collection agencies (IFPI 2009) which benefitted the publishing sector. McIntyre and Morey (2010) suggest it is thus 'reasonable to assume that publishing sector income will remain buoyant within the overall music industry' (2010, p. 5). In fact they suggest that 'there is a strongly held view that for the recording sector digital sales will eventually offset CD's decline by 2011, but this will still only return this sector of the industry to the revenues of 2004, rather than the levels achieved in the late 1990s' (ibid.). Overall, although recorded music may be threatened somewhat, live performance receipts for that sector of the music industry have remained buoyant and 'no matter which way one looks at the figures one can rightly claim that, through the distribution of publishing income alone, songs remain valuable' (ibid.). As Williamson and Cloonan suggested in 2007, although:

> the recorded music industry still represents about 70 per cent of the 'music industry', this percentage is likely to decline substantially in the coming years, largely a result of the growth of the live music

industry and the exploitation of publishing and synchronisation rights. These latter industries were estimated in 2004 at being worth $10 billion (Hardy 2005) and $3•8 billion (Enders Analysis 2002), respectively. In addition there are other growth sectors: music DVD and video is now worth $2•6 billion (IFPI 2004), and the *Financial Times* reported that music publishing has become far more interesting to venture capitalists than the recorded music industry (Hemsley 2005). Meanwhile it is estimated that the legal download industry, such as iTunes and Napster, will be worth $3•9 billion by 2008 (Informa 2003). There is also other evidence to suggest that the economic value of music industries outside of the recording sector is rising. (Williamson & Cloonan 2007, pp. 314–5)

With these sorts of income at stake, the Napster case was watched closely for its larger implications for all copyright industries, and it ultimately highlighted the fact that 'simplicity and low cost are the keys to consumer acceptance' (Pizzo 2000) in a digitised world. For example, 'iTunes has gained and maintained a reputation for being easy to use while still providing many features for obtaining, organizing, and playing media' (Wikipedia n.d.a). As Pizzo asserted in 2000, when consumers are given an undemanding and seamless method of downloading files 'at a price that will discourage piracy and encourage consumption, the whole fight will end right there and then'(Pizzo 2000).

What this legal saga implied for many actors in this case was the idea that if one allows the dissolution of copyright and thus the lawful basis for the ownership of intellectual property, the industries built on it, operating as they currently are, will cease to be. Vaidhyanathan (2001) summarised the debates that arose from this case, with some suggesting that copyright is fundamentally unworkable in the digital era, and others arguing that protection schemes would be the only way to recover costs and make profit, and still others seeing copyright as a natural right that proceeds from the act of creation by individuals who then had the right to seek to profit from their own artistic activity (Vaidhyanathan 2001, p. 183). To this point, many of these arguments have not been satisfactorily resolved for all copyright industries. Consequently, the relationship between copyright, the ability of cultural producers to exploit their own creative activity and, most importantly for us, what conception of creativity is being employed in these arguments should now be investigated a little further.

It has been argued that 'copyright law, Romantic authorship and the overpowering significance of the author were "born together" '

(Bently 1994, p. 974). The basis of copyright law developed, as did Romantic conceptions of creativity, from the idea of the autonomous, self-expressive and self-willed individual. However, the ability to question the notion of individual authorship and to see the marks of that individual in the work have been thrown open to numerous critiques by either the supposed loss of 'the aura' of the individual, its hyper-proliferation in many multimedia works or the revelation that works, especially digitised works, could come about as the result of multiple efforts from a diverse array of sources. The ability to borrow in a literally intertextual way demonstrated, as the poststructuralists claimed, that no text was original in the way Romantic authorship conceived that it should be. However, the courts, in this case those in the United States, still conceive of creativity in the Romantic sense. As Bently argues, courtesy of Jaszi, the introduction of the notion of moral rights:

> is but one example of how Romantic conception of authorship is displaying a literally unprecedented measure of ideological autonomy in legal context. Recent copyright decisions show that even as scholars of literary studies elaborate a far-reaching critique of the received Romantic concept of authorship, American lawyers are reaching out to embrace the dull range of its implications. (Jaszi quoted in Bently 1994, p. 977)

As Bently purports 'there can be little doubt that, since 1800, cultural assumptions about authorship have informed the development of copyright law' (Bently 1994, p. 979). As an example, French law, and one presumes others of those in the West, tends to connect creativity with the arts. As has been seen a little earlier, photography was not the subject of copyright in France until it was recognised, as the result of economic pressure, as Art. What this implies is that if the law can also, as Bently argues, 'invent' authors where none actually exist (1994, pp. 980–1), such as in the case of computer-generated works, then recognising a conception of creativity that still includes individuals, albeit in a slightly modified and less Ptolemaic way, such as that proposed by the systems model, should not be too difficult. The legal structure could in fact be adapted to suit these new conceptions of creativity. The case has been that copyright law has been an eminently malleable thing which it has needed to be in order to simplify questions of property rights.

> While copyright may be built on an image of creative authorship, copyright law uses that image as a point of attachment – a point

at which to ascribe a property right and by which the right can be determined. But the essence of that ascription is that it is a divestible or alienable right. In law, authorship is a point of origination of a property right which, thereafter, like other property rights, will circulate in the market, ending up in the control of the person who can exploit it most profitably. (Bently 1994, pp. 980–1)

The denial of authorial contributions by certain collaborators not legally recognised as creative agents can be seen, in part, as an instance of the law attempting to merely simplify ownership in a pragmatic way, not protect certain inalienable Romantic rights 'because a single property owner means that assignments and licences of copyright are easier and cheaper to effect' (Bently 1994, pp. 981–2). This description of the simplifying of authorship serves to reinforce the Foucauldian characterisation of the operation of certain discourses surrounding proprietorial ownership and their connection to copyright. For Michel Foucault, the way writers or authors are thought of or conceived has a function to perform that is partially necessary for the allocation of legal ownership and thus remuneration. But, as Foucault himself also recognises, a work cannot develop 'without passing through something like a necessary or constraining figure' (1977, p. 159). As Bently has argued, often that necessary or constraining figure is simply a convenient remnant of Romantic thinking and, as Becker (1982) also argues, is dependent on the context of the 'art world' the artist or writer exists in (Becker 1982, pp. 9–10).

While the Romantic author has been an implicit feature of copyright law, what has been seen as the subject of copyright has been variable over time, and this variability, from the regulator's perspective, has been an advantage in accounting for unforeseen cultural changes that may take place. In reference to the U.S. Copyright Act it is noted that 'authors are continually finding new ways of expressing themselves, but it is impossible to foresee the forms that these new expressive methods will take' (Cornell Law Institute 1999). Siva Vaidhyanathan makes the comment that there are certain uses in having the copyright system adjustable as new ideas and products and processes, the things that creativity produces, become commonly available:

What American jurists have known for centuries is that a leaky copyright system works best... a thin, leaking copyright system allows people to comment on copyrighted works, make copies for teaching and research, and record their favourite programs for later viewing.

Eventually, a copyright runs out, and the work enters the 'public domain' for all of us to enjoy at an even lower cost. But when constructed recklessly, copyright can once again be an instrument of censorship, just as it was before the Statute of Anne. (Vaidhyanathan 2001, p. 184)

Just as legislators have taken precautions about an unseen and dynamic cultural future, there is also some evidence of historical resistance to this change. For example, the persistence of the idea of individual creativity has resulted in denials of 'protection to folklore and items of cultural heritage that are valued chiefly for their fidelity to tradition rather than their deviation from it' (Bently 1994, p. 985). The cultural assumptions about creativity as solely being about innovation rather than being also deeply linked to tradition are operative here as well. So where does this leave us in relation to the more recent confluence-based conceptions of creativity?

What makes the recently devised confluence-based conceptions of creativity significant in terms of the relationship between creativity and the notion of property is the importance of the concept of patronage to the field of whatever copyright industry is being engaged with. This situation has a set of historical antecedents. For example, during the early 1400s in Florence there was an efflorescence of artistic activity. As Mihaly Csikszentmihalyi suggests, 'it is generally agreed that some of the most influential new works of art in Europe were created during that quarter century' (1997, p. 32). But he also argues that this phenomenon cannot be explained simply by looking to individuals and their greatness alone. Csikszentmihalyi asserts that the methods used by Roman builders and sculptors, those that were lost to Europe during the so-called Dark Ages, were being rediscovered through a series of informal excavations of Roman ruins all across Italy at this time. This domain of knowledge thus became available again. But why Florence in particular? Why did this city amongst all the others achieve what it did? Why not another of its rival city states? Csikszentmihalyi explains:

Florence had become one of the richest cities in Europe first through trading, then through the manufacture of wool and textiles, and finally through the financial expertise of its rich merchants. By the end of the fourteenth century there were a dozen major bankers in the city – the Medicis being only one of the minor ones – who were getting substantial interest every year from the various kings and potentate to whom they lent money. (1997, pp. 33–4)

For reasons of rivalry and a desire to stay ahead of the other cities around them, the wealthy and the citizenry of Florence decided to show off and intimidate others with their wealth. How was this accomplished? The answer is by purposely setting out to make Florence the new Athens. Csikszentmihalyi argues:

> The important thing to realise is that when the Florentine bankers, churchmen, and heads of great guilds decided to make their city intimidatingly beautiful, they did not just throw money at artists and wait to see what happened. They became intensely involved in the process of encouraging, evaluating, and selecting the works they wanted to see completed. It was because the leading citizens, as well as the common people, were so seriously concerned with the outcome of their work that the artists were pushed to perform beyond their previous limits. (1997, p. 34)

In other words the field was instrumental through its system of patronage in bringing these works to light. As far as Csikszentmihalyi is concerned, works of art don't happen in isolation from the world around them. The action of patronage is vitally important. The significant art that was produced in Florence 'didn't happen when the artists set the agenda, but when patrons insisted on certain standards that benefited them' (Csikszentmihalyi 1997, p. 325). One could argue that without patronage of one kind or another neither art nor science as it is practised in the early twenty-first century could happen. It has certainly been crucial to the development of much of what we call 'Art' in the West.

In this regard Raymond Williams (1981) has argued that there have been a set of historical social relations that have existed over time between cultural producers and the institutions they have most often interacted with. For Williams the first of these describes the association between an artist, in this case usually a poet or bard, and the formal institutions of a structured aristocratic society. In this situation, this 'instituted artist' was part of the official fabric of the social and aristocratic institution they existed in and, notably for our discussion, the work produced was the possession of the patron not the artists. The second set of interactions Williams identified was that of the relations between a chosen artist and a powerful patron, noting that there have been a variety of forms of patronage practised in this relationship. There was a transition between an official court artist attached to a prince of the realm on an ongoing basis towards one where the exchange of cultural work for patronal reward was far more temporary. The full transition occurred when artists, as individual professional workers, were placed on a retainer or travelled from patron to patron simply working for commissions typical of the Renaissance. This period was also typified by relations between artists themselves, usually in a master–apprentice relationship.

The next phase of patronage, according to Williams, was based on a form of social protection, support or recognition which aided the artist in their endeavours. This situation was typical of Elizabethan England, where the work was remunerated by a paying public but patronal protection was necessary to increase the reputations of the cultural workers, which ensured to a degree the support and attendance of the paying public. As Williams indicates, 'what was really being exchanged, within a specific kind of society marked by overt class inequalities, was a hopefully mutual reputation and honour' (1981, pp. 41–2).

The fourth form of patronage was in the form of sponsorship and took place 'within a world in which the production of works of art for sale was normal' (Williams 1981, p. 42). The fifth form was that of public patronage where revenues were raised from taxation to encourage 'the deliberate maintenance and extension of the arts as matter of general public policy' (1981, p. 43). He adds to the list a more modern type of patronage common in advanced capitalist societies. For Williams, 'certain arts which are not profitable or even viable in market terms are sustained by specific institutions such as foundations, by organizations of subscribers, and still by some private patronage' (Williams 1981, p. 55). In between these and 'fully governmental institutions are bodies wholly or significantly financed from the public revenue' (ibid.), such as the Arts Councils, or the BBC in Great Britain and the ABC in Australia. Some cultural institutions have become departments of state where producers operating within them are seen as state corporate employees.

Regardless of the system of patronage, now an essential part of the field of 'Art' in the West, 'the defining characteristic of all patronal social relations is the privileged situation of the patron' (Williams 1981, p. 43) as one who can give or withdraw their support. In the face of this often one-sided power relationship, one of the defining characteristics of artists is that they have, willingly or unwillingly, historically accommodated themselves to the market. Williams offers a typology of this relationship as well.

The first of these is typified by a producer whose work remains under their own direction, who 'offers his [sic] own work for direct sale' but is in fact 'dependent on the immediate market' (1981, p. 44). The second type of artist doesn't sell the work directly but does so through an intermediary who becomes in effect the employer of the artist. Allied to this type is the producer who sells the work to an intermediary who in this case has invested in the work to make a profit for themselves. The transformation of booksellers into publishers was a move from the former to the latter. The next type of artist Williams identifies, the third type, are the market professionals who have developed around the notions of copyright and royalty payments. This form of cultural production, the centre of our discussion here, initially developed around the reproducible technologies of print and, as has also been argued above, 'this made the question of property acute' (1981, p. 47).

This newly typical relationship between artists and the form of patronage they engaged with has a set of legal property rights at its core and it usually exists in:

> the form of a negotiated contract for a specific form or period of publication, with variable clauses on its terms and duration. As an expression of this relationship, the royalty – a specific payment on each copy of this form sold – came to replace the common earlier form of outright purchase. Thus the writer became a participant in the direct market process of the sale of his work. (Williams 1981, p. 47)

In all these types of relationships with the market the artist works not only for themselves but also for the projected demands of the structured commercial space of the market. The final category of artist Williams deals with is that of the corporate professional where artists are integrated into a corporate world where the point of origin of the work may not reside with them as individuals but sits within the combined efforts and causal processes of the commissioning corporation. In this and all the other cases outlined by Williams, the system of patronage is a fundamental part of the creative process.

The effect of patronage, or the lack thereof, can be seen in the idea that in Western culture, 'a huge number of talented and motivated artists, musicians, dancers, athletes, and singers give up pursuing their domains because it is so difficult to make a living in them' (Csikszentmihalyi 1997, p. 333); as ample evidence indicates, 'creation is jeopardised when compensation is not available' (Levinson 2006, p. 64). Without either a system of philanthropy or governmental grants of one kind or another, scientific innovation and the scientists who develop it would be hindered in their creative efforts (Sawyer 2006, pp. 263–80). The corollary argument is that without a patronage system of some sort, and the current one appears to be solidly based on copyright law, the ability to continue making artworks in various art worlds would also inevitably change. The legal industrial framework built on copyright, the source of much patronage in the West, is thus involved in an important balancing act between the desires of consumers and the needs of producers, but as Samuels argues 'copyright will continue to be important in the international legal community for as long as we want to encourage the making of creative works' (2000, p. 248).

This is not to say that all creative works should be made inaccessible to everybody simply because the notion of property, reward and profit making appears to be paramount within a discursive framework that valorises the operations of the free market. The limits on the length of copyright periods, the idea of 'public domain' that springs from it and the innovative application of ideas such as the creative commons put in place by institutions such as the BBC are attempts to suggest that creative work has a benefit apart from those envisaged by market-dominated patrons. But without some way to remunerate either artists or scientists, or indeed their patrons, what becomes public domain and held for common usage may itself be diminished (Levinson 2006, pp. 63–5).

While the ability of the current legal and ethical systems to maintain pace with technological change has been so far quite laggardly, the deep concerns over the property abuses of some using new digital media technology and the abuses of maintaining an inequitable distribution of the profits of creative activity have highlighted the necessity to investigate every implication of the introduction of new technologies. This, in our case, also applies to the laws that influenced them and are affected by them. These changes have also highlighted the current complexity of the notion of property and how far this idea has travelled since earlier hunting and gathering societies carried their possessions with them. We no longer live like that.

14
Refocusing Methods for Creative Work

In the preceding chapters we have summarised much of the literature on creativity. Then, using this research work on creativity as a wide lens, we explored various issues that have been raised within specific fields of media practice. I'd now like to see what effect the reconceptualisation of creativity that has been presented here might have on practical methods for undertaking creative practice. To begin that process I'd like to restate the idea that 'subjective impressions can be projected on to life and thereby become real to projectors' (Volkart 1951, p. 14). Proceeding from this proposition, we can see that actions taken in the world will be couched within the perceptions practitioners have of, in this case, creativity.

It would seem to me that if either the inspirationist or Romantic understandings of creativity are subscribed to by media practitioners, then it would be somewhat difficult for these creative agents to either teach or learn how to be creative? One would either possess creativity or not. This position begs the question: is it really possible to learn to be creative? Judging by the number of self-help books, courses for business administrators, school teachers following creativity-enhancing programmes and the websites dedicated to it, a number of people think this is the case. Of course this depends heavily on what you consider creativity to be. If you subscribe to the notion that only a genius can be creative, then you will be facing tremendous problems in enhancing it, especially if you don't possess the characteristics that have been constructed around the notion of genius. Similarly, if you believe that creativity is dependent entirely on genetics, then you may need to abandon the hope that you could enhance your creativity. You are either born creative or you are not. If your view of creativity is focused squarely at the individual and seen simply, for example, as being a process of

problem solving or problem finding or is entirely dependent on specific cognitive processes, then it may be possible that creativity can be
learnt. However, as we have seen, that might not be all that is involved.
Similarly, if creativity is seen as being dependent only on its acceptance by the society and culture it occurs in, that is context is seen
as all important, then the situation becomes a little more problematic
but nonetheless achievable. But rather than abandoning many of these
ideas, is it possible that each may have something to offer?

As Beth Hennessey and Teresa Amabile suggested in their recent
review of research into creativity in psychology, the field 'has grown
theoretically and methodologically sophisticated [but] investigators in
one subfield often seem unaware of advances in another' (2010, p. 569).
In order to gain a more profound understanding, they suggest that we
need to undertake 'more interdisciplinary research, based on a systems
view of creativity that recognizes a variety of interrelated forces operating at multiple levels' (ibid.). Given the significant work that has also
occurred in sociology, literary studies and philosophy, and from within
cultural and communication studies, it could be suggested that this scenario is equally applicable not only within disciplines but also across
disciplines. What I have been suggesting in the synthesis of ideas presented here is in agreement with Hennessy and Amabile's suggestion.
It also takes up the challenge from Csikszentmihalyi for those interested
in understanding creativity, and we could include media practitioners here, to move beyond a focus on the individual towards a more
encompassing perception of cultural production. I believe that the most
appropriate view of creativity is that it comes about via a confluence of
factors and one of the more encompassing views is that proposed by
the systems model itself. While this model has been largely developed
from within psychology, I believe it can be added to, complemented
and modified by the sophisticated work undertaken by Pierre Bourdieu.
To remind us of this work we can see that Bourdieu (1977, 1990, 1993,
1996) had argued, from the position of an empirical sociologist, that:

> it is the interplay between a *field of works* which presents possibili-
> ties of action to an individual who possesses the necessary *habitus*,
> partially composed of personal levels of *social, cultural, symbolic and
> economic capital* that then inclines them to act and react within
> particular structured and dynamic spaces called *fields*. (McIntyre
> 2009b, p. 161)

From this perspective, *fields* are arenas of production and circulation of
goods, ideas and knowledges and are inhabited by competitive agents

who use various levels of the forms of capital applicable to that field in their struggles to dominate the field. It is from the interplay of all of these factors that cultural production and practice arises. This explanation seems quite similar to me to the systems model of creativity developed from within psychology by Mihaly Csikszentmihalyi (1988, 1997, 1999). He proposed:

> three major factors, that is, a structure of knowledge manifest in a particular symbol system (*domain*), a structured social organisation that understands that body of knowledge (*field*), and an individual agent (*person*) who makes changes to the stored information that pre-exists them, are necessary for creativity to occur. (McIntyre, 2009b, p. 161)

The way these factors interact indicates, for me, the system's essential non-linearity as each component factor in the system, the domain, person and field, is as equally important as the others (Csikszentmihalyi 1988, p. 329). I suggest that it is a synthesis of these ideas that will give us a more Copernican view of creativity rather than the largely Ptolemaic one many practitioners have been relying and acting upon. I also propose that this process can be understood more clearly with the reiteration and clarification of three points.

Firstly, there often appears to be a misleading distinction made between the creativity ordinary people engage in and that which is seen to be extraordinary. This distinction can be resolved by looking again at Margaret Boden's (1994, 2004) conception of P- and H-creativity. As stated earlier, Boden asserts that 'there can be no *psychological* [P] explanation of this historical [H] category. But all H-creative ideas, by definition, are P-creative too' (Boden 1994, p. 77). One must firstly be P-creative prior to becoming H-creative. I believe Boden's dissolution of the hard distinctions affirms a 'mutually constitutive relation between ordinariness and exceptionality of creativity' (Negus & Pickering 2004, p. 159). This view of creativity brings the 'elevated and the mundane into conjunction [and illuminates] how the exceptional and the ordinary feed off each other' (Negus & Pickering 2004, p. 1), and it also reinforces the notion that 'the ordinary is not at odds with the exceptional, but continually open to the possibility of becoming exceptional' (ibid p. 158). From this perspective, creativity is not the result of the extraordinary operation of some universally fixed and mystically transcendent process, but is, in part, a mundane matter of a creative agent immersing themselves in a domain of knowledge and the selection and validation of the variation being socio-culturally dependent. These latter ideas 'are to be celebrated not mystified' (Negus & Pickering, 2004, p. 160), as they open the way to conceiving of exceptional creativity well away from the misleading ideas associated with the outdated conception of 'genius'.

There are, then, a number of circumstances that must be in place for anyone to perform H-creatively. These circumstances depend on temporal, spatial, psychological, biological, social and cultural circumstances coinciding for this to occur. Apart from the biological and psychological, there are all manners of societal and cultural pressures that are beyond the control of the individual which may have already been brought to bear on that person. In other words, the creative agent may have a set of environmental factors operate on them, such as sibling position, social class or educational opportunities, which predispose them to information processing strategies in an unusual way. The person may also be an unusual individual in a genetic sense, who may have been born with longer fingers than normal, which inflects their creative action, for example, in a musical setting. These individual factors may play their part, but it is certain that they are not sufficient, in and of themselves, to produce exceptional or H-creativity. It is also a truism that a creative individual is rarely creative across all domains. Just as one example, Einstein was a paradigm shifting physicist but an average piano player. These revelations tend to reinforce the notion that creativity is not an essentially innate quality possessed by gifted genius figures, who alone have the ability to undertake H-creative processes, but is grounded in a more mundane process accessible to many given the right set of circumstances.

It must also be recognised that not all creators produce on a level playing field. Some will be more adept at various aspects of the creative task than others and many will find ways to approach it differently. As Csikszentmihalyi (1997) has argued, the person involved in creativity must have access to the conventions, rules and ideas of the domain as it is their task to produce some variation in this inherited information. Access is controllable but only to a degree, in as much as whatever needs to be learnt or sought out can be seen to be dependent, once again, on the sociocultural circumstances the person finds themselves in. In addition, the person must also be able to communicate ideas and inventions to the social organisation that is concerned with the creative product. Therefore, an ability to access the field is also important. Many aspects of these above factors we have little or no control over. We cannot govern the way society will react to a revolutionary idea. We cannot govern the times we are born in. We cannot govern the family we are born into, and we certainly cannot govern the sets of genes we have acquired from that family. Therefore, at this stage, we should leave H-creativity for time and the world to pass its judgement on and concentrate on what we as creative agents involved in P-creativity can control, as the latter, in Margaret Boden's terms, may indeed lead to the former.

The second point that needs to be clarified revolves around an eluci-dation of the supposed stages of the creative process adapted by Graeme Wallas (1945, pp. 40–1). Wallas, acknowledging his debt to Helmholz, outlined four stages of creative activity. These are labelled preparation, incubation and illumination which is followed by verification. The preparation stage, according to Wallas, involves the gathering of infor-mation necessary to the process. The problem is defined as well at this early stage. Incubation is a stage where the person may not necessarily be consciously thinking about the problem. We step back from it and let our minds contemplate and work through all aspects of it. This stage may be temporally discontinuous in as much as it may occur very briefly and take mere minutes. It can be much longer-term lasting, for weeks and even years. The illumination stage consists of 'the appearance of the "happy idea" together with the psychological events which immedi-ately preceded and accompanied that appearance' (Wallas 1945, p. 41). As Ned Herrmann indicates, illuminations 'can be pieces of the whole or the whole itself.... Unlike the other stages, illumination is often very brief, involving a tremendous rush of insights within a few minutes or hours' (Herrmann 1998). As Wallas himself asserts, the final stage, ver-ification, is a period 'in which both the validity of the idea was tested, and the idea was reduced to exact form' (Wallas 1945, p. 41).

Robert Weisberg, however, contends that it is difficult to categorise each creative step in a universal set of stages, and can find little evidence, particularly of incubation, apart from self-reportage from creative indi-viduals. It should be noted however that even though Wallas's stages were based on 'his own introspection and scattered observations', they have been widely accepted by many theorists (Rothenberg & Hausman 1976, p. 69). Nonetheless, adding a fifth step of elaboration where the object is manifest in material form, Csikszentmihalyi argues 'it is essen-tial to remember...that the five stages in reality are not exclusive but typically overlap and recur several times before the process is completed' (Csikszentmihalyi 1997, p. 83). He goes on to assert:

this classic analytic framework leading from preparation to elabora-tion gives a severely distorted picture of the creative process if it is taken too literally. A person who makes a creative contribution never just slogs through the long last stage of elaboration. This part of the process is constantly interrupted by periods of incubation and is punctuated by epiphanies. Many fresh insights emerge as one is presumably just putting finishing touches on the initial insight....Thus the creative process is less linear than recursive. How many iterations it goes through, how many loops are involved, how many insights are needed, depends on the depth and breadth of the issues dealt with. Sometimes incubation lasts for years; sometimes it takes a few hours. Sometimes the creative idea includes one deep insight and innumerable small ones. In some cases, as with Darwin's formulation of the theory of evolution, the basic insight may appear slowly, in separate disconnected flashes that take years to coalesce into a coherent idea. (1997, pp. 80–1)

What can be derived for this set of critiques and assertions is that while it is difficult to convincingly provide evidence that creativity occurs in a linear, orderly sequential way, it would be equally difficult to argue that preparation, incubation, illumination, verification or elaboration do not exist as aspects of creativity. For example, in order to partake of the domain they are working with each media practitioner, or the collaborative group acting as the creative agent within the media field, has to gather information, whether that is a lifelong process of understanding the domain itself or a short-term one of gaining particular information for the specific problem they are working on. In which case, good media practitioners immerse themselves in the knowledge system pertinent to their field. They will also need to be motivated to do this. This motivation may just as readily come from alleged 'external' factors (having to do it) as well as the supposed 'internal' ones (wanting to do it) (Csikszentmihalyi 1997, pp. 22–3). There is quite a bit of evidence to show that while people feel best when the tasks they engage in are carried out on a voluntary basis, they do not feel any worse when what they do is obligatory (ibid.). In this regard, Amabile and Tighe concede that the analysis that sees extrinsic motivation leading to 'satisficing', or simply taking attention away from the task instead of exploring problems fully, may be a little misleading. They argue with some qualification that:

whatever leads a problem-solver to get deeply involved in thinking about the task will enhance creativity. Whatever draws attention away from the task, by instilling the desire to 'satisfice', will lessen creativity. (1993, p. 21)

Noting that the internal/external dichotomy itself appears to be romantically inspired (Eisenberger & Shanock 2003), one could say that the most appropriate motivator is to ignore whether you are intrinsically or extrinsically motivated. Instead, look for the challenges that are equal to your skills and make sure you start the autotelic, or flow, experience happening. There is enough evidence to suggest that this process will drive you back to the work time and time again (Csikszentmihalyi & Csikszentmihalyi 1988).

Failures will also prove to be strong motivators in stimulating creative activity. It is the case that many media practitioners are often unaware in the early stages of their careers of how many failures it took those they admire to create a success. It must be said that many successful people have produced 'their fair share of mediocre work' (Negus & Pickering 2004, p. 160). Because of the continual effort, experimentation and hard work required of them, many successful people seem to others to be resilient and 'have immense self-confidence' (Sawyer 2006, pp. 311–2), mostly borne of many failures and enough successes to have conditioned these practitioners to take risks. As Sawyer asserts, however, 'being confident isn't the same thing as being naïve. Confidence will come from years of preparation in the domain, and from additional years of hard work once you've learnt the domain' (ibid.). Therefore, preparation is an important activity in engaging with creativity.

Incubation is of course, as mentioned above, the most problematic of Wallas's stages with very little evidence to suggest that, as described by Wallas, it is a vital stage in the process (Weisberg 1993). But cogitation of some form does take place. In addition, the existence of illumination has, however, been documented widely. The mistake made here is that this step has often been assumed to be the whole process and as such provided a basis for the notion that creativity is simply a 'bolt from the blue'. However, if the notion of intuition is substituted for both incubation and illumination, then a great deal of evidence can be produced for the existence of this phenomenon.

Tony Bastick asserts that intuition has been perceived in a number of ways. It has been variously theorised, like the related concepts of 'the muse' and 'genius', as a mystical metaphysical process. Linked to this is the view that intuition can be seen as a telepathic process linked to parapsychological phenomena (Bastick 1982, pp. 1–20). On the other hand, intuition has also been contrasted to linear, analytical processes of logic and it has also been seen as dependent on prior experience, as in the case of spontaneous intuition after a period of preparation and incubation. Bastick however asserts that intuition can be more accurately described as a form of non-linear parallel processing of global multi-categorised information (1982, p. 215). With evidence mounting from neuropsychology of the global processing of information occurring in the brain, the concept of intuition put forward by Bastick becomes a more reasonable one to use in this case. In fact, Bastick claims that Wallas's first three stages (preparation, incubation and illumination) can be incorporated 'into the one phase of "intuition" so that the creative process may be thought of as just two stages, *viz.* intuition followed by verification' (1982, pp. 310–1). It may well be that verification could be collapsed into intuition as well, but I will return to the question of intuition in a moment.

If creativity is defined as an idea that is novel or unique, a decision has to be made about the work's novelty or originality. Verification is thus important as creators and the fields they work inside make judgements about what to keep, what not to keep, whether an edit is 'working', whether this word is better to use in this context or not and so on. As Gardner states, 'a creative individual is one who regularly solves problems, fashions products, and/or poses new questions in a domain in a way which is initially considered novel but which is ultimately accepted in at least one cultural setting' (Gardner 1993b, p. 32). He adds that 'no person or work or process can be considered creative unless it is so deemed by relevant social institutions' (ibid.). Verification then becomes important through the actions of the field in two ways; they, firstly, confirm, encourage and facilitate the actions of the creative agent and, secondly, verify that the process or product created fits the domain. Elaboration is a feature of creativity where an idea is manifest as an object. Quite simply, creative products do get made. In this case media practitioners must gain a working understanding of the complex relationship that exists between themselves as creative agents and the structural aspects of the field and domain they engage with in order to ensure their work is produced and accepted.

This brings us to the third point of clarification. It involves reflecting again on the question of the dynamic relationship between agency and structure. John Tulloch has argued that 'the relationship between "agency" and the "bounds" of social structure is always a dynamic one ("subjects" are in other words, never simply "positioned" as "effects" of structure)' (1990, p. 13). As I have also suggested a number of times, the arguments that spring from the bipolar oppositions that underpin many of the assumptions made about creativity in the media can be resolved once it is realised that these dichotomies are complementary rather than oppositional (Kelso & Engstrm 2008). In this case media practitioners don't have to eschew a set of constraints to be creative. They can become creative by assimilating into their being the codes, conventions and knowledge frameworks their particular media engages with and taking on board the way the social organisation of the field they deal with makes decisions. Once these structured processes become intuitive to a practitioner, as described above, the ideas and actions that spring from them will follow. These necessary structures can be embraced more fully, with obvious caution, once it is realised that structures not only inhibit and constrain creativity but they, at one and the same time, just as readily encourage and enable it. To reinforce this point Boden has argued that constraints, usually seen in the perception of generative systems or collaborative processes, sometimes construed as interference from members of the field, 'far from being opposed to creativity – make creativity possible' (1994, p. 79). Both Giddens and Bourdieu have presented similar propositions. Giddens argues that 'structure is not to be equated with constraint but is always both constraining and enabling' (1984, p. 25). According to David Swartz, Bourdieu argues against:

> conceptualising human action as a direct, unmediated response to external factors, whether they be identified as micro-structures of interactions or macro-level cultural, social, or economic factors. Nor does Bourdieu see action as the simple outgrowth from internal factors, such as conscious intentions and calculations, as posited by voluntarists and rational-actor models of human action.... Bourdieu wants to transcend this dichotomy by conceptualizing action so that micro and macro, voluntarist and determinist dimensions of human activity are integrated into a single conceptual movement rather than isolated as mutually exclusive forms of explanation. (Swartz 1997, p. 9)

In short, agency and structure are interdependent. Furthermore, Janet Wolff has argued, as we have seen, that all action 'arises in the complex conjunction of numerous structural determinants and conditions' (Wolff 1981, p. 9). Given this, one can also argue that the presence of external structures, that is the presence of the field and the domain, will not just detract from but will also lead to creative activity.

Considering this view of the interdependence of agency and structure, it is obvious by now that conceptualising creativity as a set of elements that occur in stages that are discrete and linear may not be overly accurate or indeed entirely useful. It may be better to see them conceptually as part of a non-linear system with any and all of them occurring at various times and even coincidentally. In which case we can again declare that creativity is an activity where some process or product, one that is considered to be unique and valuable in at least one social setting, comes about from a set of antecedent conditions through the located actions of a creative agent. Each factor belongs to a system in operation and creativity emerges from that system in operation.

Given that I suggested earlier that there are multiple factors involved in creativity and many of these we have little or no control over, I would reinforce the idea that there are still, nonetheless, a multiplicity of factors we can do something about. For example, as Keith Sawyer (2006, p. 307) suggests, an individual can actively choose a domain, a body of knowledge existent in a field of works, out of the ones on offer to them that they will feel comfortable working with. It may also be necessary to focus on one domain for extended periods as most practitioners spend years internalising it and building relevant skills until it becomes part of their daily practice. This advice is linked to the notion of global processing suggested by Bastick above in his definition of intuition as a form of non-linear parallel processing of global multi-categorised information (Bastick 1982, p. 215). It also supports, in part, Donald Schon's contention that practitioners utilise a 'feel' for the work they engage in.

Schon asserts that in setting aside the idea that practice is an application of knowledge, we can readily observe that the spontaneous behaviour of skilful practice is, according to Chester Barnard, a form of non-logical process which is often 'not capable of being expressed in words or as reasoning, and which are only made known by a judgement, decision or action' (Schon 1983, p. 51). These processes may occur so rapidly that it is difficult to analyse by those involved in them. Schon argues, via Barnard, that our bias towards logical analytical thinking 'blinds us to the non-logical processes which are omnipresent in effective practice' (Schon 1983, p. 52). He also argues, this time via Polanyi (1967), that the manifestation of tacit knowledge is one of these processes. It is reliant on the acquisition of a skill and is manifest in the feelings we acquire in repetitive exercise of the practice we are engaged in, 'of which we are initially aware become internalised in our tacit knowing' (Schon 1983, p. 52). He contends that 'we can often recognise and correct the "bad fit" of a form to its context, but that we usually cannot describe the rules by which we find a fit bad or recognise the corrected form to be good' (Schon 1983, p. 52). As media practitioners we just know that 'it works' in that 'we can recognise and describe deviations from a norm very much more clearly than we can describe the norm itself' (Polanyi quoted in Schon 1983, p. 53). Schon goes on to suggest that 'there are actions, recognitions, and judgements which we know how to carry out spontaneously; we do not have to think about them prior to or during their performance' (1983, p. 54); secondly, 'we are often unaware of having learned to do these things – we simply find ourselves doing them' (ibid.); thirdly, we may have been once cognisant of the understandings which we then 'internalised in our feeling for the stuff of action. In other cases, we may never have been aware of them. In both cases, however, we are usually unable to describe the knowing which our action reveals' (ibid.). It is this process that Schon describes as practitioners 'finding the groove' or having a 'feel' for their material (Schon 1983, p. 55).

For me, these ideas correspond in a number of ways to the propositions on self-directed anticipative learning (SDAL) put forward by Christensen and Hooker (2004) in their research into complex adaptive systems and they also match well with Pierre Bourdieu's concepts. He argues that in order for a person to become a practitioner utilising the knowledge base, the internalised codes and manner of thought of the maker, that person must firstly acquire the cultural capital pertinent to their area of concern. In acquiring this cultural knowledge they undergo a long process of inculcation or immersion in the knowledge, developing a 'feel' for it, or a sense of how it operates. Bourdieu calls this feel for the way things are done 'habitus'. Just to remind us, Johnson has described habitus in the following way:

> a 'feel for the game', a 'practical sense' (*sens practique*) that inclines agents to act and react in specific situations in a manner that is not always calculated and that is not simply a question of conscious obedience to rules. [It] is the result of a long process of inculcation, beginning in early childhood, which becomes a 'second sense' or a second nature. (Bourdieu 1993, p. 5)

In this case immersing oneself in a domain of knowledge would be an extremely good idea. Equally importantly, immersing oneself in the way a field works would also be very beneficial. Either way it is necessary to immerse yourself in the world you wish to become creative in. In this case we can say that creativity requires work.

The well-worn adage that creativity is 1 per cent inspiration and 99 per cent perspiration is borne out by an examination of creative individuals both at the P-level and the H-level. One need only look at the people regarded in the West as highly creative and note the effort they put into their area of work before they were recognised as being creative. Howard Gardner's study of important creators of the modern era where he examined the life and work of Eliot, Einstein, Picasso, Stravinsky, Martha Graham, Gandhi and Freud (1993a) provides an illustration. To support this idea Robert Weisberg also gives several accounts of the mundanity of ongoing creative activity for some of the same significant creators (Sternberg 1988). Similarly, Walberg also argues that 'distinguished accomplishment seems partly a matter of continuous and concentrated effort over a decade or more' (Sternberg 1988, p. 345). This evidence refutes, to a degree, the Romantic ideal and the concept that creativity only results from inspiration or a bolt from the blue. In the end, sitting around and waiting for inspiration, as the sole activity designed to bring on the creative process, may only result in sitting around and waiting for inspiration. The 'A-ha' experiences only come about after considerable immersion in the domain. In this case we can say that creativity is an activity. It requires both short- and long-term effort.

In any endeavour to become creative, according to Robert Weisberg, what is required is a commitment to and an acquisition of expertise in the chosen domain. Commitment for many creative people 'provides sufficient time for the small changes that occur as one gathers experience in some domain to evolve into something truly original and innovative' (Sternberg 1988, p. 173). Weisberg comments on this accumulation of expertise by stating that:

> These two aspects of creative work, commitment and expertise within one's own area, are neither profound nor novel. All scientists and artists have extensive training, either formally or informally, and very few individuals make a mark in the world without a relatively long commitment to an area beyond their actual training. (ibid.)

The seemingly obvious downside to all this acquisition of particular knowledge is the widespread belief that if rules are internalised, then thinking will be bound by them and the creative process will become inevitably habitual and thus non-creative. Sharon Bailin, as mentioned prior, argues that the reverse may be true in as much as the evidence suggests that creation, even of the paradigm shifting sort, 'is usually less radical a departure from the existing framework than we tend to believe' (1988, p. 89). She suggests that 'one never breaks all the rules, since to do so would be to abandon the discipline' (Bailin 1988, pp. 96–7).

What the above tends to indicate though is that certain individuals have seen the necessity to go beyond habitual thought process.

As a result they have produced a set of novel ideas that have been extrapolated from the conventions of the domain, indicating that one must understand these traditions in the first place. As Negus and Pickering have argued, rather than seeing tradition and innovation as the antithesis of each other:

> we want to consider tradition and innovative forms and practices as informing and supporting each other. It is only by thinking about their interrelationship that we can understand processes of creativity and cultural change. Creativity doesn't emerge out of a vacuum, but builds on one or more existing cultural traditions. This is true of poetry, architecture, film-making, styles of singing and any number of other examples. In this sense creative talent requires a tradition so that it can learn how to go further within it or beyond it. Innovation should be understood by rejecting those approaches which set it squarely against tradition and established cultural practice. (2004, p. 91)

Not only is there a deep connection between creative activity and a recognition and use of the rules, conventions and techniques pertinent to a domain, but the codes, conventions, values and mores of a field are necessary knowledges for a creative agent to acquire.

Keith Sawyer (2006, pp. 307–8) suggests that a creative agent should by necessity become involved in the field, the social organisation that understands and makes decisions about the domain they work in and one that suits their particular needs. He also advises that some fields will require lots of networking. The media is no exception. The ability to engage in consultation, collaboration, negotiation and conflict resolution are highly prized within this field of cultural production since fields are, according to Bourdieu (1993), arenas of social contestation where struggles for dominance take place. Cultural, symbolic, social and economic capital are employed in a variety of ways by *all* active players in the field of cultural production, specifically the media industries, sometimes called culture industries and increasingly referred to as creative industries, so it is important to realise that some connection and interaction with the field will be necessary in order to gain support to enable the creative work to take place and for the agent to continue that creative activity. In this case there is an imperative to focus outwards. Sawyer (2006) asserts that a useful way to begin the journey towards being creative is to examine the structure of the field, find out how it makes decisions and how it structures the selection processes it uses to discern novelty. This information will help you negotiate your entry into and survival in this active arena of social contestation. As Sawyer states, 'the most successful creative people are very good at introducing their ideas to the field' (2006, p. 309) and many successful creative operatives in the media are adept at collaboration.

As has been argued elsewhere (Kerrigan & McIntyre 2010), Paulus and Nijstad (2003) have collated much of the research into group creativity and identified various aspects of the way collaborative groups function, such as those typically found in the production of media. While they seem to favour a somewhat linear explanation, that is, they set out a model of collaboration that is based on a cyclic process, qualified with heavily recursive and iterative aspects, similar arguments can be made as the ones set out above in regard to the staged process of creativity. In short, from the model they develop 'it can be seen that the movement of ideas, knowledge sharing and critical feedback on processes and products is comparable to the systems model in that it also identifies individual, field and domain interactions necessary to produce artefacts' (Kerrigan & McIntyre 2010, p. 125). As mentioned previously, Csikszentmihalyi (2004) has used the systems model to explain the collaborative production of films and Sawyer (2006), who adapted the model and renamed it the sociocultural approach, has used it to illustrate the collaborative activity of improvisatory drama groups, jazz ensembles and the way creativity works within corporate settings (Sawyer 2007). It can also be seen from the other chapters in this book that this situation is equally applicable to radio, television, film and popular music. In other words collaboration in the media, the work of many people acting together, is systemic. This is especially the case, as argued earlier, if the conception of a creative agent encompasses both the way this term is used in actor network theory (Callon 1987, Latour 2005) and those varied collective enterprises media practitioners deal with on a daily basis are also seen as creative agents. This is a difficult proposition to accommodate if you still adhere to the Romantic myths ingrained as common sense within Western culture, but what it indicates for me, on a practical level, is that a very pragmatic approach is required in undertaking creative work inside various media institutions be they traditional or those emerging and competing with them via digitisation.

As Sawyer (2006, p. 311) advises, media practitioners should not be afraid of collaboration. It is inevitable that many colleagues in the media will not only be able to contribute well to collaborative work but when they do they will invest their own reputation, their own hard-earned cultural and social capital, in any solution they also have faith in. In this case a network of like-minded people is crucial to the development of possible creative activity. The desire for credit most media practitioners feel is understandable given the focus on the individual in the West, noting that this is not the case for all cultures across the globe (Niu & Sternberg 2006), and it is also understandable in terms of a desire for adequate remuneration within a system of intellectual property allocation that has itself 'adopted a "romantic" model of authorship' (Bently 2009, p. 192). However, there is ample evidence to suggest that a fear of not being sufficiently remunerated could prevent a critical collaboration. One adage that seems to ring true is that 50 per cent of something appears better than 100 per cent of nothing. Furthermore, it can be confirmed that creative ideas, processes and products are often enhanced by collaboration (Sawyer 2006, p. 311). The obvious caution is that, given the possible rewards at stake, one must proceed by assessing the field wisely. Choose those collaborators who can be trusted to push both you and the work you are all creating to its maximum potential. In other words, get to know the field as well as you know the domain. Immerse yourself in both.

In summing up, I want to reiterate the idea that creativity is systemic. It comes about when a domain of knowledge intersects with a social organisation that can affect that domain of knowledge and both of these intersect at the same time with a creative agent who possesses an idiosyncratic yet shared set of attributes and circumstances. This is the case whether that creative agent is seen as a single person or a collective enterprise. As well as the daily application of everybody's ordinary creative abilities, it seems obvious to me that extraordinary work can take place within this system. We may not be able to use the word 'genius' in quite the same way anymore, but you can be guaranteed that exceptional and extraordinary work will continue to emerge out of this dynamic system in operation. In a similar way the notion of 'Art', as conceived and applied in the West, may also be highly problematic, but it is also certain that the making of aesthetically pleasing and meaningful objects will be a prime feature of the lives of media practitioners as they continue to engage with the dynamic aspects of creativity and cultural production.

Holding this set of ideas in mind, I want to return briefly to a proposition suggested by Csikszentmihalyi in 1988 (p. 336). He appealed for those involved in understanding cultural production to let go of what he called the Ptolemaic view of creativity. If we, as scholars and practitioners, continue to locate the individual in the centre of a radius of creative activity, we may be in danger of not grasping the entirety of the picture and risk much that is to be derived from reconceptualising creativity as systemic. Shifting our gaze away from a person-centred view allows us to see that there are other equally important factors at play; factors that are just as necessary for creativity to occur. This shift in thinking does not mean we need to lose appreciation for what individuals do. When Copernicus set humanity on the road to conceiving of the earth as part of a much larger solar system in operation, not a great deal changed as far as the earth was concerned. The people on this planet still carried on doing much of what they had always done. They got up in the morning, worked and fought as they felt the sun go overhead and then rested and prepared for the evening as they watched it settle in the West. But now they know that everything doesn't revolve around themselves and the globe they exist on. Now they know there is much more to it than that. And that has changed everything.

Bibliography

ABC (1985) 'The Role of a National Broadcaster in Contemporary Australia: ABC position paper', *Australian Broadcasting Corporation* (Sydney: ABC Corporate Relations Department).

——(1987) 'Current Editorial & Programming Practices in ABC Radio and Television', *Australian Broadcasting Corporation* (Sydney: ABC Corporate Relations Department).

——(2000) 'The ABC's Charter', *Australian Broadcasting Corporation*, http://www.abc.net.au/corp/charter.htm, date accessed 6 December 2000.

Adams, J. (1976) *Conceptual Blockbusting: A Pleasurable Guide to Better Problem Solving* (San Francisco: San Francisco Book Co.).

Adorno, T. (1941) 'On Popular Music', *Studies in Philosophy and Social Science*, 9, 17–48.

Alexander, V. (2003) *Sociology of the Arts: Exploring Fine and Popular Forms* (Malden, MA: Blackwell).

Allan, R. (ed.) (1990) *The Concise Oxford Dictionary of Current English Usage* (Oxford: Clarendon Press).

Allen, R. & Hill, A. (eds) (2004) *The Television Studies Reader* (London: Routledge).

Alvarado, M. & Buscombe, E. (1978) *Hazell: The Making of a TV Series* (London: British Film Institute).

Amabile, T. (1983) *The Social Psychology of Creativity* (New York: Springer-Verlag).

——(1996) *Creativity in Context* (Boulder, CO: Westview Press).

Amabile, T. & Tighe, E. (1993) 'Questions of Creativity', in J. Brockman (ed.) *Creativity: The Reality Club 4* (New York: Touchstone), pp. 7–27.

Ang, I. (1990) 'Culture and Communication: Towards an Ethnographic Critique of Media Consumption in the Transnational Media System', *European Journal of Communication*, 5, 239–260.

Ang, I. (1991) *Desperately Seeking the Audience* (New York: Routledge).

Anthony, L. (1998) 'Radio Heads', in T. Creswell (ed.) *Juice*, (April) (Sydney: Terraplane Press).

APRA/AMCOS (2010) 'An Overview of APRA and AMCOS' 2010 End of Year Financial 13Results', *APRA/AMCOS*, http://issuu.com/apraamcos/docs/2010yearinreview, date accessed 14 October 2001, 12–13.

Archer, M. (2000) *Being Human: The Problem of Agency* (New York: Cambridge University Press).

——(2003) *Structure Agency and the Internal Conversation* (Cambridge: Cambridge University Press).

ARIA (2006) 'Australian Recorded Music Sales for 6 Months to 30 June 2006: Digital Music and Strong Album Sales Drive Local Music Market', *ARIA News webpage*, http://www.aria.com.au/pages/httpwww.aria.com.aupagesnews-ARIAhalfyearResults.htm, date accessed 24 October 2006.

Aristotle (1960) *Metaphysics* (Ann Arbor: Michigan University Press).

Ashby, F., A. Isen & Turken, U. (1999) 'A Neuropsychological Theory of Positive Affect and Its Influence on Cognition', *Psychological Review*, 106(3), 529–50.

Bailin, S. (1988) *Achieving Extraordinary Ends: An Essay on Creativity* (Dordecht: Kluwer Academic Publishers).

Barker, H. & Taylor, Y. (2007) *Faking It: The Quest for Authenticity in Popular Music* (New York: W.W. Norton & Co.).

Barthes, R. (1970) *S/Z* (Paris: Éditions du Seuil).

———(1977) 'The Death of the Author', in *Image, Music, Text* (New York: Noonday Press), pp. 142–53.

———(1990) 'The Grain of the Voice', in S. Frith & A. Goodwin (eds) *On Record: Rock, Pop, and the Written Word* (London: Routledge), pp. 293–300.

Bastick, T. (1982) *Intuition: How We Think and Act* (Chichester UK: John Wiley and Sons).

Baxter, J. (1996) *Steven Spielberg: The Unauthorised Biography* (London: Harper Collins).

Beavers, S. (2002) '*The West Wing* as a Pedagogical Tool', *Political Science & Politics*, 35, 213–16.

Becker, H. (1982) *Art Worlds* (Los Angeles: University of California Press).

Bendix, R. (1997) *In Search of Authenticity: The Formation of Folklore Studies* (Madison, WL: University of Wisconsin Press).

Benjamin, W. (1970) 'The Work of Art in the Age of Mechanical Reproduction', in H. Arendt (ed.) *Illuminations* (London: Jonathan Cape), pp. 219–26.

Bently, L. (1994) 'Copyright and the Death of the Author in Literature and Law', *The Modern Law Review*, 57, 973–86.

———(2009) 'Authorship of Popular Music in UK Copyright Law', *Information, Communication & Society*, 12(2), 179–204.

Berger, A. (1994) *Popular Culture Genres: Theories and Texts* (London: Sage).

———(1995a) *The Essentials of Mass Communication Theory* (Thousand Oaks, CA: Sage).

———(1995b) *Cultural Criticism: A Primer of Key Concepts* (Thousand Oaks, CA: Sage).

Bergquist, C. (2006) 'A Comparative View of Creativity Theories: Psychoanalytic, Behaviouristic and Humanistic', *Vantage Quest*, http://www.vantagequest.org/trees/comparative.htm, date accessed 19 March 2007.

Berman, M. (1970) *The Politics of Authenticity: Radical Individualism and the Emergence of Modern Society* (New York: Atheneum).

Bhaskar, R. (1979) *The Possibility of Naturalism: A Philosophical Critique of the Contemporary Human Sciences* (Brighton: Harvester Press).

Bihali-Merin, O. (1984) *World Encyclopedia of Naive Art* (London: Frederick Muller).

Boden, M. (1994) *Dimensions of Creativity* (Cambridge, MA: MIT Press).

———(2004) *The Creative Mind: Myths and Mechanisms*, 2nd edn (London: Routledge).

Bordwell, D. & Thompson, K. (1990) *Film Art: An Introduction*, 3rd edn (New York: McGraw-Hill).

———(1997) *Film Art: An Introduction*, 5th edn (New York: McGraw-Hill).

———(2004) *Film Art: An Introduction*, 7th edn (Boston: McGraw-Hill).

Bourdieu, P. (1977) *Outline of a Theory of Practice* (Cambridge: Cambridge University Press).

———(1984) *Distinction: A Social Critique of the Judgement of Taste* (Cambridge, MA: Harvard University Press).

———(1986) 'The Forms of Capital', in Richardson, J. (ed) *Handbook of Theory and Research for the Sociology of Education* (New York: Greenwood Press), pp. 241–58.

———(1990) *The Logic of Practice* (Cambridge: Polity Press).

———(1993) *Field of Cultural Production*, ed. R. Johnson (New York: Columbia University Press).

———(1996) *The Rules of Art: Genesis and Structure of the Literary Field* (Cambridge: Polity Press).

———(1998) *On Television and Journalism* (London: Pluto).

———(2005) 'The Political Field, the Social Science Field and the Journalistic Field', in R. Benson & E. Neveu (eds) *Bourdieu and the Journalistic Field* (Cambridge: Polity Press), pp. 29–47.

Brennan, P. (n.d.) 'Timeline: A History of Copyright in the U.S.', http://arl.cni.org/info/frn/copy/timeline.html, date accessed 25 May 2001.

Brockman, J. (ed.) (1993) *Creativity: The Reality Club 4* (New York: Touchstone).

Brode, D. (1995) *The Films of Steven Spielberg* (New York: Citadel).

Brown, A. (ed.) (1982) *History of Rock* (Scarborough: Orbis Publishing).

Buscombe, E. (1981) 'Ideas of Authorship', in J. Caughie (ed.) *Theories of Authorship: A Reader* (London: Routledge & Kegan Paul).

Byrne, M. (1999) 'Music Directors Place in the Radio Station: Notes for Guest Lecture', *CMNS2050 Radio Industry Studies*, University of Newcastle, 17 May.

Callon, M. (1987) 'Society in the Making: The Study of Technology as a Tool for Sociological Analysis', in W. Bijker et al. (eds) *The Social Construction of Technological Systems* (London: MIT Press), pp. 83–103.

Campany, D. (ed.) (2003) *Art and Photography* (London: Phaidon).

Caputo, J. & Yount, M. (eds) (1993) *Foucault and the Critiques of Institutions* (Pennsylvania: Pennsylvania University Press).

Castaneda, C. (1968) *The Teachings of Don Juan; a Yaqui Way of Knowledge* (Berkeley: University of California Press).

Castells, M. (1996) *The Rise of the Network Society, The Information Age: Economy Society and Culture Vol 1* (Oxford: Blackwell).

Chatman, S. (1978) *Story and Discourse: Narrative Structure in Fiction and Film* (Ithaca NY: Cornell University Press).

Christensen, W. & Hooker, C. (2004) 'Self-Directed Agents', *Complex Adaptive Systems Research Group*, University of Newcastle, http://www.newcastle.edu.au/centre/casrg/publications/C&HfV10.pdf, date accessed 29 October 2004.

Clark, K. (1969) *Civilisation: A Personal View* (London: British Broadcasting Corporation).

Collingwood, R. (1963) *The Principles of Art* (Oxford: Clarendon Press).

Cornell Law Institute (1999) 'U.S. Code: Title 17, Section 102 (a)(2), Legal Information Institute', *Cornell Law Institute*, http://www4.law.cornell.edu/uscode/17/102.html, date accessed 25 January 1999.

Corner, J. & Hawthorn, J. (1993) *Communication Studies: An Introductory Reader* (London: Edward Arnold).

Cottle, S. (2007) 'Ethnography and News Production: New(s) Developments in the Field', *Sociology Compass*, 1(1), 1–16.

Csikszentmihalyi, M. (1988) 'Society, Culture and Person: A Systems View of Creativity', in R. Sternberg (ed.) *The Nature of Creativity: Contemporary Psychological Perspectives* (New York: Cambridge University Press), pp. 325–9.

———(1990) 'The Domain of Creativity', in M. Runco & R. Albert (eds) *Theories of Creativity* (Newbury Park, CA: Sage), pp. 190–212.

———(1991) *Flow: The Psychology of Optimal Experience* (New York: Harper Perrenial).

———(1997) *Creativity: Flow and the Psychology of Discovery and Invention* (New York: Harper Collins).

———(1999) 'Implications of a Systems Perspective for the Study of Creativity', in R. Sternberg (ed.) *Handbook of Creativity* (Cambridge: Cambridge University Press), pp. 313–35.

———(2004) 'Creativity across the Life-span: A Systems View', http://www.ditd. org/Cybersource/record.aspx?sid=10559&scat=902&stype=110&sort=SrcCat% 2cSrcCod%2cSourceName%2c+SourceARRating%2c+lastUpdated+DESC, date accessed 17 December 2004.

Csikszentmihalyi, M. & Csikszentmihalyi, I. (eds) (1988) *Optimal Experience: Psychological Studies of Flow in Consciousness* (New York: Cambridge University Press).

Cunningham, S. & Turner, G. (eds) (1993) *The Media in Australia: Industries, Texts, Audiences* (Sydney: Allen & Unwin).

Dacey, J. & Lennon, K. (1998) *Understanding Creativity: The Interplay of Biological, Psychological, and Social Factors* (San Francisco: Jossey-Bass).

de Bono, E. (1971) *Lateral Thinking for Management* (New York: McGraw-Hill).

de Bono, E. (1992) *Serious Creativity: Using the Power of Lateral Thinking to Create New Ideas* (New York: Harper Collins).

de George, R. & de George, F. (1972) *The Structuralists: From Marx to Levi-Strauss* (New York: Doubleday).

Demers, J. (2006) *Steal This Music: How Intellectual Property Law Affects Musical Creativity* (Athens, Georgia: University of Georgia Press).

Deutsch, E. (1982) *Personhood, Creativity and Freedom* (Honolulu: University of Hawaii Press).

Dissanayake, E. (1995) *Homo Aestheticus: Where Art Comes From and Why* (Seattle: University of Washington Press).

Easthope, A, & McGowan, K. (eds.) (1992) *A Critical and Cultural Theory Reader* (North Sydney: Allen & Unwin).

Eckstein, L. (2006) 'Torpedoing the Authorship of Pop: A Reading of Gorillaz' "Feel Good Inc." ', *Popular Music*, 28(2), 239–55.

Edwards, B. (1979) *Drawing on the Right Side of the Brain: A Course in Enhancing Creativity and Artistic Confidence* (New York: St. Martin's Press).

Eisenberger, R. & Shanock, L. (2003) 'Rewards, Intrinsic Motivation, and Creativity: A Case Study of Conceptual and Methodological Isolation', *Creativity Research Journal*, 15(2–3), 121–30.

Eliasmith, C. (n.d.) 'Dualism', *Dictionary of Philosophy of Mind*, http://philosophy. uwaterloo.ca/MindDict/dualism.html, date accessed 16 April 2010.

Ellis, J. (2004) 'Television Production', in R. Allen & A. Hill (eds) *The Television Studies Reader* (London: Routledge), pp. 258–66.

Erickson, M. (n.d.) 'Pay Lars', http://www.paylars.com/more_info.asp, date accessed 25 September 2006.

Evans, P. & Deehan, G. (1988) *The Keys to Creativity* (London: Grafton Books).

Feldman, D., Csikszentmihalyi, M. & Gardner, H. (1994) *Changing the World: A Framework for the Study of Creativity* (Westport, CT: Praeger).

Ferguson, O. (1979) 'Before the Cameras Roll', in G. Mast & M. Cohen (eds) *Film Theory and Criticism: Introductory Readings*, 2nd edn (New York: Oxford University Press).

Field, S. (1988) *Screenplay: The Foundations of Screenwriting* (Los Angeles: Dell).

Finke, R. (1989) *Principles of Mental Imagery* (Cambridge, MA: MIT Press).

Fiske, J. (1987) *Television Culture* (London: Methuen).

———(1990) *Introduction to Communication Studies* (London: Routledge).

Flew, T. (2005) *New Media: An Introduction* (South Melbourne: Oxford University Press).

Florida, R. (2002) *The Rise of the Creative Class* (New York: Basic Books).

Foster, A. & Blau, J. (1989) *Art and Society: Readings in the Sociology of the Arts* (New York: State University of New York Press).

Foucault, M. (1977) *Language, Counter-Memory, Practice: Selected Essays and Interviews*, ed. D. Bouchard (Ithaca NY: Cornell University Press).

———(1979) 'What Is an Author', in J. Harare (ed.) *Textual Strategies: Perspectives in Post-structural Criticism* (New York: Cornell University Press), pp. 141–60.

———(1980) *Power/Knowledge: Selected Interviews and Other Writings, 1972–1977*, ed. C. Gordon (Brighton, Sussex: Harvester Press).

Freud, S. (1959) 'The Relation of the Poet to Daydreaming', in J. Strachey (ed.) *Collected Papers*, Vol. 4, (Hogarth: London).

Frith, S. & Goodwin, A. (eds) (1990) *On Record* (New York: Pantheon Books).

Frow, J. & Morris, M. (1993) *Australian Cultural Studies: A Reader* (Sydney: Allen & Unwin).

Fulton, J. (2008) 'Print Journalism and the Creative Process: Traditional versus Digital', *Conference on Comparative Journalism Studies 2008*, Hobart, Tasmania: University of Tasmania, http://www.utas.edu.au/ejel/journalsimstudies/documents/CJS08%20Fulton%20revised%20paper.pdf, date accessed 8 April 2008.

———(2010) 'Print Journalism and the Creative Process: The Social Organisation of Journalism and Its Influence on Print Journalists' Creative Practices', *Media, Democracy & Change: Refereed Proceedings of the Australian and New Zealand Communications Association Annual Conference*, Australian and New Zealand Communication Association, Old Parliament House, Canberra, 7–9 July 2010, http://www.canberra.edu.au/anzca2010/attachments/pdf/Print-journalism-and-the-creative-process.pdf, date accessed 15 November 2010.

Galton, F. (1892) *Hereditary Genius* (London: Watts).

———(1950) *Hereditary Genius: An Inquiry into Its Laws and Consequences* (London: Watts & Co.).

Gamson, J. (1994) *Claims to Fame: Celebrity in Contemporary America* (Berkeley: University of California Press).

Gardner, H. (1993a) *Creating Minds: An Anatomy of Creativity Seen through the Lives of Freud, Einstein, Picasso, Stravinsky, Eliot Graham and Gandhi* (New York: Basic Books).

———(1993b) 'Seven Creators of the Modern Era', in J. Brockman (ed.) *Creativity: The Reality Club 4* (New York: Touchstone), pp. 28–47.

Gardner, H., Csikszentmihalyi, M. & Damon, W. (2001) *Good Work: When Excellence and Ethics Meet* (New York: Basic Books).

Giddens, A. (1979) *Central Problems in Social Theory: Action, Structure and Contradiction in Social Analysis* (London: Macmillan Press).

———(1984) *The Constitution of Society: Outline of the Theory of Structuration* (Cambridge: Polity Press).

———(1990) *Sociology: A Brief But Critical Introduction* (London: Macmillan).

Gitlin, T. (1994) *Inside Prime Time* (London: Routledge).

Glover, D. (2011) *The Art of Great Speeches and Why We Remember Them* (Cambridge: Cambridge University Press).

Gorny, E. (2007) *Dictionary of Creativity: Terms, Concepts, Theories & Findings in Creativity Research*, http://creativity.netslova.ru/Matthew_effect.html, date accessed 20 April 2011.

Gould, C. (1988) *Rethinking Democracy: Freedom and Social Cooperation in Politics, Economy and Society* (New York: Cambridge University Press).

Gray, P. (1998) 'Amid the Mass Market Noise, These Writers Made Themselves Heard', *Time*, 23, June, 78.

Green, L. (2010) *The Internet: An Introduction to New Media* (Oxford: Berg Publishers).

Greenfield, S. (2008) 'Creating Creative Brains', *Creating Value: Between Commerce and Commons Conference*, 25 June–27 June (Brisbane: Centre for Creative Industries and Innovation QUT) http://cultural-science.org/creatingvaluesusan1.html, date accessed 29 July 2009.

Grenfell, M. & James, D. (1998) *Bourdieu and Education: Acts of Practical Theory* (London: Falmer Press).

Griffin, E. (1997) *A First Look at Communication Theory*, 3rd edn (New York: McGraw-Hill).

———(2000) *A First Look at Communication Theory*, 4th edn (New York: McGraw-Hill).

———(2006) *A First Look at Communication Theory*, 6th edn (New York: McGraw-Hill).

Gross, L. (ed.) (1995) *On the Margins of Art Worlds* (Boulder, CO: Westview Press).

Gruber, H. (1988) 'The Evolving System Approach to Creative Work', *Creativity Research Journal*, 1, 27–51.

Guildford, J. (1950) 'Creativity', *American Psychologist*, 5, 444–54.

———(1970) 'Creativity: Retrospect and Prospect', *The Journal of Creative Behaviour*, 4(3), 149–68.

Guthrie, W. (1967) *The Greek Philosophers: From Thales to Aristotle* (London: Methuen).

Hall, S. (1980) 'Encoding/Decoding', in S. Hall et al. (eds) *Culture, Media, Language: Working Papers in Cultural Studies, 1972–79* (London: Hutchinson), pp. 128–38.

Haralambos, M. & Holbern, M. (1995) *Sociology: Themes and Perspectives*, 4th edn (London: Collins).

Harding, R. (1979) *Outside Interference: The Politics of Australian Broadcasting* (Melbourne: Sun).

———(1987) *Superstructuralism: The Philosophy of Structuralism and Post-Structuralism* (London: Methuen).

Harris, T. (2000) 'Board Stacking a Party Custom', *The Australian*, December 4, p. 2.

Hartcher, E. (1985) *Art as Culture: An Introduction to the Anthropology of Art* (New York: University Press of America).

Hartley, J. (ed.) (2005) *Creative Industries* (Malden, MA: Blackwell).

Haynes, D. (1997) *The Vocation of The Artist* (Cambridge: Cambridge University Press).

Hayward, P. (ed.) (1991) *Culture, Technology and Creativity (in the Late Twentieth Century)* (London: J. Libbey).

Hayward, S. (1996) *Key Concepts in Cinema Studies* (London: Routledge).

Hellige, J. (1993) *Hemispheric Asymmetry: What's Right and What's Left* (Cambridge, MA: Harvard University Press).

———(2001) *Hemispheric Asymmetry: What's Right and What's Left*, 2nd edn (Cambridge, MA: Harvard University Press).

Hendy, D. (2000) *Radio in the Global Age* (Cambridge: Polity Press).

Hennessey, R. & Amabile, T. (2010) 'Creativity', *Annual Review of Psychology*, 61, 569–98.

Herrmann, N. (1998) 'Theories of Brain Organisation', *The Creative Brain*, http://www.ozemail.com.au/~caveman/Creative/Brain/herrmann.htm, date accessed 28 July 1998.

Hesmondhalgh, D. (2002) *The Cultural Industries* (London: Sage).

———(2006) 'Bourdieu, the Media and Cultural Production', *Media, Culture and Society*, 28(2), 211–31.

Hill, S. (1988) *The Tragedy of Technology* (London: Pluto Press).

Holbert, L., Pillion,O., Tschida, D., Armfield, G., Kinder, K., Cherry, K. & Daulton, A. (2003) '*The West Wing* as Endorsement of the U.S. Presidency: Expanding the Bounds of Priming in Political Communication', *Journal of Communication*, 53(3), 427–43.

Holloway, J. (1975) *Radio in Australia* (Sydney: Reed Education Publications).

Howe, M. (199) *Genius Explained* (London: Cambridge University Press).

Hume, D. (1952) *An Enquiry Concerning Human Understanding* (London: Routledge and Kegan Paul).

IFPI (2003) 'Music: One of the Great Global Industries', *International Federation of Phonographic Industries*, http://www.ifpi.org/, date accessed 29 May 2003.

———(2009) 'Recorded Music Sales 2008', *International Federation of Phonographic Industries*, http://www.ifpi.org/content/section_statistics/index.html, date accessed 27 October 2009.

Isaacson, W. (2009) 'How to Save Your Newspaper', *Time*, 173(8), p. 30.

Jarvie, I. (1987) *Philosophy of the Film: Epistemology, Ontology, Aesthetics* (New York: Routledge & Kegan Paul).

Jervis, B. (1987) *News Sense* (Adelaide: Advertiser Newspapers Limited).

Jordan, G. & Weedon, C. (1995) *Cultural Politics: Class, Gender, Race and the Postmodern World* (Oxford: Blackwell).

Kansas City Star, 'Style Guide', *Kansas City Star*, http://www.kcstar.com/hemingway/ehstarstyle.shtml, date accessed 10 May 2010.

Kant, I. (1982) *The Critique of Judgement* (Oxford: Clarendon Press).

Kapur, S. (2007) 'Elizabeth: The Golden Age' (Dir. Interviewed, *Asia Today*), BBC World Service radio broadcast, 11:33 am, 15 September.

Kaspersen, L. (2000) *Anthony Giddens: An Introduction to a Social Theorist* (trans. S. Sampson) (Oxford: Blackwell).

Kavolis, V. (1972) *History on Art's Side: Social Dynamics in Artistic Efflorescences* (New York: Cornell University Press).

Kelly, O. (1984) *Community, Art and the State: Storming the Citadels* (London: Comedia).

Kelso, J. & Engstrm, D. (2008) *The Complementary Nature* (Cambridge, MA: MIT Press).

Kerouac, J. (1972) *Lonesome Traveller* (London: Grafton Books).

Kerrigan, S. (2006) 'Reflecting on Documentary Video Practice', in R. Vella (ed.) *Speculation and Innovation: Applying Practice Led Research in the Creative Industries*, Queensland, University of Technology, viewed 4 August 2006, http://www.speculation2005.net.

———(2008) 'Collaborative and Creative Documentary Production in Video and Online', in I. Hoofd, M. Tan & K. Ying (eds) *Proceedings of ISEA2008: The 14th International Symposium on Electronic Art* (Singapore: ISEA), pp. 265–7.

———(2011) 'Creative Documentary Practice: Internalising the Systems Model of Creativity – A Case Study into Video and Online Documentary Practice', PhD Thesis, University of Newcastle.

Kerrigan, S. & McIntyre, P. (2010) 'The 'Creative Treatment of Actuality': Rationalising and Reconceptualising the Notion of Creativity for Documentary Practice', *Journal of Media Practice*, 11(2), 111–30.

Koch, C. & Joel Davis (eds) (1994) *Large-Scale Neuronal Theories of the Brain* (Cambridge, MA: MIT Press).

Lane, R. (1994) *The Golden Age of Australian Radio Drama: 1923–1960* (Melbourne: Melbourne University Press).

Latour, B. (2005) *Reassembling the Social: An Introduction to Actor-Network-Theory* (Oxford: Oxford University Press).

Levinson, P. (2006) 'Electronic Watermarks: A High Profile for Intellectual Property in the Digital Age', in P. Cobley (ed.) *Communication Theories: Critical Concepts in Media and Cultural Studies* (London: Routledge), pp. 53–66.

Locke, J. (1956) *The Second Treatise of Government (An Essay Concerning the True Original, Extent and End of Civil Government), and, A Letter Concerning Toleration*, ed. J. Gough (Oxford: Blackwell).

Lombroso, C. (1891) *The Man of Genius* (New York: C. Scribner's Sons).

———(1984) *The Man of Genius* (New York: Garland Publishing).

Long Lance, B. (1976) *Long Lance: The Autobiography of a Blackfoot Indian Chief* (London: Abacus).

Love, C. (n.d.) 'Digital Downloads', http://www.holemusic.com/digihollywood.html, date accessed 23 September 2006.

Lovejoy, M. (1990) 'Art, Technology, and Postmodernism: Paradigms, Parallels, and Paradoxes', *Art Journal*, 49(3), 257–65.

Lull, J. (1987) *Popular Music and Communication* (Newbury Park, CA: Sage).

———(1992) *Popular Music and Communication*, rev. edn (Newbury Park, CA: Sage).

Maddock, K. (1990) 'Aboriginal Customary Law', in Andrew Fraser (ed.) *LAW112 History and Philosophy of Law: The Ancient World and the Origins of the Western Legal Tradition* (Sydney: School of Law, Macquarie University), pp. 14–15.

Marcus, G. (1980) 'The Beatles', in J. Miller (ed.) *The Rolling Stone Illustrated History of Rock* (New York: Random House).

Marlow, K. (1995) *The Crucial Role of Radio in the Music Industry* (Melbourne: Ausmusic).

Marr, A. (2001) 'In the Zone: A Behavioural Theory of the Flow Experience', *Athletic Insight: The Online Journal of Sport Psychology*, 3(1), viewed 10 April 2006, http://www.athleticinsight.com/Vol3Iss1/Commentary.htm.

Martindale, C. (1999) 'Biological Bases of Creativity', in R. Sternberg (ed.) *Handbook of Creativity* (Cambridge: Cambridge University Press), pp. 137–52.

Marx, K. (1980) *Grundisse der Kritik der Politischen Okonomie*, 2nd edn, D, McLellan (ed.) (London: MacMillan).

Maslow, A. (1968) *Toward a Psychology of Being* (Princeton, NJ: Van Nostrand).

Mast, G. & Cohen, M. (eds) (1979) *Film Theory and Criticism: Introductory Readings*, 2nd edn (New York: Oxford University Press).

Maugham, W. (1963) *The Razor's Edge* (Harmondsworth: Penguin).

McIntyre, E. (2004) 'Facilitating the Script: Creativity and Cultural Production for the Screen', Honours Thesis, University of Newcastle.

McIntyre, P. (2006a) 'Radio Program Directors, Music Directors and the Creation of Popular Music', in S. Healy, B. Berryman & D. Goodman (eds) *Radio in the World: Radio Conference 2005* (Melbourne: RMIT Publishing), pp. 449–60.

———(2006b) 'Paul McCartney and the Creation of "Yesterday": The Systems Model in Operation', *Popular Music*, 25(2), 201–19.

———(2007) 'Copyright and Creativity: Changing Paradigms and the Implications for Intellectual Property and the Music Industry', *Media International Australia Incorporating Cultural Policy*, 123, 82–94.

———(2008) 'Creativity and Cultural Production: A Study of Contemporary Western Popular Music Songwriting', *Creativity Research Journal*, 20(1), 40–52.

———(2009a) 'Rethinking the Idea of the Mainstream/Alternative Dichotomy in Contemporary Western Popular Music in the Light of Recent Research into Creativity', in C. Strong & M. Phillipov (eds) *Stuck in the Middle: The Mainstream and Its Discontents, Selected Proceedings of the 2008 IASPM-ANZ Conference*, Brisbane, 28–30 November 2008, pp. 142–51.

———(2009b) 'Rethinking Communication, Creativity and Cultural Production: Outlining Issues for Media Practice', in T. Flew (ed.) *Communication, Creativity and Global Citizenship: Refereed Proceedings of the Australian and New Zealand Communications Association Annual Conference*, Brisbane, July 8–10, http://www.proceedings.anzca09.org, date accessed 12 April 2010.

———(2011) 'Systemic Creativity: The Partnership of John Lennon and Paul McCartney', *Musicology Australia: Journal of the Musicological Society of Australia*, 33 (2), 239–252.

McIntyre, P. & McIntyre, E. (2007) 'Rethinking Creativity and Approaches to Teaching: The Systems Model and Creative Writing', *International Journal of the Book*, 4(3), 15–22.

McIntyre, P. & Morey, J. (2010) Section 1.01, ' "Working out the Split": Creative Collaboration and Assignation of Copyright across Differing Musical Worlds', *The Sixth Annual Art of Record Production Conference 2010*, Leeds Metropolitan University, Leeds, UK, 3–5 December 2010.

McQuail, D. (1994) *Mass Communication Theory: An Introduction* (London: Sage).

McQueen, D. (1998) *Television: A Media Student's Guide* (London: Arnold).

MENSA (2010) 'About Mensa International', *Mensa International*, http://www.mensa.org/about-us#what-goals, date accessed 26 March 2010.

Mensch, E. (1990) 'The Colonial Origins of Liberal Property Rights', in Andrew Fraser (ed.) *LAW112 History and Philosophy of Law: The Eighteenth Century Constitution* (Sydney: School of Law, Macquarie University), pp. 918–31.

Merton, R. (1968) *Social Theory and Social Structure* (New York: Free Press).

Metallica (n.d.) 'News', http://www.metallica.com/news/2000/000501a.html, date accessed 18 May 2000.

Meyers, J. (1985) *Hemingway: A Biography* (London: Macmillan).

Miles, B. (1997) *Paul McCartney: Many Years From Now* (London: Secker and Warburg).

Mitchell, N. (2004) 'Left Brain Right Brain: Fact or Fiction?', *All in the Mind* (ABC Radio National podcast), http://www.abc.net.au/rn/science/mind/stories/s1137394.htm#links, date accessed 28 July 2004.

Mittell, J. (2004) 'A Cultural Approach to Television Genre Theory', in R. Allen & A. Hill (eds) *The Television Studies Reader* (London: Routledge), pp. 258–66.

Moran, A. (1982) *Making a TV Series: The Bellamy Project* (Sydney: Currency Press).

———(ed.) (1992) *Stay Tuned: An Australian Broadcasting Reader* (Sydney: Allen & Unwin).

Moran, A. & Hill, A. (2004) 'The Pie and the Crust: Television Program Formats', in R. Allen & A. Hill (eds) *The Television Studies Reader* (London: Routledge), pp. 258–66.

Morley, D. (1993) 'Active Audience Theory: Pendulums and Pitfalls', *Journal of Communication*, 43(4), 13–19.

Moxey, K. (1994) *The Practice of Theory: Poststructuralism, Cultural Politics, and Art History* (Ithaca, NY: Cornell University Press).

Natoli, J. (1997) *A Primer of Postmodernity* (London: Blackwell).

Negus, K. (1992) *Producing Pop: Culture and Conflict in the Popular Music Industry* (London: Edward Arnold).

———(1996) *Popular Music in Theory: An Introduction* (Cambridge: Polity Press).

Negus, K. & Pickering, M. (2004) *Creativity, Communication and Cultural Value* (London: Sage).

Neill, K. (2000) 'Hook, Line & Singer! Essential Criteria for Maximising the Playlist Potential of New Zealand Music on Commercial Radio: A Programme Directors' Perspective', Masters Thesis, Massey University, Palmerston North NZ.

Nemiro, J. (2004) *Mapping Out the Creative Process and Work Design Approach* (San Francisco: Pfeiffer).

Newberg, A. & D'Aquili, E. (2000) 'The Creative Brain/The Creative Mind', *Zygon*, 35(1), 53–79.

Nichols, B. (ed.) (1976) *Movies and Methods* (Berkley: University of California Press).

Niu, W. & Sternberg, R. (2006) 'The Philosophical Roots of Western and Eastern Conceptions of Creativity', *Journal of Theoretical and Philosophical Psychology*, 26, 18–38.

O'Boyle, M. & Singh, H. (2004) 'Interhemispheric Interaction during Global-Local Processing in Mathematically Gifted Adolescents, Average-Ability Youth, and College Students', *Neuropsychology*, 18(2), 371–7.

OED (2010a) 'Genius', *Oxford English Dictionary Online*, http://0-dictionary.oed.com.library.newcastle.edu.au/cgi/entry/50093688?single=1&query_type=word&queryword=genius&first=1&max_to_show=10, date accessed 26 March 2010.

————(2010b) 'Freedom', *Oxford English Dictionary Online*, http://0-dictionary. oed.com.library.newcastle.edu.au/cgi/entry/50089657?query_type=word&que ryword=freedom&first=1&max_to_show=10&sort_type=alpha&result_place= 1&search_id=ypmJ-i5IsDW-2857&hilite=50089657, date accessed 26 March 2010.

Orvell, M. (1989) *The Real Thing: Imitation and Authenticity in American Culture, 1880–1940* (Chapel Hill, NC: Carolina University of North Carolina Press).

Osborn, A. (1953) *Applied Imagination* (New York: Scribners).

Osborne, H. (1968) *Aesthetics and Art Theory: An Historical Introduction* (London: Longmans).

Paddison, M. (1982) 'The Critique Criticised: Adorno and Popular Music', *Popular Music*, 2, 201–18.

Page, W. & Carey, C. (2009) 'Adding up the Music Industry for 2008', *Economic Insight*, 15, http://www.prsformusic.com/creators/news/research/Documents/ Will Page and Chris Carey (2009) Adding Up The Music Industry for 2008.pdf, date accessed 20 July 2009.

Passmore, J. (1991) *Serious Art: A Study of the Concept in All the Major Arts* (London: Duckworth).

Paton, E. (2008) 'Creativity and the Dynamic System of Australian Fiction Writing', PhD Thesis, University of Canberra, Australia.

Paulus, P. & Nijstad, B (eds) *Group Creativity: Innovation through Collaboration* (Oxford: Oxford University Press), pp. 304–25.

Penley, C. & Ross, A. (eds) (1991) *Technoculture* (Minneapolis: University of Minnesota Press).

Perkins, V. (1972) *Film as Film* (Baltimore: Penguin).

Peterson, R. (1982) 'Five Constraints on the Production of Culture: Law, Technology, Market, Organizational Structure and Occupational Careers', *Journal of Popular Culture*, 17, 143–53.

————(1985) 'Six Constraints on the Production of Literary Works', *Poetics*, 14, 45–67.

————(1997) *Creating Country Music: Fabricating Authenticity* (Chicago: University of Chicago Press).

Petrie, D. (1991) *Creativity and Constraint in the British Film Industry* (London: MacMillan).

Pizzo, S. (2000) 'Napster and MP3: La Revolucion or La Larceny', *O'Reillynet*, http://www.oreillynet.com/pub/a/network/2000/05/12/PizzoFiles.html, date accessed 18 May 2000.

Plato (1937) *The Dialogues of Plato* (New York: Random House).

————(1971) *The Collected Dialogues of Plato, Including the Letters* (Princeton, NJ: Princeton University Press).

Pojman, L. (1998) *Classics of Philosophy: Vol.1 Ancient and Medieval* (New York: Oxford University Press).

Polanyi, M. (1967) *The Tacit Dimension* (London: Routledge & Keegan Paul).

Poole, M. (1990) 'Do We Have Any Theories of Group Communication?', *Communication Studies*, 41, 237–47.

Pope, R. (2005) *Creativity: Theory, History, Practice* (New York: Routledge).

Pratt, A. (2008) 'Creative Cities: The Cultural Industries and the Creative Class', *Geografiska Annaler: Series B, Human Geography*, 90(2), 107–17.

Propp, V. (1968) *The Morphology of the Folktale* (Austin: University of Texas Press).

Read, H. (1965) *The Origins of Form in Art* (London: Thames and Hudson).

Real, M. (1996) *Exploring Media Culture: A Guide* (Thousand Oaks, CA: Sage).

RIAA (2003) 'Tracking Music Trends in America', *Recording Industry Association of America*, http://www.riaa.com/MD-Tracking.cfm, date accessed 29 May 2003.

Rohthenbuhler, E. (1985) 'Commercial Radio as Communication', *Journal of Communication*, 46(1), 125–43.

———(1987) 'Commercial Radio and Popular Music: Processes of Selection and Factors of Influence', in J. Lull (ed.) *Popular Music and Communication* (Newbury Park, CA: Sage).

Rollins, P. & O'Connor, J. (eds) (2003) *'The West Wing': The American Presidency as Television Drama* (New York: Syracuse University Press).

Roth, A. & Altshuler, T. (1969) *Writing Step by Step: Exercises in Structured Creativity* (Boston: Houghton Mifflin).

Rothenberg, A. (1979) *The Emerging Goddess: The Creative Process in Art, Science and Other Fields* (Chicago: University of Chicago Press).

Rothenberg, A. & Hausman, C. (eds) (1976) *The Creativity Question: A Reader* (Durham, NC: Duke University Press).

Runco, M. (2004) 'Creativity', *Annual Review of Psychology*, 55, 657–87.

———(2007) *Creativity: Theories and Themes: Research, Development and Practice* (New York: Elsevier Academic Press).

Runco, M. & Pritzker, S. (1999) *Encyclopedia of Creativity* (San Diego: Academic Press).

Ryan, B. (1991) *Making Capital from Culture: The Corporate Form of Capitalist Cultural Production* (Berlin: de Gruyter).

Samuels, E. (2000) *The Illustrated Story of Copyright* (New York: Thomas Dunne Books).

Sardar, Z. & Van Loon, B. (1998) *Introducing Cultural Studies* (Cambridge: Icon Books).

Sawyer, K. (2006). *Explaining Creativity: The Science of Human Innovation* (Oxford: Oxford University Press).

———(2007) *Group Genius: The Creative Power of Collaboration* (New York: Basic Books).

Sayer, A. (2000) *Realism and Social Science* (London: Sage).

Schiffer, L. (ed.) (1996) 'Definitions', *Creative Basics*, http://www.ozemail.com.au/~caveman/Creative/Basics/definitions.htm, date accessed 28 July 1998.

Schirato, T. & Yell, S. (1996) *Communication and Cultural Literacy: An Introduction* (Sydney: Allen & Unwin).

Schon, D. (1983) *The Reflective Practitioner: How Professionals Think in Action* (New York: Basic Books).

Seidman, S. (1994) *The Postmodern Turn: New Perspectives on Social Theory* (Cambridge: Cambridge University Press).

Sewell, W. (1990) 'Work and Revolution in France: The Language of Labour from the Old Regime to 1848', in Andrew Fraser (ed.) *LAW112 History and Philosophy of Law: The Eighteenth Century Constitution* (Sydney: School of Law, Macquarie University), pp. 913–7.

Sheridan-Burns, L. (2002) *Understanding Journalism* (London: Sage).

Shusterman, R. (ed.) (1999) *Bourdieu: A Critical Reader* (Oxford: Blackwell).

Silverman, S. (1992) *David Lean* (New York: Harry N. Abrams Inc.).

Simonton, D. (1975) 'Sociocultural Context of Individual Creativity: A Transhistorical Time-series Analysis', *Journal of Personality and Social Psychology*, 32, 1119–33.

——(1976) 'The Causal Relation between War and Scientific Discovery: An Exploratory Cross-national Analysis', *Journal of Cross-Cultural Psychology*, 7, 133–144.

——(1980) 'Techno-Scientific Activity and War: A Yearly Time-Series Analysis, 1500–1903 A.D.', *Scientometrics*, 2, 251–5.

——(1994) 'Individual Differences, Developmental Changes and Social Context', *Behavioural and Brain Sciences*, 17, 552–3.

——(1996) 'Individual Genius and Cultural Configurations: The Case of Japanese Civilization', *Journal of Cross-Cultural Psychology*, 27, 354–75.

——(2003) 'Creative Cultures, Nations and Civilisations: Strategies and Results', in P. Paulus & B. Nijstad (eds) *Group Creativity: Innovation through Collaboration* (Oxford: Oxford University Press), pp. 304–25.

Sinclair, A. (1979) *John Ford* (London: Allen & Unwin).

Smith, B. (1988) *The Death of the Artist as Hero: Essays in History and Culture* (Melbourne: Oxford University Press).

Smith, G. (2002) 'Response to the Keynote Address by James Akenson', *The First Annual Australian Institute of Country Music Conference*, Gympie Qld., August 23–25.

Smith S., Ward, T. & Finke, R. (eds) (1995) *The Creative Cognition Approach* (Cambridge, MA: MIT Press).

Sorkin, A. (2002) *'The West Wing': Script Book* (New York: Newmarket Press).

Sorokin, P. (1937) *Social and Cultural Dynamics* (New York: American Books).

——(1941) *The Crisis of Our Age: The Social and Cultural Outlook (Based upon Four Volumes of the Author's 'Social and Cultural Dynamics')* (New York: Dutton).

Sperry, R. (1974) 'Lateral Specialization in the Surgically Separated Hemispheres', in F. Schmitt & F. Worden (eds) *Third Neurosciences Study Program* (Cambridge: MIT Press), pp. 3, 5–19.

Sporre, D. (1987) *An Introduction to the Arts in Western Civilisation* (Sydney: The Book Company).

Stein, M. (1953) 'Creativity and Culture', *The Journal of Psychology*, 36, 311–22.

——(1974) *Stimulating Creativity: Volume One, Individual Procedures* (New York: Academic Press).

Sternberg, R. (ed.) (1988) *The Nature of Creativity: Contemporary Psychological Perspectives* (New York: Cambridge University Press).

——(ed.) (1999) *Handbook of Creativity* (Cambridge: Cambridge University Press).

Sternberg, R. & Davidson, J. (eds) (1995) *The Nature of Insight* (Cambridge, MA: MIT Press).

Sternberg, R. & Lubart, T. (1991) 'An Investment Theory of Creativity and Its Development', *Human Development*, 34, 1–32.

——(1992) 'Buy Low and Sell High: An Investment Approach to Creativity', *Current Directions in Psychological Science*, 1(1), 1–5.

Stillinger, J. (1991) *Multiple Authorship and the Myth of Solitary Genius* (Oxford: Oxford University Press).

Stokes, M. (1994) *Ethnicity, Identity and Music: The Musical Construction of Place* (Oxford: Berg Publishers).

Storey, J. (1994) *Cultural Theory and Popular Culture: A Reader* (New York: Harvester Wheatsheaf).

Storey, J. (2006) *Cultural Theory and Popular Culture: A Reader*, 3rd edn (New York: Harvester Wheatsheaf).

Strachey, J. (ed.) (1953) *The Standard Edition of the Complete Psychological Works of Sigmund Freud* (London: Hogarth Press).

Sullivan, H. (1955) *Conceptions of Modern Psychiatry* (London: Tavistock).

Suzuki, D. (1994) *The Brain: Our Universe Within (pt 5: The Subconscious Mind and Creativity)* (videorecording), Original Production NHK/NHK Creative Inc., c1994, series broadcast SBS TV, 28 July 1996.

Swartz, D. (1997) *Culture and Power: The Sociology of Pierre Bourdieu* (Chicago: University of Chicago Press).

Sykes, J. (ed.) (1983) *The Concise Oxford Dictionary of Current English* (Oxford: Clarendon Press).

Tannebuam, R. (1998) *Theoretical Foundations of Multimedia* (New York: W.H. Freeman).

Teichmann, J. & Evans, K. (1991) *Philosophy: A Beginners Guide* (Oxford: Basil Blackwell).

Thomas, A. (1992) Extract from 'The Politicisation of the ABC in the 1930s', reprinted in A. Moran (ed.) *Stay Tuned: An Australian Broadcasting Reader* (Sydney: Allen & Unwin), pp. 66–70.

Thomas, W. (1967) *The Unadjusted Girl: With Cases and Standpoint for Behavioral Analysis* (London: Harper & Row).

Thompson, R. (1990) *Adventures on Prime Time: The Television Programs of Stephen J. Cannell* (New York: Praeger).

Thussu, D. (2000) *International Communication: Continuity and Change* (London: Arnold).

———(2006) *International Communication: Continuity and Change*, 2nd edn (London: Hodder Arnold).

Todorov, T. (1977) *The Poetics of Prose* (Oxford: Blackwell).

Tokoro, M. & Mogi, K. (eds) (2007) *Creativity and the Brain* (Hackensack, NJ: World Scientific).

Torrance, E. (1974) *Torrance Tests of Creative Thinking* (Lexington, MA: Personnel Press).

Toynbee, J. (2000) *Making Popular Music: Musicians, Creativity and Institutions* (London: Arnold).

Truax, B. (1984) *Acoustic Communication* (New Jersey: Ablex Publishing).

Tschmuck, P. (2006) *Creativity and Innovation in the Music Industry* (Berlin: Springer).

Tulloch, J. (1990) *Television Drama: Agency, Audience and Myth* (London: Routledge).

Tulloch, J. & Alvarado, M. (1983) *Doctor Who: The Unfolding Text* (London: Macmillan Press).

Tulloch, J. & Moran, A. (1986) *A Country Practice: Quality Soap* (Sydney: Currency Press).

Vaidhyanathan, S. (2001) *Copyrights and Copywrongs: The Rise of Intellectual Property and How It Threatens Creativity* (New York: New York University Press).

Vernon, P. (ed.) (1970) *Creativity: Selected Readings* (Harmondsworth: Penguin).

Volkart, E. (ed.) (1951) *Social Behavior and Personality: Contribution of W.I. Thomas to Theory and Social Research* (New York: Social Research Council).

von Oech, R. (1983) *A Whack on the Side of the Head: How to Unlock Your Mind for Innovation* (New York: Warner Books).

von Oech, R. (1986) *A Kick in the Seat of the Pants: Using Your Explorer, Artist, Judge and Warrior to Be More Creative* (New York: Perennial Library).

Walker, J. (1983) *Art in the Age of Mass Media* (London: Pluto Press).

———(1994) *Art in the Age of Mass Media*, 2nd edn (London: Pluto Press).

Wallas, G. (1945) *The Art of Thought* (London: C.A. Watts & Co.).

Ward, T., Smith, S. & Vaid, J. (1997) (eds) *Creative Thought : An Investigation of Conceptual Structures and Processes* (Washington, DC: American Psychological Association).

Watson, P. (2001) *A Terrible Beauty: The People and Ideas That Shaped the Modern Mind: A History* (London: Phoenix).

———(2005) *Ideas: A History from Fire to Freud* (London: Weidenfeld & Nicolson).

Weber, M. (1946) *Essays in Sociology*, ed. Gerth H. and Wright Mills, C. (Oxford: Oxford University Press).

Webb, M. (1981) 'Radio On: Music in the Air', in Beilby & Roberts (eds) *The Australian Music Directory* (Melbourne: AMD P/L).

Weisberg, R. (1993) *Creativity: Beyond the Myth of Genius* (New York: W.H. Freeman and Co.).

———(2006) *Creativity: Understanding Innovation in Problem Solving, Science, Invention and the Arts* (Hoboken, NJ: John Wiley).

Wells, L. (ed.) (2004) *Photography: A Critical Introduction*, 3rd edn (London: Routledge).

West, D. (1996) *An Introduction to Continental Philosophy* (Cambridge, MA: Polity Press).

Wicke, P. (1990) *Rock Music: Culture, Aesthetics and Sociology* (Cambridge: Cambridge University Press).

Wiesner, M., Ruff, J. & Wheeler, W. (1993) *Discovering the Western Past: A Look at the Evidence* (Boston: Houghton Mufflin).

Wikipedia (n.d.a) 'Steven Spielberg', http://en.wikipedia.org/wiki/Steven_Spielberg, date accessed 12 September 2009.

———(n.d.b) 'iTunes', http://en.wikipedia.org/wiki/Itunes, date accessed 25 October 2006.

Wikstrom, P. (2009) *The Music Industry: Music in the Cloud* (Cambridge: Polity Press).

Williams, R. (1961) *The Long Revolution* (London: Chatto and Windus).

———(1981) *Culture* (London: Fontana Press).

Williamson, J. & Cloonan, M. (2007) 'Rethinking the Music Industry', *Popular Music*, 26(2), 305–22.

Wodak, R. (2009) *The Discourse of Politics in Action: Politics as Usual* (Basingstoke: Palgrave Macmillan).

Wolff, J. (1981) *The Social Production of Art* (London: MacMillan).

———(1993) *The Social Production of Art*, 2nd edn (London: MacMillan).

Wollen, P. (1969) *Signs and Meaning in the Cinema* (London: Secker & Warburg).

Zelizer, B. (2004) *Taking Journalism Seriously: News and the Academy* (London: Sage).

Zolberg, V. (1990) *Constructing a Sociology of the Arts* (Cambridge: Cambridge University Press).

Index